We Will Teach!

Channel Island Women
who Trained in Salisbury
1841–1978

Jenny Head & Anne Johns

ELSP

Published by ELSP in 2019

www.ex-librisbooks.co.uk

Origination by Ex LIbris Press
Bradford on Avon, Wiltshire

Printed by Gomer Press
Llandysul Enterprise Park
Llandysul
Ceredigion Wales
SA44 4JL

ISBN 978-1-912020-55-3

CHALKE VALLEY HISTORY FESTIVAL

'We Will Teach' is dedicated to the Channel Island women who trained and taught during the Occupation years, 1940-1945. Their devotion to their vocation was immeasurable.

Contents

Foreword

by Adrian Green, Director of Salisbury Museum

Salisbury Museum is based in the King's House which was formerly the home of the Salisbury Diocesan Training College, later known as The College of Sarum St Michael. This important chapter in the history of the building is still evident in the property today – for example the door to our social history store still has the words Upper Lecture Room painted on it. Our own lecture hall was the Chapel of the Holy Angels and has stained glass windows dedicated to the students.

Former students still gather in large numbers for an annual reunion at the King's House. Meeting the people who lived and worked in the college – and then went off to successful careers in education has been very inspiring. I have also learnt lots of trivia about the building – for example, the Milky Way was the name given to the back corridor where students used to line up for their cocoa in the dining room (now our Wessex Gallery of Archaeology)!

A lively and accessible source of information about the history of the College is the excellent Inspired to Teach by former students Jenny Head and Anne Johns. We Will Teach is the eagerly anticipated sequel and delves into the fascinating stories of the students and staff from the Channel Islands who attended the College.

At first this may seem a specialised subject – however hundreds of students studied at the College because it was for many years the nearest training establishment. This was a strong bond that went back to 1843 when the first student arrived, only two years after the College was founded!

This link continued during the Second World War. During the Occupation of the Channel Islands, existing students were cut off from home, whilst former students who returned to the islands lived under Nazi rule. Jenny and Anne explore the profound impact this had on those students.

The well-deserved success of Inspired to Teach encouraged Anne and Jenny to produce this new book. We Will Teach continues to show that the students at the Salisbury Diocesan Training College were a significant part of the life of the city for 137 years.

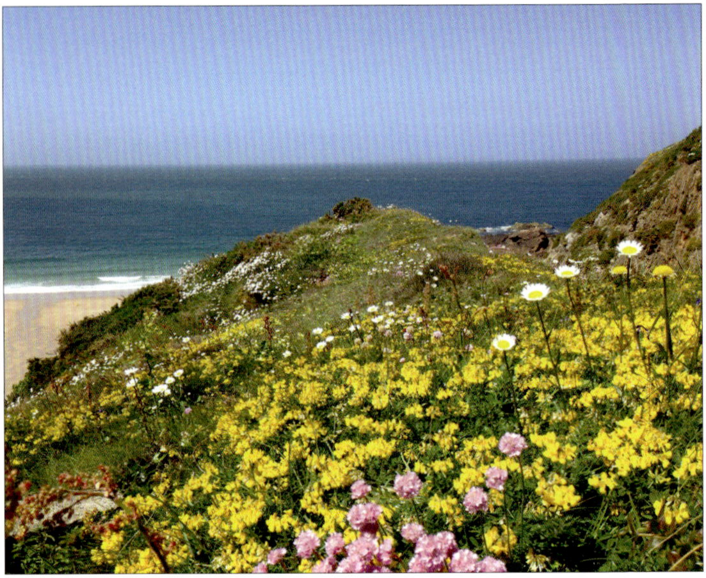

Fig. B Cliff flowers in Guernsey

Introduction

Salisbury Diocesan Training College was founded in 1841. It had the honour and prestige of being the first Church of England Training College for women teachers. During its 137 years of existence, thousands of students received an excellent training there, including hundreds who came from the Channel Islands.

Eliza Smith, a student from Guernsey, arrived in 1843 and in 1859 two students from Jersey made the long journey from there. Over the decades a strong link was established with the Channel Islands, as Salisbury was the nearest College.

The location of the College in the Cathedral Close had a special impact on the students, with its unique atmosphere and sense of calm spirituality. The Cathedral gave strength to the students in difficult times of war and during the Occupation of the Channel Islands.

Archive material has inspired us to celebrate the unique link between the Channel Islands and Salisbury. Our book provides a lasting record of the lives and times of women from Guernsey and Jersey who chose to train in Salisbury. In the words of John Say, former College lecturer '… they trained in what was probably the best and most beautiful of all training college sites in the country.'

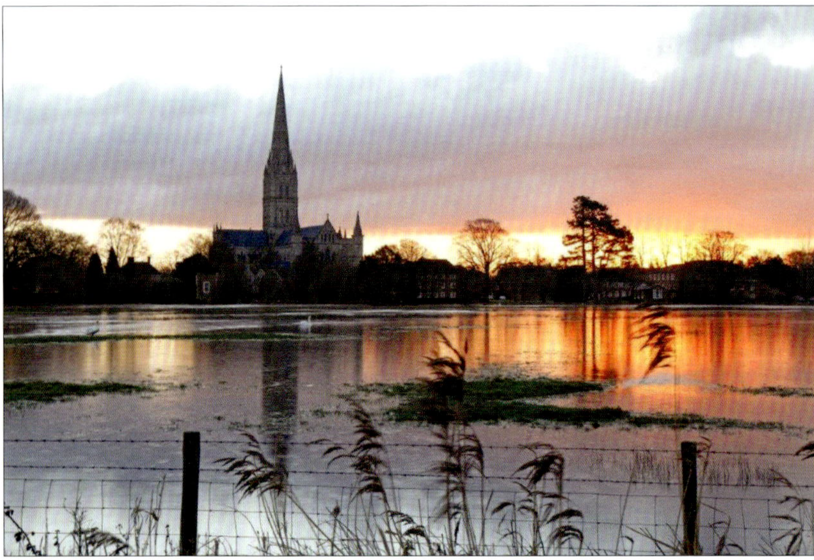

Fig. C Sunrise over Salisbury Cathedral and the former College from the flooded water meadows in 2013

1 Our Story

Our story is about a significant and surprising link between the Channel Islands and Salisbury.

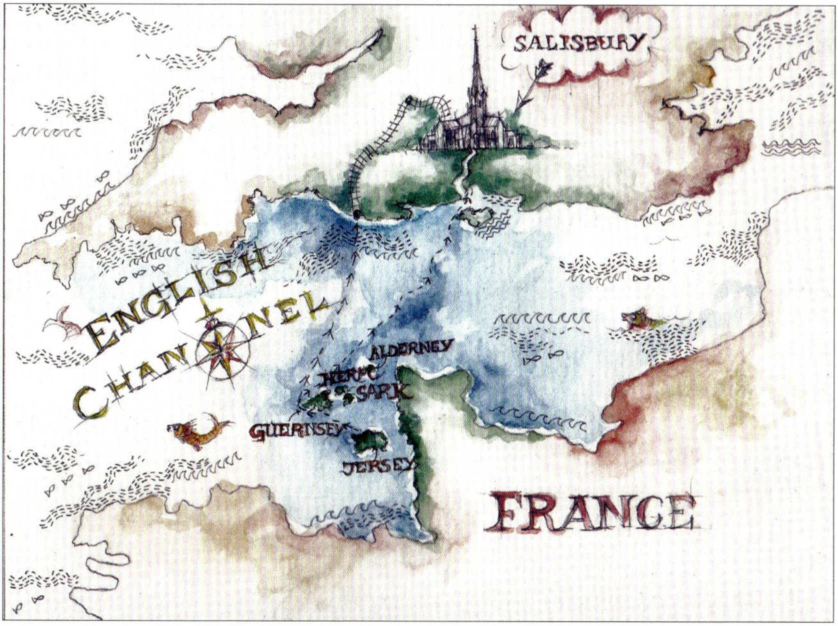

Fig 1.1 The Channel islands and Salisbury

The Channel Islands lie off the coast of Normandy in France, about 100 miles from Southampton. Jersey is the largest island and is approximately 18 miles from Guernsey. The Bailiwick of Guernsey includes the islands of Alderney, Sark and Herm. Victor Hugo described the Channel Islands as 'portions of France which have fallen into the sea and been picked up by England'. Historically, it was France that did the 'picking up' when

William, Duke of Normandy, defeated Harold at the Battle of Hastings in 1066 and became King of England. Even today, islanders like to think that England belongs to them, rather than the reverse. The islands are not part of the United Kingdom or European Union, but are possessions of the British Crown and those who live there are British citizens. The islands have independent administrations and are self-governing. They are very different from one another and cherish their individuality.

What was life like in these far-flung islands in the 19th century?

Jersey has an area of 45 square miles. The island has twelve parishes which are named after the saints to whom their parish churches are dedicated. The formation of the parishes was complete by 1087, possibly by 1066. Jersey's government is called the States of Jersey and is presided over by the Bailiff. It comprises 49 elected members, made up of Senators, Constables and Deputies. Each Constable is the civic head of one of the island's 12 parishes, as well as being head of the Honorary Police of that parish. There are also five members appointed by the Crown: the Bailiff, the Lieutenant Governor, the Dean of Jersey, the Solicitor General and the Attorney General. The Queen is represented in the island by the Lieutenant Governor. The Parish of St Helier contains the island's principal town and capital.

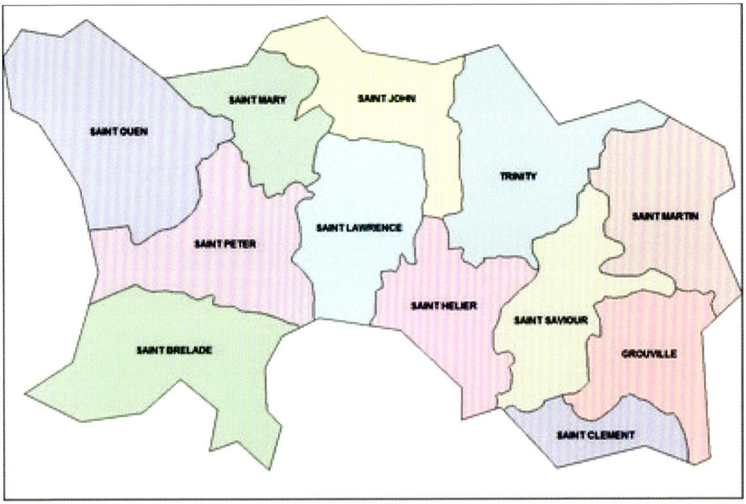

Fig. 1.2 Jersey and its twelve parishes

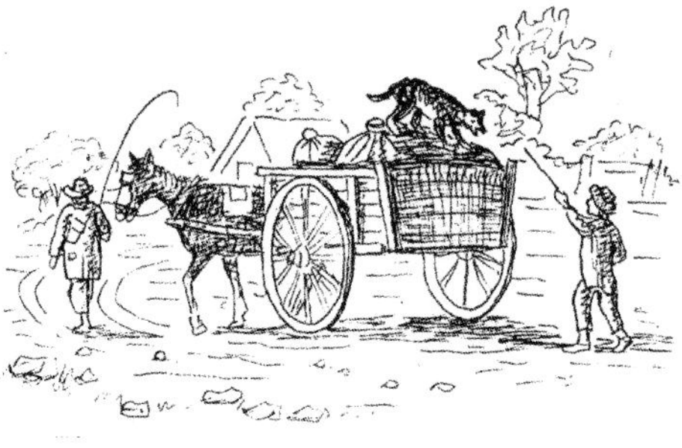

Fig. 1.3 A country road

In the early part of the 19th century some of the residents in the rural, furthermost parish of St Ouen might not even have ventured as far as St Helier. The country roads were rough and difficult and lives were often lived out in home parishes.

As the 19th century progressed and incomers arrived in Jersey, the population grew and was approximately 47,500 in 1850. Significant numbers of English speaking people settled in the island, attracted by:

> 'The mildness of the climate, the moderate prices of the necessaries of life and the extreme cheapness of its luxuries, the thoroughly English comforts of residence, the English society, the inexpensive facilities of education for which Jersey is pre-eminent – to say nothing of the extreme beauty of its natural aspect, both inland and seaward'.
>
> *Redstones Guernsey and Jersey Guide* 1843

The island also had the great financial advantage of freedom from tax. Hotels began to spring up and tourism was beginning. Farming was prospering as never before and wheat, apples, cider, potatoes, cows and butter were being exported. Occupations at this time included church ministry, law, medicine, manufacture, commerce and trade, as well as fishing and farming. There were ship owners, merchants, mariners and fishermen.

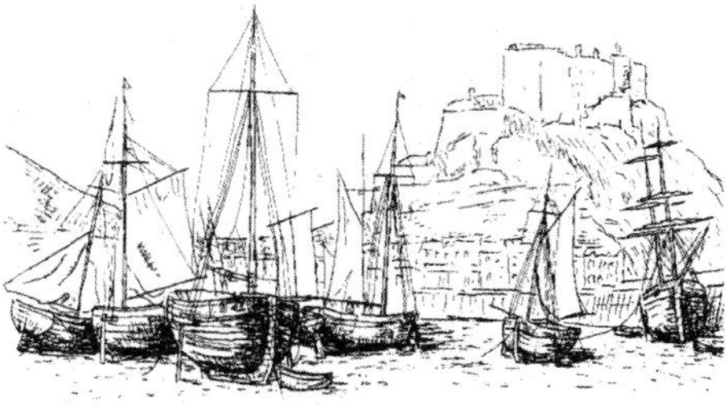

Fig. 1.4 Small oyster boats and a two-masted ship at Gorey in the 1840s.

There was a strong feeling amongst many Jersey people that the French origins of their way of life should be preserved and that children should be taught French from an early age. In 1800 almost everyone spoke Jersey-Norman French (*Jerriais*) and most people also spoke and understood French. However, by 1900 nearly everyone spoke English, some spoke *Jerriais* and most people understood both French and English. This change was brought about by the influx of English people who settled in the island, mainly in and around St Helier, during the 19th century. English gradually became incorporated into the island's culture, politics and life.

Schools differed as to which language was used for instruction. In St Brelade in 1815, few children could read English, but during the next fifty years English was introduced to successive generations in the parish and by 1859 was well established. At Trinity School however, children were taught in French until 1882, when the master was reprimanded for not using English as the teaching medium. Reception class teachers at rural schools, well into the 20th century, retained the ability to teach in Jerriais, French and English, depending on which language their new pupils spoke.

Since the late 18th century, Church of England schools had been set up in each of the twelve parishes. Classes were often held in the parish churches, which were the only public buildings at this time. By the mid-19th century the church monopoly of education had ended and there were also at least 75 private schools. Many of these were dame schools, which were run by women from their own homes. They were fee paying and whilst some were inadequate, others provided pupils with a good foundation in the basic skills.

By 1863, eleven Church of England schools had been built, as well as one Roman Catholic school and one Wesleyan. The schools were dependent on private initiative and the generosity of individuals.

Grouville Central School opened in 1858. The population in the area had grown considerably, mainly due to the flourishing oyster trade at Gorey. The school provided two large classrooms and a third room in which the headmaster taught the senior pupils. There were three other schools in the parish.

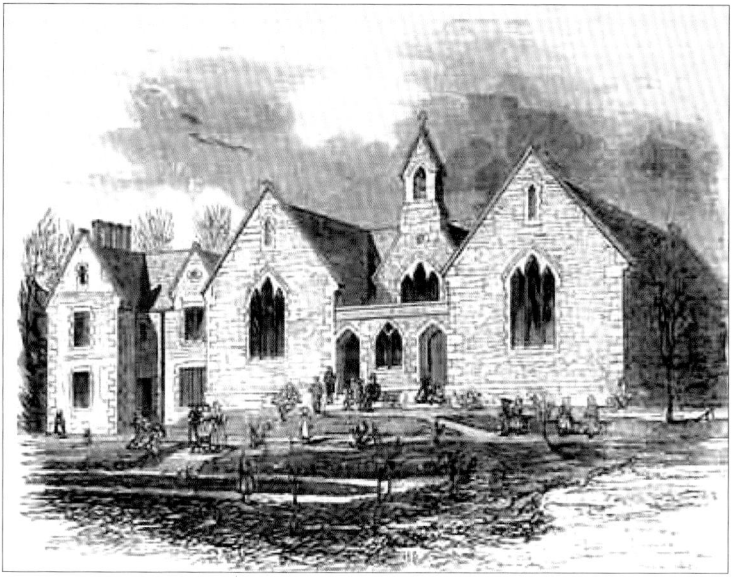

Fig. 1.5 A drawing of the new Central School in Grouville, 1858

There were at least eight public elementary schools in St Helier, as well as other schools attached to churches in the town. A Ragged School existed for the benefit of children whose parents could not afford any fees.

John Le Marquand, former President of the Education Committee, said that:

> 'Little interest was shown in the need to teach children of the poorer classes. We were, predominantly, a peasant community depending so much on family child labour at times of harvest, when absenteeism emptied the classrooms in the country schools. This must have been a factor in weakening the community sense of the need for schooling'.
>
> J. Le Marquand: *Elementary education 1870–1912*

The part played by Her Majesty's Inspectors in the development of island elementary education was vital. Although the 1870 Education Act did not apply to Jersey, the English government was willing to continue inspecting schools, but the States had to pay for the service and the schools that were inspected had to fulfill the requirements of the 1870 Act. The report of Her Majesty's Inspector in the late 1880s stated that island schools were generally below the standard of that required by the 1870 Education Act. There was no compulsory provision of new schools in Jersey and there was a serious deficiency in eleven of the twelve parish schools.

Jersey's standard of education was below that of England. The States took notice and were spurred on to make more effort, but there was still a long way to go. Free compulsory education started in Jersey in 1899, 29 years after England.

Guernsey is the second largest of the Channel Islands. It is approximately 30 miles from France and 125 miles from the south of England. It has an area of 25 square miles. The ten parishes of Guernsey were established in the 11th century. Each parish had its own church. Guernsey has its own parliament: the States of Guernsey. Its Deputies pass legislation which broadly follows that of the United Kingdom. Although Guernsey is part of the Commonwealth, it has its own traditions, laws and character.

What was the state of education in Guernsey? During the years 1800–1839 there was little direct intervention in Guernsey's education system from the British Government. Rose-Marie Crossan in her monograph 'The retreat of French from Guernsey Primary Schools, 1800–1939' explains that Guernsey's education system was relatively well developed in the early nineteenth century, in comparison with England and France. By 1820, each of the parishes had its own school under the supervision of Parochial Rectors and financed by charitable endowments, parish rates and moderate fees.

By 1821 the population of Guernsey was 20,302 with around 50 per cent of people living in St Peter Port. Guernsey was a 'society in transition', with an increasing percentage of English migrants. There was a 53% increase in the population of St Peter Port between the years 1821–1851. In Guernsey, at this time, there was significant poverty, especially in the country areas. Although quarrying and horticulture had increased rural work opportunities, many families lived a very difficult hand-to-mouth existence. In St Peter Port there was a minority of more affluent families, but as it was the garrison town and main port there were many social problems.

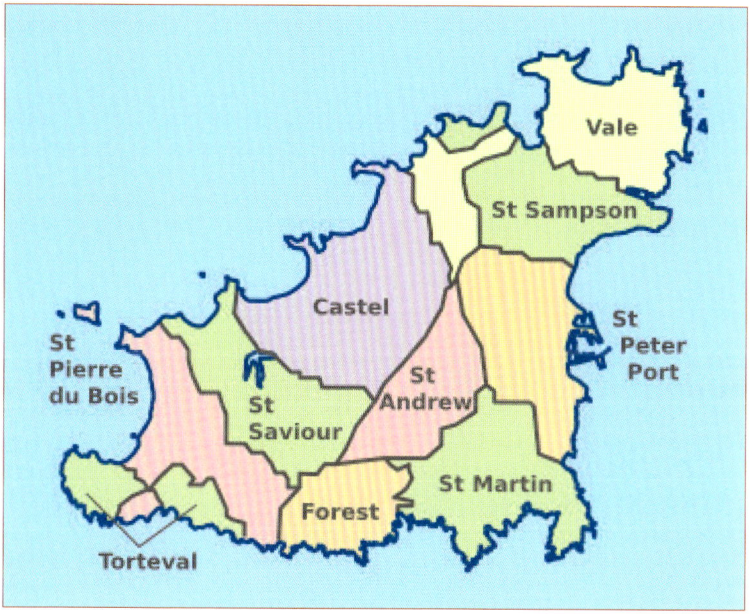

Fig. 1.6 Guernsey and its ten parishes

The majority of poorer children received their education at Sunday Schools or at the St Peter Port National School, founded in 1812. At this time Old Norman French was still spoken by many of the population. The amount of French spoken gradually decreased – partly due to the increase in English migrants, particularly in St Peter Port.

Ragged Schools for the poorest children were founded in Britain in the 1830s. There was a Ragged School situated in Berthelot Street, St Peter Port from 1853 until 1899. This provided a basic education for the poorest town children and also hot meals.

A Prayer said by the Children of the Ragged School before Morning School:

> O God! We thank thee for bringing us here to learn thy Word and way to Heaven. Teach us how to pray and what to pray for. Pardon our sins for Jesu's sake. Wash them away in His Precious Blood. Give us grace to obey our teachers and all that have rule over us. Keep the door of our

lips: set a watch before our mouth, that we tell no lies. Help us to keep our hands from stealing. Convert our parents. Be pleased to give us food and clothing and bless the instruction that may be given us. Do it all for Jesu's sake. Amen.

Extract from the First Annual Report of the Ragged School, St Peter Port May 26th 1851

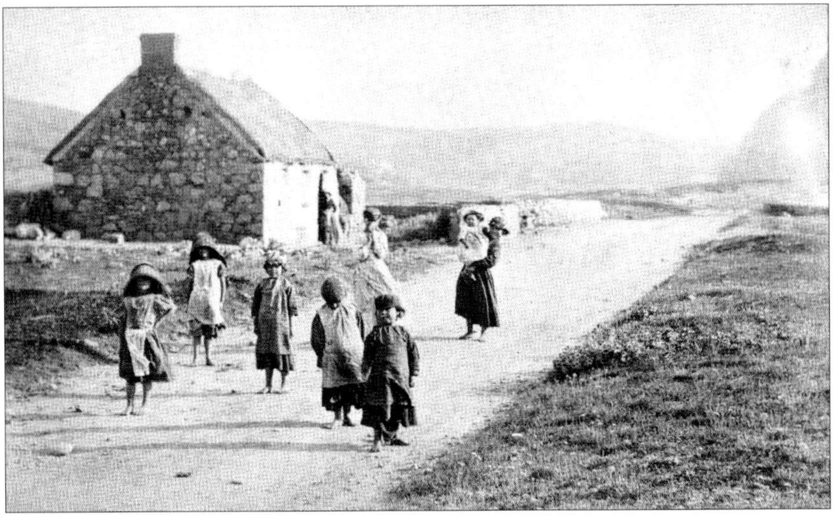

Fig. 1.7 Pauper children in the late 19th/early 20th century

The demand for education increased and in 1838 another National School was erected at St John's, which by 1858 accommodated boys and girls. By this time, the majority of children at the National School in St Peter Port were of English parentage and therefore instruction was provided mainly in English. This was much less the case in rural schools where some tuition in French continued. St Peter Port also had several private schools. Rural families who could afford it sent their children there on a daily basis to receive instruction in English.

In 1842, a 'British School' opened, which admitted children of all religious denominations. It was claimed that the National Schools were intended for the children of members of the Established Church.

Until the late 1840s Guernsey National Schools had received no grants from the British Government. In 1847, the St Peter Port Central School applied to Sir James Kay-Shuttleworth for a grant. This was the beginning of grants and HMI inspections in Guernsey. School masters on the island received extremely low pay. Grants were now offered to masters who were willing to instruct the most competent pupils to become pupil-teachers as a form of training. Stipends were also given to the apprentices themselves.

Elizabeth College, founded by Queen Elizabeth I in Guernsey in 1563, was a major factor in Guernsey education. In the early 19th century, although there was a headmaster, there were no pupils. Following an enquiry a beautiful new building was commissioned and new life was breathed into the establishment. In the early 20th century pupil-teachers, including those who later trained in Salisbury, went to Elizabeth College for some initial training.

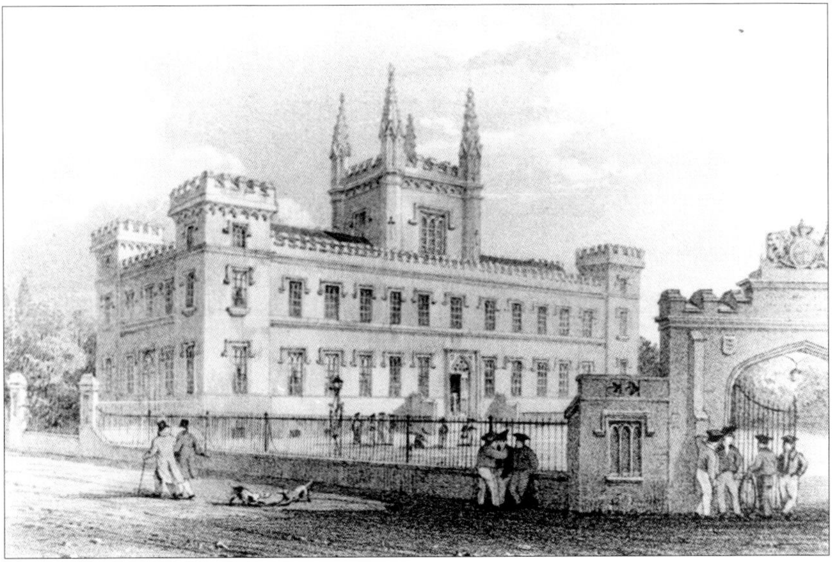

Fig. 1.8 Elizabeth College 1840

By 1900, the Guernsey population had doubled and prosperity increased. Many men arrived in Guernsey to work in the quarries and glasshouses. Shipbuilding had declined by 1880, as island shipbuilders were unable to compete with those in England and Scotland who were producing large numbers of iron ships. Guernsey's maritime industry was also in decline by 1900, with fewer locally owned and registered ships. Quarrying had increased, as Guernsey granite was in high demand. London Bridge was built from Guernsey granite and several London roads were paved with it. Horticulture was increasing and grapes, flowers and tomatoes were grown under glass. Tourists were discovering Guernsey's many delights. Having beautiful beaches and gorgeous countryside, Guernsey was a popular holiday destination with a long and fascinating history.

Alderney is the third largest of the Channel Islands with an area of three square miles. There is evidence of a school being built there in 1790. There is no trace of any students from Alderney, Sark or Herm attending Salisbury Training College, although in 1925 Doris Noel, a former College student from Jersey, was sent there to improve the school.

The sea that separates the Channel Islands from southern England is a physical and psychological barrier. Even today, when the journey by air can be as little as 40 minutes, the islands feel far away from the mainland and vice versa. How hard it must have been for those early island students who came to train as teachers in Salisbury. Eliza Smith, the first one, arrived from Guernsey as early as 1843. Over the next 130 years she was followed by hundreds of other students from the Channel Islands. How did they hear about the Training College and why did they want to come? First and foremost, they were embarking on a great adventure. It is likely that, for many, it was their first visit to this unknown place that locals still refer to today as 'the mainland'. Enterprise, a desire to 'get on in life' and a spirit of adventure must surely have flooded the veins of those who wanted to cross the sea to England.

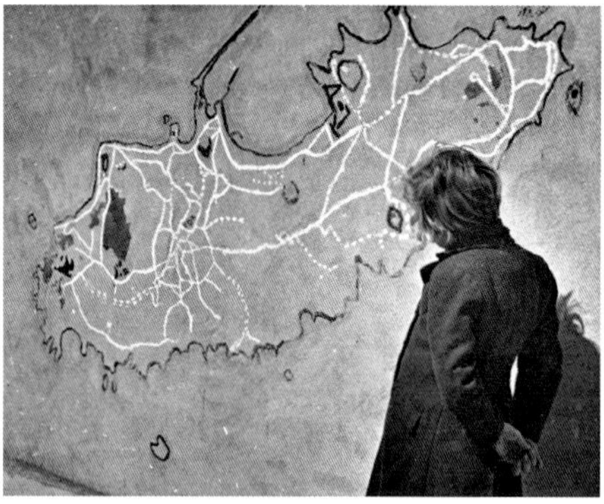

Fig. 1.9 A map of Alderney in a school playground

Salisbury, renowned for its beautiful 13th century Cathedral, is in south Wiltshire, about an hour by road from Southampton on the south coast. In the early 19th century it was still a boisterous medieval market city. The 1834 Poor Law Report described the Crane Street Workhouse as 'a scene of filth and misrule'. The last public execution was in 1855, but the execution stocks remained in the market square until 1858. Change, however, was on its way. Railways were spreading across the country and in 1847 the London and South Western line reached Salisbury, linking the city with Southampton and London. Further rail links followed, opening the city up to trade and creating jobs and prosperity. The resulting huge increase in population led to a great demand for housing. In 1849 the city suffered a serious cholera epidemic as a result of contaminated water. This led to a new drainage system being dug in the 1850s. Salisbury was slowly becoming a safer and healthier place to live.

Educational provision at this time included Sunday Schools, private schools of different sizes and the Song School, as it was then known, in the Cathedral Close. St Martin's, which opened in 1811, was the first school to be established in Salisbury by the 'National Society for Promoting the Education of the Poor in the Principles of the Established Church' (The National Society). The school subsequently developed strong links with the Diocesan Training College, as it was used for teaching practice.

By the late 1830s education was becoming a 'hot topic' in England. Schools were there for those who could afford it, but people began to reflect on the plight of the children of the poor, who were frequently growing up in ignorance and neglect. These children needed to be given 'secular instruction sufficient to guide them through life in their proper station'. Reading, 'Riting and Rithmetic' would be taught and so too would the fourth 'R' of Religion. This was the principle of the National Society, which founded the first system of universal education in England and Wales.

Edward Denison was the Bishop of Salisbury from 1837 until 1854. Dora Robertson, writing in 'Sarum Close', explained that the Bishop had a tremendous interest in religious education and that Salisbury owed the existence of the Training College for Schoolmistresses to him.

Acting quickly to the request from the National Society that each diocese should provide a Training School for teachers, the Bishop and the newly formed Diocesan Board of Education agreed that Salisbury would train women teachers, whilst Winchester took the men. Mrs Duncan was appointed as the Lady Superintendent.

Salisbury Training School opened in North Walk in the Cathedral Close in January 1841 with just one student, Martha Gibson, but within a year she had been joined by eleven others.

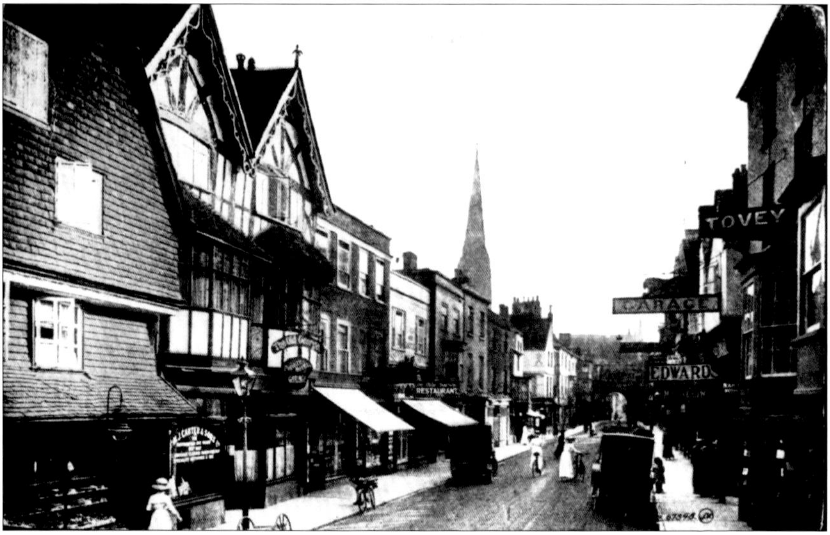

Fig. 1.10 An early photograph of Salisbury High Street looking towards the Cathedral. Many Channel Island students would have walked this way.

Enter the lively hustle and bustle and savour the smells and sounds of mid-Victorian Salisbury. There were breweries, bakeries and inns, wagons and stage-coaches, open water channels and traders, craft workers, farmers and butchers – and much more. Imagine this scene:

> 'The thoroughfares about the market-place being filled with carts, horses, donkeys, garden-stuff, meat, tripe, pies, poultry and huckster's wares of every description'.
>
> Charles Dickens: *Martin Chuzzlewit*

As the students stepped into the Cathedral Close through the High Street Gate, they entered a world of seclusion and genteel privacy. A common sight would have been that of clergymen, deep in conversation, walking to the Cathedral across land that was described by John Byng in 1782 as being 'like a cow-common, as dirty and neglected'. By now this land has been raised, flattened and 'tidied up' by the controversial architect, James Wyatt. Even in the 1840s, The Close was not always tranquil and the Cathedral choristers could be exceptionally unruly. College students, escorted by governesses on their daily walks, were enlivened by the sight of the boys running along the stone walls, dashing in and out of The Close and playing vigorous games that ended with the crashing of glass.

Salisbury Training College lived out its days in the Cathedral Close. Many Channel Islanders can be counted amongst the successive generations of students whose lives were influenced and inspired by their experiences of living and working in the precinct of the Cathedral. The life of every Channel Island student is part of the wider historical story that links the islands and Salisbury.

2 Eliza Smith – The First of Many! Guernsey to Salisbury in 1843

Eliza Smith was born in Dublin in 1825 when her father Henry DeLaporte Smith was 33 years old and her mother, Maria, was 21. Queen Victoria had reigned for six years: it was a time of change in England and throughout the world. The family travelled to England where Eliza's six brothers and sisters were born. By 1841 they had moved to St Peter Port, Guernsey where they lived at Vauvert Cottage, Vauvert Road, with four other occupants. Eliza's eldest brother John was eleven years old and the youngest was two years old. Sadly, Eliza's mother died just before the Census in 1841. By June of that year, Henry had remarried. However, things took a disastrous turn for the worse!

In February 1942 Henry was sentenced to transportation by the Royal Court, Guernsey, for 'forging and uttering bills of exchange for £530 to defraud the bank of Ireland, Messrs Kinhan, of this city, and the Guernsey Commercial Bank'. He was sentenced in Gosport, Hampshire and immediately transferred to the *York* a prison hulk in Gosport, whilst awaiting transportation. Ships which were considered unseaworthy were reconfigured to accommodate prisoners before transportation. Most were located in harbours which made them convenient for their purpose. Henry faced unhealthy and overcrowded conditions with very little ventilation on board.

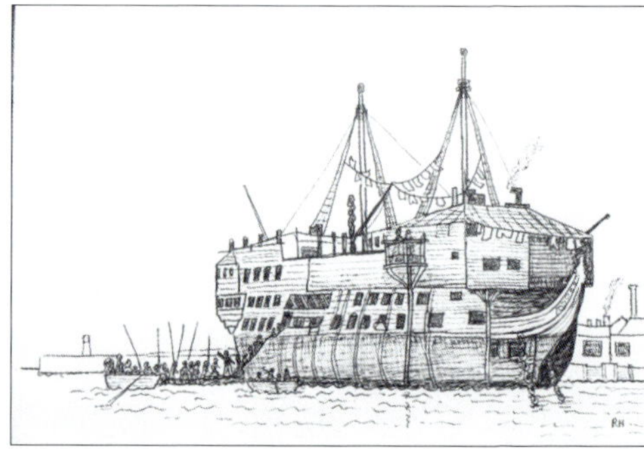

Fig. 2.1 The *York* prison hulk

Henry's sentence of seven years was viewed as lenient, as the average sentence was eleven years. At this time Henry, now aged 50 is described as a provision merchant. In March 1842 he joined 250 men on the convict ship *Candahar* and sailed to Van Dieman's Land, later known as Tasmania, a large island situated off the south east coast of Australia. The journey, in terrible conditions, took four months. Henry survived and his behaviour as a convict appears to have been good as he was later given positions of responsibility. Life on Van Dieman's Land at that time was often tough and brutal. Henry remained in Australia, where he died in 1877 aged 85.

It was a dreadful time for Eliza and we can imagine her longing to escape from the traumatic events at home. In 1843, at the age of eighteen, she set out alone on a long and hazardous journey to Salisbury with the ambition of training to teach. It was extremely brave for a single young woman to make this journey into the unknown.

She was admitted to Salisbury Training College in July 1843, but why did she choose Salisbury and how did she get there? She was recommended to the College by the Revd J. Hawtrey, who was the Minister of St James's Church in St Peter Port. He would certainly have known about Salisbury Training College and its foundation in 1841 as the first residential teacher training college for women.

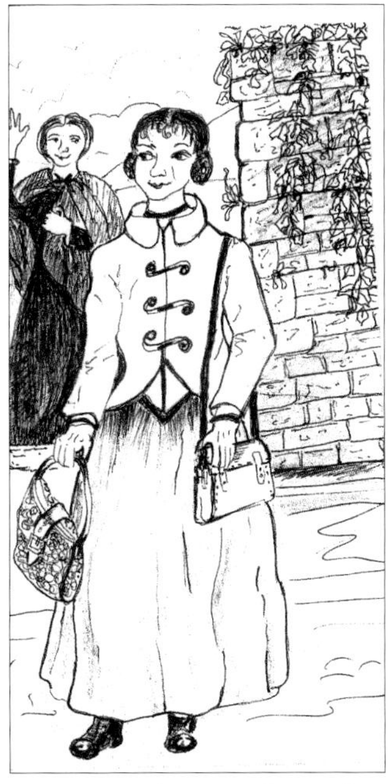

Fig. 2.2 Eliza says farewell to Guernsey

The link with Salisbury began in 1818 when (in place of the Bishop of Winchester) Bishop John Fisher, the Bishop of Salisbury, came to St Peter Port in Guernsey, to consecrate the church. St James was once the British Garrison church in St Peter Port, where services could be held in English; in the Town Church they were in French. The beautiful church of St James was sketched by JMW Turner in 1832. The church is about a six minute walk from Eliza's home in Vauvert, so it is very likely that she attended services there. Redstone's Guide to Guernsey and Jersey of 1843, written by Louisa Lane Clarke, describes classes held there every Sunday and Wednesday by Revd J. Hawtrey.

As an older pupil she possibly worked as a monitor or pupil-teacher in a local school and it is certain that she had a discussion with Revd J. Hawtrey, applied for Salisbury Training College and was accepted. In summer 1843 she set sail on the next stage of her life.

Her journey was a major undertaking. Eliza boarded a steamship to Southampton. Steamships bringing visitors to the island commenced in 1824 with the paddle steamer *Ariadne*. At this time Southampton was developing as a port. By the time of Eliza's arrival the wooden Royal Victoria Pier had been built, which provided berths at all depths. By 1843, the Channel Islands to Southampton route operated once a week in winter and three times a week in the summer. The journey, often in extremely rough seas, took at least fourteen hours in uncomfortable and crowded conditions. Hopefully Eliza would not have had to spend the journey on deck!

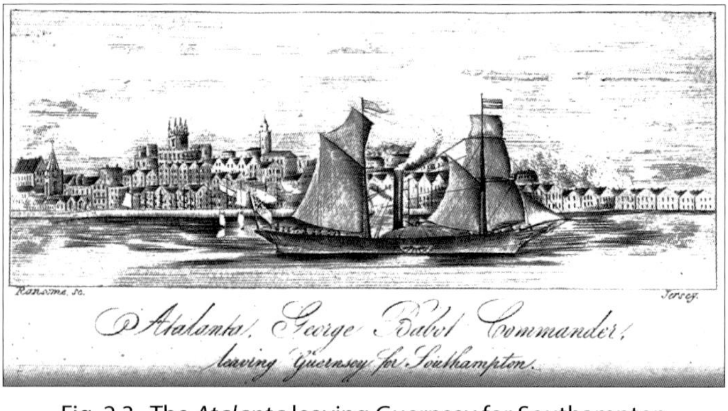

Fig. 2.3 The *Atalanta* leaving Guernsey for Southampton

What a shock Eliza would have had on arrival at Southampton! The railway line to London from Southampton had opened in 1840 and she would have found the sight of a roaring steam engine for the first time overwhelming. How frightening all the sounds, smells and noises of the port and city would have been!

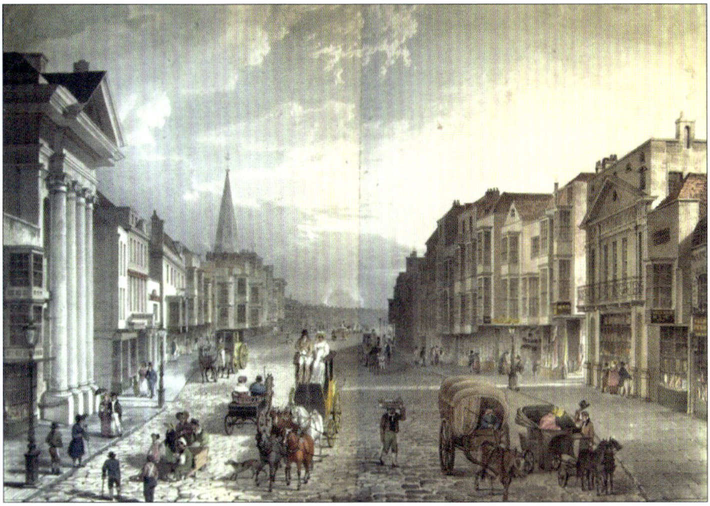

Fig. 2.4 A Southampton Street Scene 1828

Eliza did not give up, her future was at stake. The journey of about 22 miles continued by stage coach from Southampton to Salisbury, and probably took about four hours with stops.

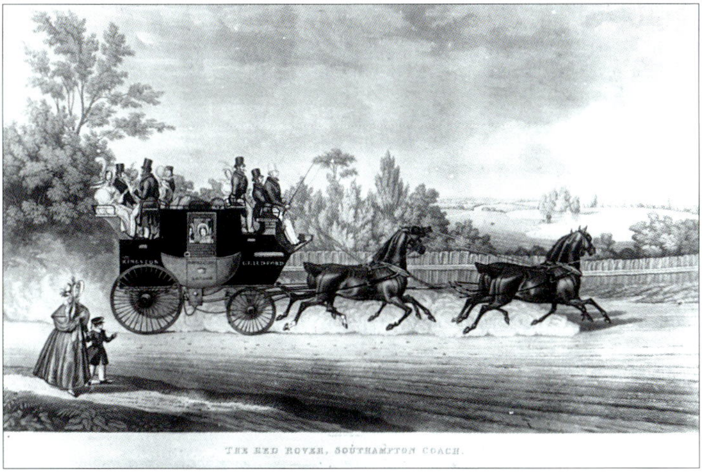

Fig. 2.5 The Red Rover Stagecoach

After a rough, bumpy and very lengthy journey, the spire of Salisbury Cathedral would have been seen. Eliza had arrived! Salisbury had many coaching inns at this time. How delighted Eliza would have been to alight and be almost at the end of her long and tiring journey. The Red Lion Inn, a well known coaching inn, was just around the corner from the Cathedral Close and the College.

In 1843 the College was situated in two adjoining houses, numbers 8 and 9 Bishop's Walk. Eliza found the accommodation reasonable: her room would have had a fireplace, a clothes-closet and possibly shutters at the windows. In 1891 Canon Edward Steward published 'The Red Book' about the Training School, as the College was then known,. He lists seventeen entrants in 1843 and includes reminiscences from a student in 1843:

> 'Candidates are examined in reading, writing, and spelling; in the first four rules of arithmetic; in the history of the O. and N. Testament, and in the Church Catechism. An elementary knowledge of Grammar and Geography will be generally expected. They must be well skilled in plain needlework and knitting'.

It was a hard life with lessons beginning at 7 a.m. Every evening the students studied from seven to eight, followed by a Scripture lesson for an hour. The students then went to bed 'supperless and often very hungry'.

Food was sparse and the cook at this time was described as 'a very slovenly and illiterate person, but she excelled in burnt pea soup and rice milk'.

Enjoyment was gained from the Cathedral services. The cook was the only servant who was employed by the College and students were required to assist in household tasks. Each year in June the examinations were held, followed by six weeks holiday. Eliza probably returned to Guernsey during these weeks, but as at Christmas there was only one week holiday, she would have stayed in College 'in the charge of the Second Mistress'. At least Eliza enjoyed a substantial meal. A student remembered:

> 'The Christmas festivities consisted of a dinner of roast beef and plum pudding; two puddings were made, and special orders left that one only was to be eaten at Christmas, the other on New Year's Day'.

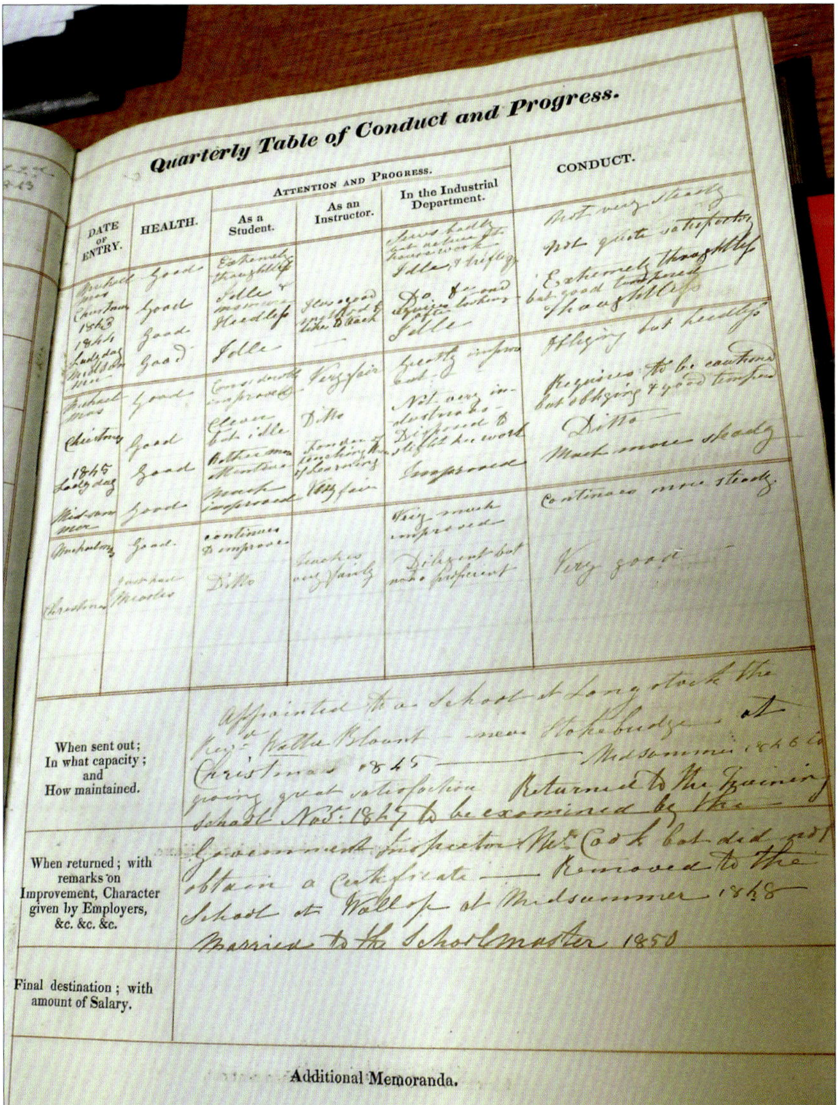

Fig. 2.6 College Log Book

Mrs Duncan was the Lady Superintendent during Eliza's training:

> 'The vision of Mrs Duncan, with the little velvet band over her hair, going her rounds to see if we were all in bed, holding up her little brass candlestick and peering under it at the sleepers. She was very strict with us. How well I remember being arraigned with others in the Schoolroom and having to confess that we had picked up some windfall apples in the garden, into which entrance was always forbidden'.

Eliza's entry record to College has survived and gives fascinating information about her College years and afterwards. By the time she reached Salisbury, it seems that Eliza had forgotten much of what she had learnt at church and school. Her 'State of Acquirement' on entry to College states:

> 'A very limited knowledge of the Bible, and though she had received a tolerable education as a child, it was nearly all forgotten'.

Her health during her college years was always good. She was very fortunate as conditions were tough and many students became ill. When the Revd F.C. Cook inspected the college in 1847 he noted that in the previous 20 months two students had died and five were so weak that there was no hope they could ever take up the teaching profession.

Fortunately, as Eliza progressed through College her 'acquirement' improved! Eliza's report shows that initially as a student she was 'idle and insincere', but this improved over time. As an instructor she was described as having 'a good understanding and likes to teach'. Her work in the 'industrial department' such as cleaning, was initially described as idle, but by the end of her training was much improved. As for her conduct, in the early years it was 'not very steady' but by the final term was 'much more steady'. Eliza seems to have had a difficult start, but gradually applied herself to College life.

At Christmas 1845 she was appointed to a school at Longstock in Hampshire. In November 1847 she needed to return to college to be examined by Revd F.C. Cook, in order to qualify. This occasion was described in reminiscence by a student:

'In 1847 came the greatest change of all, the visit of H.M.I. the Revd FC Cook. It was a day never to be forgotten; old Students had been recalled from their schools. Imagine the consternation on the eventful morning; everyone expecting as usual a viva voce examination when this great man (he was rather small in stature) arrived with his rolls of papers and questions, everything looking formidable; one crying here, another shaking there. However, by the end of the week we had on the whole acquitted ourselves fairly well. I remember Mrs Duncan telling me that Bishop Denison had remarked to her that many of the questions were more difficult than those given to undergraduates at Oxford'.

Revd F.C. Cook made several positive comments about the students:

'The pupils read with singular ease and good taste. Their intonation is perfectly free from vulgarity and affectation... Many of their papers in Religious Knowledge prove that they have a really comprehensive knowledge of religious subjects. I have remarked in many, and more or less in nearly all, the presence of those qualities which are most essential to a teacher: good temper, shown under very trying circumstances; an unaffected yet self-possessed deportment, such as acts upon children, both as an example and a governing principle; and lastly, good sense in what they attempted and what they omitted'.

Eliza did not obtain her teaching certificate. Only four of the former pupils who were examined were successful. This inspection was crucial to the College's development, as the Revd F.C. Cook advised that numbers should increase from 30 to 60. The Board agreed and 'King's House' in the Cathedral Close was purchased, where the College remained until its closure in 1978.

In Midsummer 1848 Eliza returned to teaching, as an uncertificated teacher at Nether Wallop School in Hampshire. Nether Wallop Endowed Church of England School was built in 1838 and enlarged in 1854 as numbers grew. Eliza taught there for two years before marrying the headmaster David Hill in 1850.

Not long after their marriage, David and Eliza moved to a newly built national school in Soberton, Hampshire. In 1850 Eliza gave birth to her son James. Ten years later the family remained in Soberton, with three children. They continued to live in this village, where David remained as school master into his sixties.

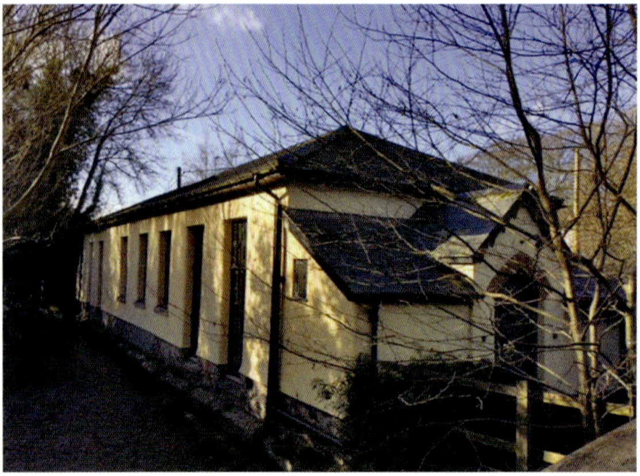

Fig. 2.7 The old school at Nether Wallop

By 1901, when David was 81 and Eliza 75, they had moved to Winchester. Born in Dublin, brought up in Guernsey and trained to teach in Salisbury – what a fascinating life! During her long life Eliza witnessed so many changes in education, in society and throughout the world. Although she only taught for a few years, Eliza appears to have been dedicated to supporting her family and her husband, the village schoolmaster, for many fruitful years.

Eliza's life ended sadly. The 1911 Census shows that Eliza Hills, born in Dublin around 1826 was by now a patient in the Bromley Union Workhouse and Infirmary at Farnborough, Kent. Records were not always completely accurate but it does seem likely that this is 'our' Eliza. She is recorded as a widow having 'no occupation'. Eliza is likely to have been a patient in the infirmary where 80 females where located in 12 rooms. Conditions would have been poor and Eliza probably ended her days here. Why was that? She may well have become too ill and infirm to care for herself after her husband's death. Her daughter Harriet had died at the age of 39 and Eliza's son James was probably unable to care for his mother. In 1921 James was admitted to the workhouse in Bermondsey. Many records of deaths in the workhouse have been lost. If there was no one able to care for Eliza, then there was no other option at that time except the workhouse. What a miserable and tragic ending to Eliza's life!

3 Bound for Salisbury!

The Journey Begins

Between the years 1850–1870 students who were determined to train as teachers in Salisbury faced a long and arduous journey. However, by 1870 their journey time had reduced because of the expansion of the railways from Southampton and Weymouth.

Paddle steamers continued to plough their way across the English Channel. Over the years, several operators and owners had sought to provide ferry services. There were numerous closures, amalgamations of companies and stiff competition for custom. The steamers from Southampton were seen by the owners of the London and South Western Railway as a natural extension of the railway service from Southampton. They set up the South Western Steam Packet Company because an Act of Parliament did not allow the LSWR Company to operate ships. In 1845 they won the contract to carry mail to the Channel Islands, which increased the importance of the routes and also led to better ships. The paddle steamers for Southampton left from Jersey calling at Guernsey on their way across the Channel. St Peter Port harbour was enlarged in 1864 to accommodate increasing traffic. On 1 January 1870, the Channel Island service was increased to three times a day, except on Sundays.

Salisbury's first railway was a London and South West Railway (LSWR) branch from the main line at Bishopstoke (later known as Eastleigh) and terminating at Milford, Salisbury. It was situated in Tollgate Road on the southern edge of Milford Hill, quite close to St Martin's Church and school. The line opened for goods early in 1847 and later that year for passengers. It linked Salisbury to Bishopstoke which enabled a London connection. During the following years the College had strong connections with Eastleigh and many of the schools there were used for teaching practice. One can imagine the anxious students boarding the train at Milford wondering what awaited them!

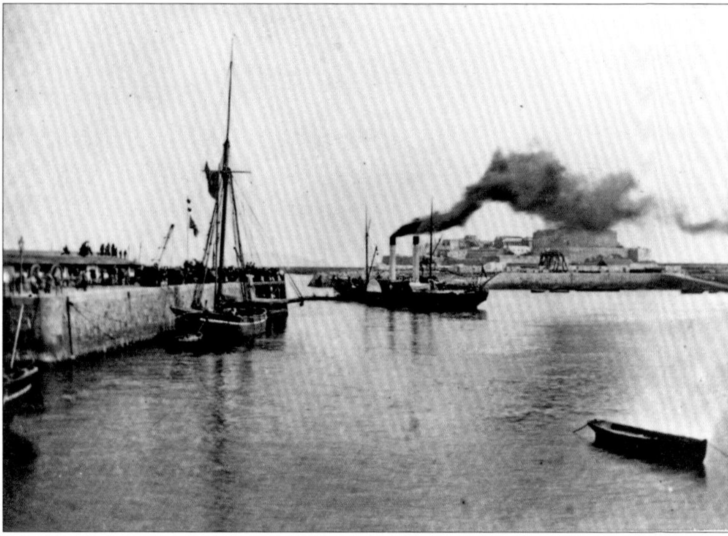

Fig. 3.1 The Weymouth and Channel Island Steam Packet *Cygnus* leaving St Peter Port harbour in 1864

There were great hopes in Salisbury that the coming of the railway would bring prosperity to the city. On 17 January 1847 the *Salisbury and Winchester Journal* reported great excitement as a goods train entered the Salisbury Station south of Milford. One citizen proclaimed that 'Salisbury might become the Manchester of the south!'

The Member of Parliament for Salisbury, Mr W.J. Chaplin, was also chairman of the LSWR. There was much poverty and hardship in Salisbury at this time and many poorer citizens were grateful for the 50 tons of coal which were distributed to them by Mr Chaplin.

The station had large coal bunkers which led to plenty of dust on the roads. The Railway Inn, also named The Dust Hole, is situated close to where the station would have been. The weary, thirsty and hungry students who arrived by train would have passed the doors of The Dust Hole, but of course they never entered the pub!

For nearly ten years Milford was the only station in Salisbury. It was now possible for the Channel Island students to disembark at Southampton and reach Salisbury by train from Bishopstoke on the LSWR. How much quicker this was than to travel by stagecoach just a few years earlier!

Milford continued to be used as a busy goods station with many cattle trucks arriving full of sheep and cows. The animals would then be driven through the city to the Market Place and on more than one occasion they escaped, causing havoc. Nothing remains of the station at Milford, as it was demolished in 1967.

In 1857 a link from Andover to Milford Junction was introduced providing a more direct route up and down to London. In May 1859 the LSWR opened Fisherton station, to coincide with the opening of the Salisbury and Yeovil railway. As services increased the station was extended. The GWR established its own terminus station adjacent to the LSWR initially to serve the Westbury line. From 1948 the GWR and LSWR stations were in common ownership under British Rail.

The Royal Mail had been shipped to the Channel Islands since 1791 in sailing cutters based at Weymouth, later changing to steamships. Passengers had also been accommodated, which enabled several Dorset families to settle in the Channel Islands. For many years Channel Islanders had called for a passenger service from Weymouth, as this route had a shorter sea crossing than Southampton and it was less likely to suffer from fog, which frequently delayed the ships on the Southampton route.

It was possible to travel by ship to London from Jersey and Guernsey, but the voyage was longer and more expensive. In 1863 an advertisement in the Jersey Almanac announced the service by the Weymouth and Channel Islands Steam Packet Company with its three steamships, the Aquila, the Brighton and the Cygnus. The reliability of the early steamships was a problem and it was necessary to have a good-sized fleet. Tickets cost 31 shillings first class from London to either Guernsey or Jersey and 21 shillings second class.

The disadvantage of the ferry link to Weymouth had been the lack of a railway connection. With the arrival of the Great Western Railway (GWR) line from Westbury in January 1857, this obstacle was removed and a regular passenger service between the islands and Weymouth began. It did not immediately become the most favoured port and there were disagreements between companies for nearly thirty years until in 1889 the GWR took over the Weymouth to Jersey and Guernsey route. In 1857, students who had taken the ferry to Weymouth could have taken the train on the GWR via Yeovil and Castle Cary to Westbury and then changed for Salisbury.

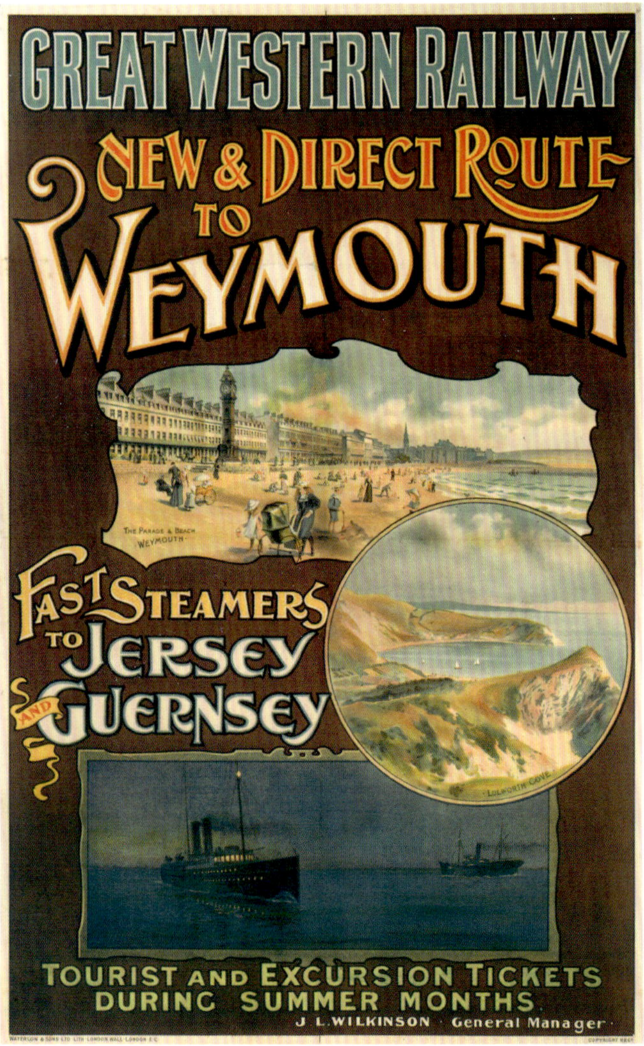

Fig. 3.2 GWR Poster 1922–47

The GWR opened their broad gauge line from Westbury to Salisbury on 30 June 1856. The brick-built station (designed by Isambard Kingdom Brunel) was on the west side of Fisherton Street in Salisbury.

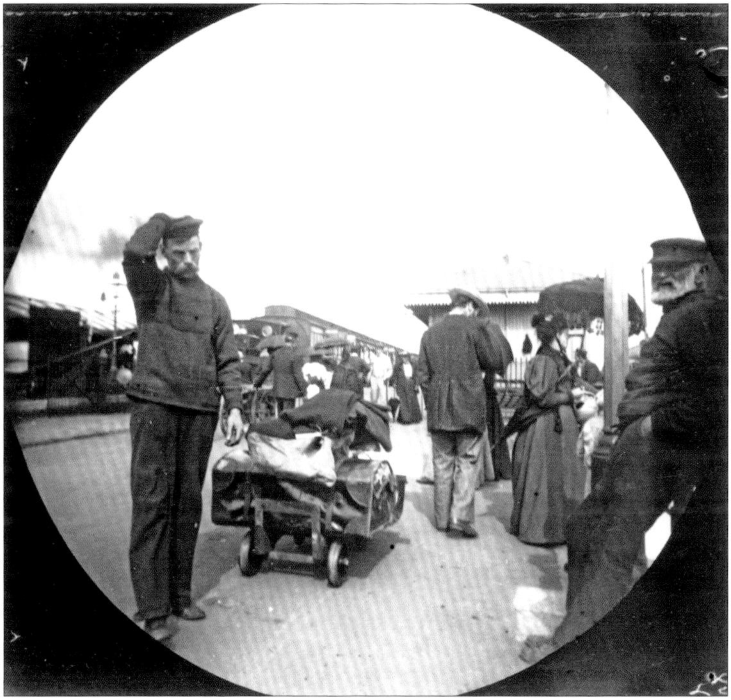

Fig. 3.3 A GWR 'boat train' meets the Channel Island ferry at Weymouth Quay c 1900. Is this a Salisbury student embarking?

The building of the railway and its extensions would have had a significant impact on the lives of Salisbury students and was of great use to those students coming from outside the city. Their journey to Salisbury was over, but an even more difficult journey was about to begin, as they embarked upon their rigorous training.

1856–1857 Mary Ann Beavan
A sixteen year-old student

Early retirement? This was certainly out of the question for Mary Ann Beavan who was still teaching in Guernsey aged 71, in 1911. Her teacher training in Salisbury, which she began in 1856 at the early age of sixteen, stood her in good stead and she had a long and industrious career in education.

Her father, Lawrence Crew Beavan, was born in London in 1778 in St Martin-in-the-Fields. Her parents moved to Guernsey and Mary Ann was born in St Peter Port, Guernsey on 23 April 1840. At this time the family resided at Les Amballes. She was baptised at St Peter Port Parish Church (The Town Church).

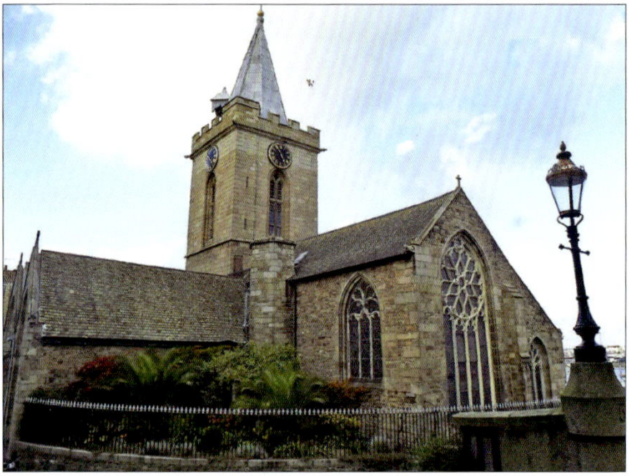

Fig. 3.4 St Peter's Church (The Town Church) St Peter Port

Why did her parents move to Guernsey from London? During the years 1841–1851 many people emigrated from England to Guernsey, possibly because the cost of living in Guernsey was lower at this time. The majority settled in St Peter Port. Mary Ann's father had been a baker in St Martin's Lane, London, and maybe her parents thought that this would be a great boon in their new life in Guernsey where they ran a lodging house.

Mary Ann's College entry form from 1856 confirms that her parents remained in St Peter Port and that her father had died in 1850. In 1851, when Mary Ann was ten, the family, which included her mother and three siblings, still lived in St Peter Port. Mary Ann's mother continued to run the lodging house. Mary Ann was educated at a school in St Peter Port which was supported and run by the Anglican Church. What type of education would Mary Ann have received? She probably attended the National School that opened in the St John's district in 1838–39, as she had close links with this parish. This school was enlarged in 1858 and accommodated boys and girls. In 'Education in Guernsey', Peter J. Girard described the school environment:

> 'The boys' school consisted of one room 45 feet by 30 feet and the girls' school was of the same size and situated above the boys' school whilst in 1841 an infant school was added. Essentially one large classroom was used where the Head, seated on a dais, could keep the whole school in view'.
>
> 1977 Report of the Societe Guernesiaise

Course of Instruction for the Guernsey Parochial Schools for the year 1861

First Class

Scripture History The subject to be chosen by the Rector
Catechism To be learnt by heart, with simple explanation
Reading English and French
Grammar French Parsing; English Parsing; Translations from French into English and from English into French
Arithmetic Mental Tables; Weights and Measures; Simple and Compound Rules with Multiplication and Division by one, two and three figures; Reduction Proportion Practice
Geography Map of the World. The boys will draw the map of Guernsey from memory

Mary Ann's education must have been at least satisfactory as her College record states 'Fair, reads better than most'.

Prior to the late 1840s, the National Schools in Guernsey received no grants or funding from the British Government. However, a successful grant application by St Peter Port Central School led to further grants and HMI (Her Majesty's Inspectorate) inspections in other Guernsey schools. The teaching of French was a condition of a financial subsidy to St John's National School, by the States (Guernsey Government) in 1849. Later, awards were not dependent on the teaching of French, although several schools undertook voluntary teaching of the subject. In 1850 a States Parochial Education Committee was set up to oversee funding and exert some influence over the public schools in the nine country parishes. The parishes were also expected to make a financial contribution to the running of the schools.

Mary Ann may have been a monitor at St John's School from the age of ten and then promoted to a pupil-teacher at thirteen. The pupil-teacher scheme was originally set up by Dr J. Phillips Kay (later Kay-Shuttleworth). Carefully selected pupils aged thirteen or above who fulfilled certain moral, scholastic and physical conditions could be apprenticed to headteachers for five years. They taught the younger pupils throughout the day, usually drilling them in the basic subjects, in which they themselves had been drilled. They received instruction from the Headteacher for at least one and a half hours either before or after school. Every year they faced an examination by HMI. If this was satisfactory they received payment of approximately £10 for boys and £7 for girls. At the end of their apprenticeship, the pupil-teachers were able to take an examination leading to a Queen's Scholarship which would finance their entrance to Training College. They received a maintenance grant of £25 for men and £20 for women and were known as 'Queen's Scholars'. In 1856 these scholars were required to agree that they would teach for a certain number of years, or they had to repay the grant.

What kind of a reception did the students from a pupil-teacher background receive at Salisbury? A student's reminiscence from 'The Red Book' in 1860 makes interesting reading:

> 'As yet Pupil Teachers were a novelty – I think there were about two in our number, and these excellent of their kind–but as they began to pour in, in great numbers, in the following year, we regarded their coming rather as an intrusion to our family party, and we did not readily take to each other. While they despised us for want of a knowledge of

technicalities which they were familiar with, we on our part thought them "one-idea'd", wanting in general knowledge and in some cases pedantic and conceited.'

Evidence over time indicates that gradually the students from a pupil-teacher background were accepted and became part of the College family.

There were numerous private schools in Guernsey for the minority that could afford them. In 1849, Brouard's *Guernsey Almanack* listed fifty schools of different sizes including some which were both boarding and day schools. Mrs Spurgeon planned to open her school in 1854.

BOARDING AND DAY SCHOOL FOR YOUNG LADIES,
conducted by Mrs S SPURGEON

Mrs SPURGEON hopes to enjoy a measure of public patronage, in consequence of her long experience and particular method of imparting instruction, it being eminently calculated to draw out the minds of the young and make them think and enquire after cause and effect. This end once accomplished, it is astonishing to see the rapid progress a child makes. The pupils will be examined annually in the presence of their parents and friends.

Hours of attendance, from 9 till 3 o'clock,
with an hour's relaxation at noon.

NB No communication whatever with Mr Spurgeon's pupils,
there being separate entrances.

At the tender age of sixteen, Mary Ann left St Peter Port and travelled to Salisbury. What a journey to make at that young age! Salisbury Training College placed high importance on religious knowledge and Mary Ann would have faced a lengthy grilling in regard to this on entry.

How did she pay her fees? As she was only sixteen years old Mary Ann would have been a 'private scholar'. She was recommended by the Reverend C.P. Carey who also paid her premium. The Reverend Carteret Carey was vicar of St John the Evangelist Church in Les Amballes, St Peter Port, from 1846–1858. The Church was opened in 1838 in order to provide for the rapidly increasing population of the island. By

1843, the church was already too small as the population of the area had increased to 3,000 and the church could only seat 600. Money was raised to enlarge the church.

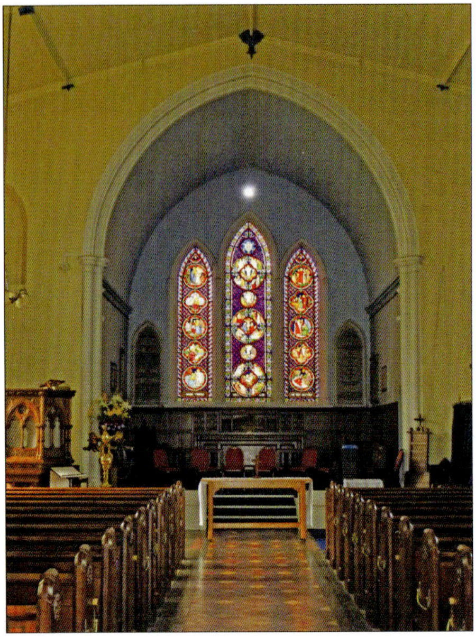

Fig. 3.5 St John's Church where Mary Ann worshipped

When Mary Ann arrived at College she was said to be in very good health. Sadly this was far from true for many of Guernsey's residents at this time. There were many social problems particularly in St Peter Port. The population in town was higher than that of all the other island parishes together. There were many immigrants from Ireland, England and France and the other Channel Islands. The 1851 Census shows that the migrants from England and Ireland comprised 21 per cent of the island's total population. There were many single women in St Peter Port whose husbands were at sea and who therefore found it hard to make ends meet. There were numerous pubs in the town and alcohol was 'cheap and plentiful' according to *The Star*, a Guernsey newspaper. Food was expensive and wages low both in the town and in the country. *The Star* described the mid 1840s as 'the famine period'. Many homes in town were cramped and insanitary and there was another cholera outbreak in 1849 following the earlier one in 1832.

Bands of unruly urchins were said to roam the streets. People were often forced to use the second-hand shops in the town and use pawnbroking as a way of having just enough money to survive. Those who could not survive in these ways were admitted to the Town Hospital (Workhouse). The average annual admission in this period was about 200. In 1850, 75 per cent of St Peter Port residents owned no property.

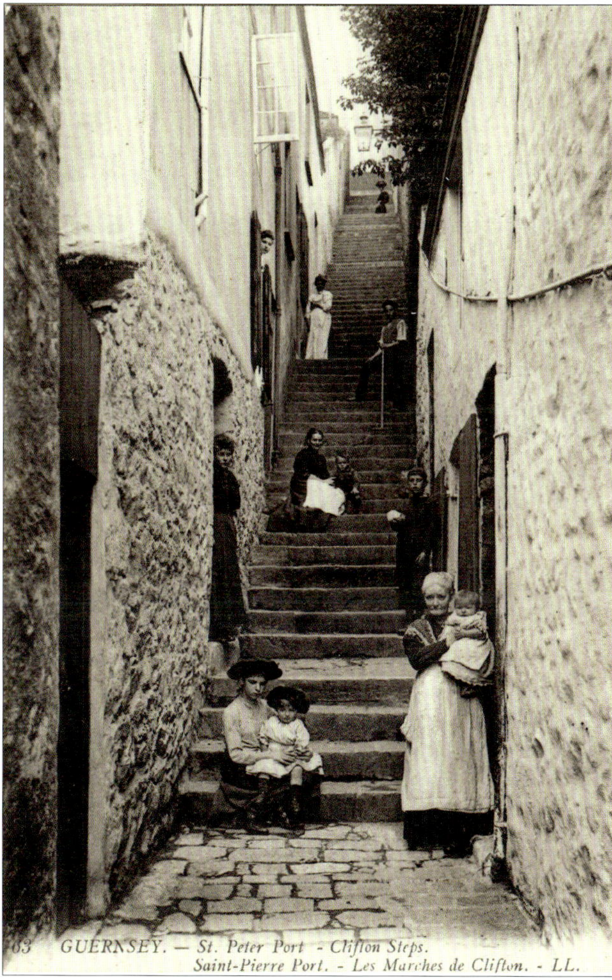

Fig. 3.6 Clifton Steps St Peter Port circa 1909

The Priaulx Library contains fascinating memoirs of the town at this time. The *Evening Press* of 1940 included an interesting memoir looking back to 1860:

> 'The Town Church was almost swamped beneath an encroaching growth of tenements and buildings stretching almost up to the porch of the North Door. Even the South and East sides of the church were built around until it almost seemed smothered in a sea of houses'.

The town lamplighter would have been a welcome sight for Mary Ann. The memoir continues:

> 'What I remember most vividly, however, was the nightly visit of the lamplighter, who brought his ladder over his shoulder to reach the street light. Although gas was then in use, the lamplighter carried a lamp from which he lit a spill or match, and afterwards there was always the thrill of watching him slide down the ladder to earth again'.

The interviewee recalled common disorderly scenes at night at that time. 'Street fights between the garrison and civilians and the stone-workers and anyone who would oblige them, kept the town Police force busy'.

Would Mary Ann have met Victor Hugo, one of Guernsey's most famous residents? The famous novelist and poet was exiled from France and lived on the island from 1856 until his return to France in 1870. He loved Guernsey, enjoying walks along the beautiful coastline and picnics on the beach with his family, especially at Cobo Bay. He loved Guernsey for 'its breath of ocean and breath of flowers'. Victor Hugo lived in Hauteville House, St Peter Port and it was here that he entertained friends and family. He repudiated the idea of deserving any merit for what he was doing, as it was merely a 'simple and positive duty'.

Victor Hugo was concerned that so many children were seriously ill and severely undernourished. He selected 40 children and made sure they were given some fresh meat and a small glass of wine each fortnight which ensured that the health of the children was much improved. It was whilst he lived in Guernsey that his famous novel *Les Miserables* was completed. Perhaps he based some of the children and people he created upon those that he met. He set his book *Toilers of the Sea* on

Guernsey and dedicated it to the inhabitants: 'The rock of hospitality and freedom…the island of Guernsey, severe yet gentle, my present refuge'.

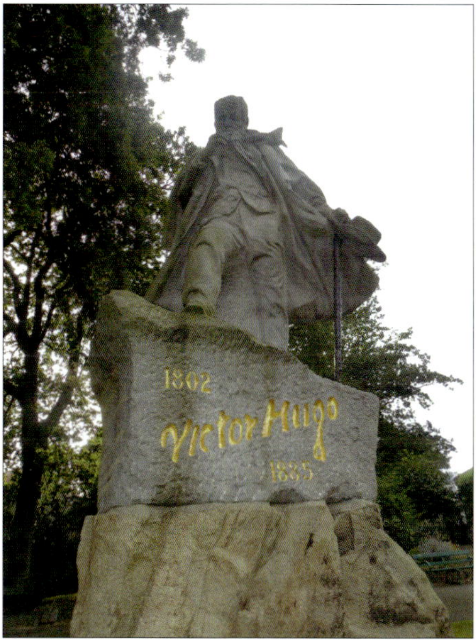

Fig. 3.7 Statue of Victor Hugo in Candie Gardens Guernsey

In 1851, the Beavan family were living in Amballes, St Peter Port and by 1861 had moved to 37 St John's Road, just a few doors away from the vicar at number 42. It was the vicar of this parish who found a teaching post for Mary Ann when she returned to the island from College.

It was 13 years since Eliza Smith arrived at College from Guernsey in 1843 and there had been many changes to College life during that time. By now the Training College had moved into its new home 'The King's House' in Salisbury Cathedral Close. In 1856 thirty students were admitted. Canon Steward recorded that:

> 'The College accommodation was now increased to 60 students, and the success of the year was 'entirely exceptional and unprecedented.' In Mr Inspector Cook's words 'seven out of fifteen second year students being placed in the first class, a proportion not only larger by far than in any former year at Salisbury, but exceeding the largest proportion from any other institution'.

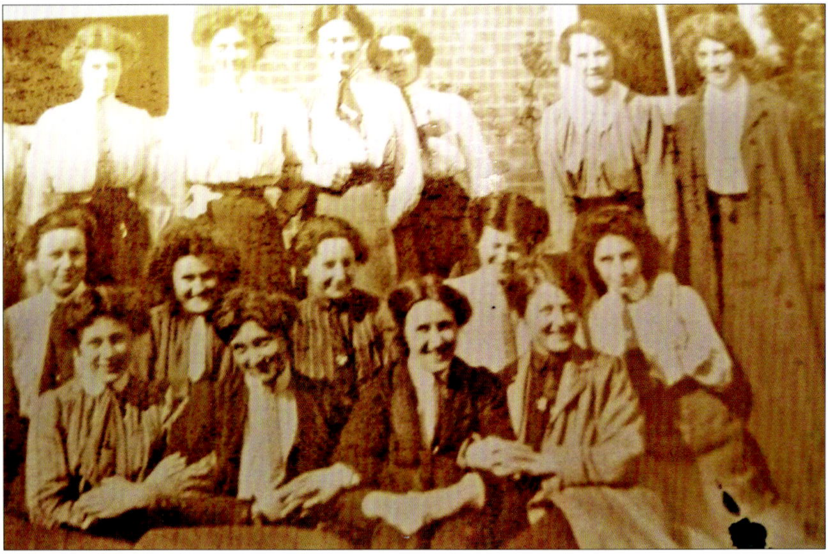

Fig. 3.8 Some of the College students

A student at the College in 1854 described her time there which would have been very similar to that of Mary Ann just two years later. Students practised giving lessons in the Model School situated at the College and also at local schools such as St Martin's. Examinations, inspections and tests were regular and rigorous. The student listed the College curriculum:

> 'Scripture, Church History, English Grammar, Reading: '1st year Milton, 2nd year Cowper (Even now I shudder to think of what that ordeal was, to read aloud before Mrs Duncan), Domestic Economy, English History, Geography, Music, both theory and singing. One harmonium in Schoolroom, which was generally used to accompany our evening hymn. An old piano in the Class-room, needlework, five mornings a week, from 9 to 10 in winter; during summer in the afternoons'.

Mary Ann's health remained 'good' throughout her time at College. The entry form shows that her progress varied. She was said to have 'a peculiar temper', but perhaps this was because of her young age and being so far from family and friends at home. For someone so young, the conditions at College must have been especially tough. She left College at Christmas 1858: 'The clergyman of her own Parish to find her a situation in Guernsey'.

In 1861, aged 21, Mary Ann was working as a schoolmistress and living in the family home at St Peter Port with her mother and sisters. Ten years later she remained as a schoolmistress living at the same address. The Revised Code of 1862 had enormous impact in Guernsey and Jersey, as it did in England. In 1864 the States insisted that French be re-introduced as a subject. Teaching was not an easy option!

In the 1881 Census, Mary Ann is shown as the head of the house and working as a 'public school mistress'. By 1891, she lived at Staverton House, St John's, Guernsey, with a lodger, Martha Finch, who was a tobacconist's assistant. In 1901 Mary Ann was teaching at the Girls' Central School. At this time numbers on roll at the school were judged to be too low and it was felt that younger teachers were required. Mary Ann left the school and from then on gave private lessons from home. The 1911 Census shows she was still teaching from home at this time. After a long and full life in education, Mary Ann Beavan died at the age of 75 at Staverton House on 17 August 1915, from abdominal cancer.

1859 – 1860 Emma Jane de Gruchy
Jersey born and bred

It was not until some years later that other Channel Island students followed the example of Eliza Smith and crossed the sea to train as teachers in Salisbury. During the late 1850s and early 1860s students started arriving from Jersey.

The College Register shows that Emma Jane de Gruchy entered Salisbury Training College in January 1859. Emma was born in the country parish of Trinity in the north of the island in 1839. The 1841 Census records the family as living in New Street, St Helier where Emma's father, Philip, was a shoemaker. By 1851 they were living in Trinity again. Perhaps they had left the town because there was too much competition for business. Setting up a workshop in a village may have been more profitable. Another possibility is that Emma's mother, Mary, wanted to return to Trinity, where she had been born. It is likely that some of her family lived in this parish.

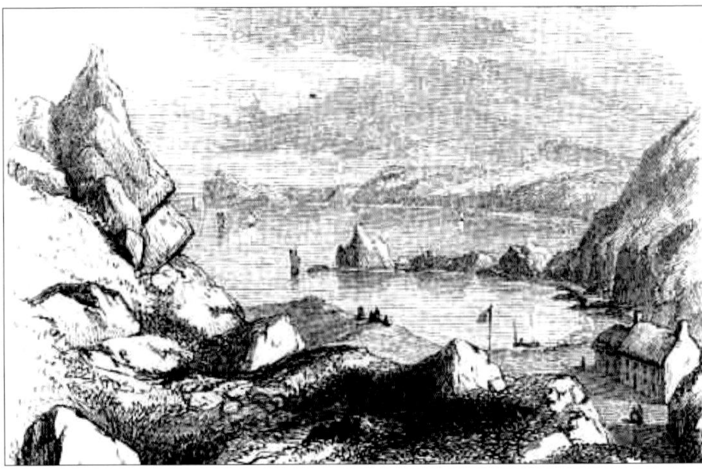

Fig. 3.9 Bouley Bay from an 1856 guide book

Emma's childhood in the mid-1800s would have revolved around the parish of Trinity. Let's step back and see what life was like.

Horse-drawn carriages clattered through the narrow lanes, taking early tourists on sight-seeing trips. *Vraic* (seaweed) gatherers returned from the beaches at Grouville and St Ouen, their carts heavily laden with the seaweed that would manure their fields. Most people in the parish had small plots of land, and in addition to spreading vraic, they would have dried it, before burning it on their fires, with the salty smell filling their houses. Perhaps we can glimpse eleven year old Emma hurrying through the leafy lanes and down a steep track into Bouley Bay to watch the fishermen bring in their catch. There may have been some ormers and conger eels, both of which were considered to be delicacies. Emma's family probably enjoyed the fruits of low-water fishing and collected and ate local shellfish such as limpets, cockles, scallops and razor-fish. Dried cod from Newfoundland was also popular but the once thriving cod trade was by now decreasing.

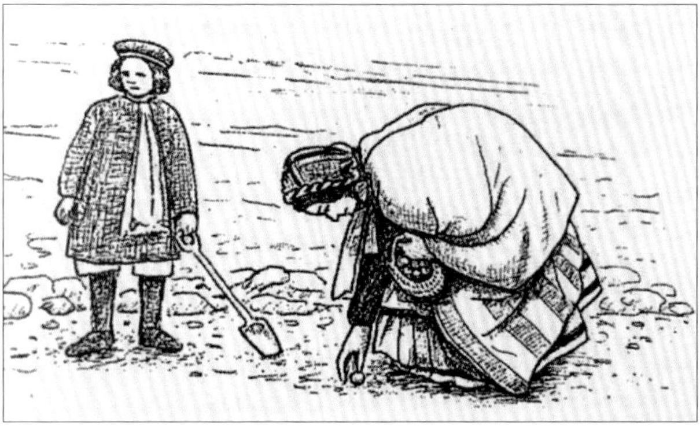

Fig. 3.10 Searching for cockles

Children were expected to take their turn at household chores and Emma would have taken her turn at cooking. If the family kept a pig, then pork would have been a mainstay of their diet. The family probably enjoyed Jersey bean crock, which is a slow cooked mixture of dried beans and pork. Pork fat would have been clarified and used as lard for making pastry and for cooking the rich and crumbly *merveilles* (Jersey wonders). Apples, as well as soft fruit and vegetables, were plentiful, and apple pie was frequently enjoyed.

The family probably took their cabbage loaves (traditional Jersey bread that is baked between cabbage leaves) to the village baker, to be cooked on Saturday nights.

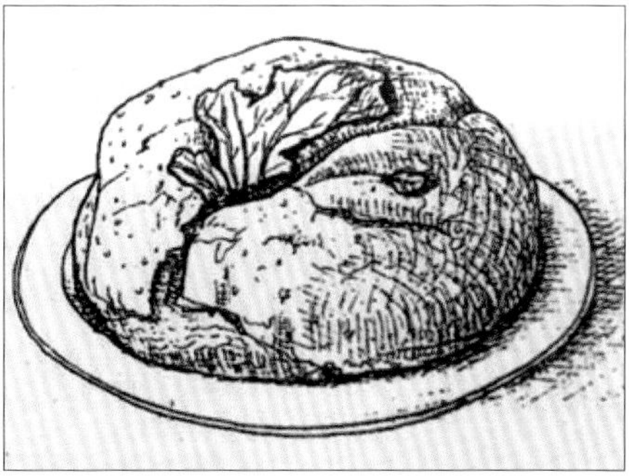

Fig. 3.11 Jersey cabbage loaf

The Revd William du Heaume, a strong supporter of education, was appointed the Rector of Trinity in 1850. He had considerable influence on Emma's life. The parish was already paying for a schoolmaster to teach its children and the new rector was willing for the school to be

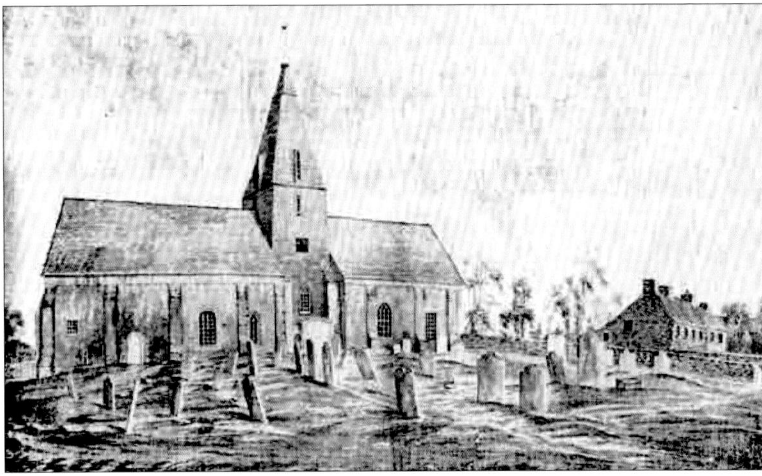

Fig. 3.12 Holy Trinity Church

run in the church. Emma and the other pupils would have attended classes that were held either behind a curtain or in the vestry. Absences were frequent due to bad weather, illness and people being unable to pay the weekly fee of one or two pennies. At certain times of the year, families kept their children at home to help on the farms with potato planting and vraic-gathering and spreading.

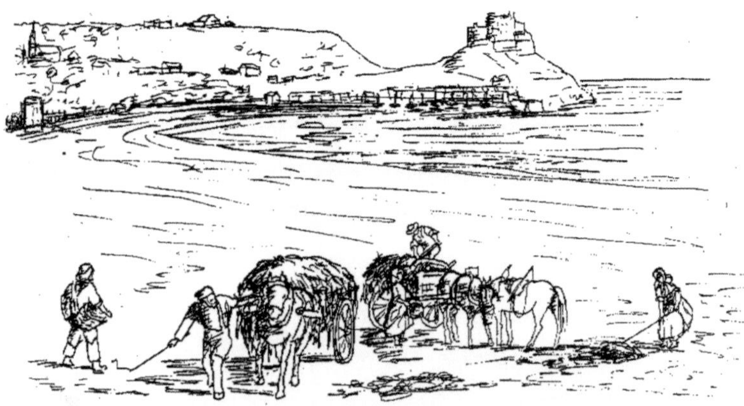

Fig 3.13 Gathering *vraic* at Grouville

The Revd William du Heaume campaigned for a proper school building and Trinity Parish School, which opened in 1854, was one of the earliest parish schools. These schools were founded through the support of the National Society. In Jersey, parents paid a small weekly charge and the States of Jersey paid an annual grant of £10 to each school. This was raised to ten or eleven shillings per child in 1909.

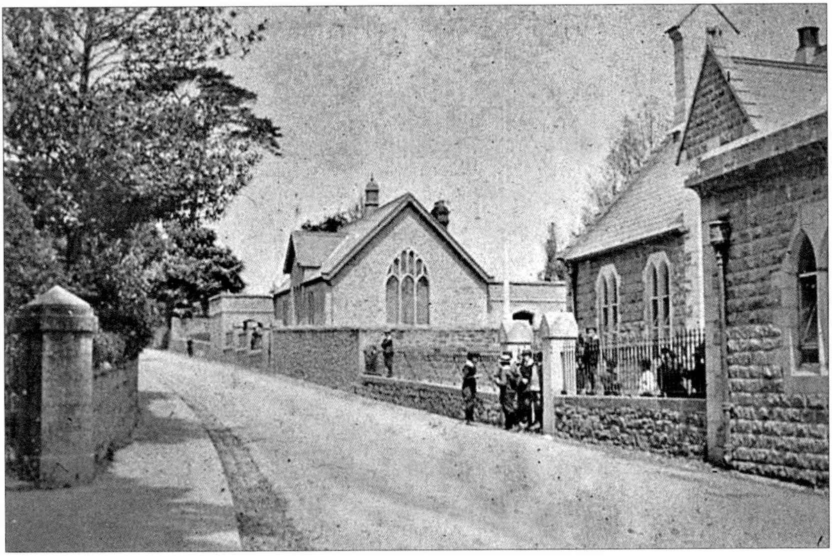

Fig. 3.14 Trinity School

Emma may not have attended Trinity Parish School in its fine new building. By 1854 she was 15 years old and a pupil-teacher at a 'school for girls' in St Helier. She probably lodged in the town as daily journeys would have been long and expensive. In 1859, she was 'recommended' to Salisbury Training College by the Revd Christopher Heath (the vicar of St Mark's Church) and her fees were 'paid by the government'. Emma started at the same time as Maria Verner, another student from Jersey and the daughter of a 'superannuated coastguard'. We can imagine that Emma and Maria probably felt both excited and apprehensive as they bade farewell to their proud parents and embarked on the boat that would take them to England. It was mid-winter and perhaps not the best time of year for a sea voyage, but the College year started in January. There were 61 students at the College in 1859.

Emma's 'state of acquirement' was described on her college registration form as 'fair'. Her health was 'generally good but subject to headaches'. During her two years in Salisbury she worked hard and comments on her progress were consistently 'good'. This was at a time when life at College was hard, so she certainly deserved the commendations. Reminiscences from a student who was at College in the 1850s were recorded in Canon Steward's Red Book and help us to imagine what life was like for Emma:

> 'On weekdays we were in the Schoolroom at 6.45am, Sundays at 7.45, and retired to bed at 9pm. Mistresses always in turns putting out gas at 10. Of course we began and ended the day with prayers'. Students attended services in the Cathedral with often three times a day on a Sunday. The students were also expected to help with domestic work. 'There was a great deal of unnecessary drudgery in those days. Three hours washing and six hours with a heavy mangle, or ironing in a hot laundry, in one week was too much, and keep up our lessons as well. This work came once a half year'.

> 'We never had luxuries in the way of food and for growing girls not always necessaries. We had two slices of bread and butter each for breakfast and tea; no more, hungry or not. No supper; but from 6pm to 8pm was too long to fast so it led to us having things from home. We were always allowed to have a hamper on our birthday. I slept in No 20 room but we kept more than 20 birthdays. We were all very united and happy, and shared every scrap of our birthday goodies...we had pudding on Fridays and Saturdays only, either suet or rice; no other kind was ever given us'.

Although life was very hard, lifelong friendships were made.

> 'Training was not all work, even in those days, and good laughs would some of us have in talking over our holiday evenings, Easter gatherings, Mrs Duncan's birthday party, our charades and musical evenings, our picnic to Stonehenge, our occasional long walks, blackberrying and watercress gathering.'

A lasting memory was the daily service of Communion in the Cathedral when students found peace and tranquillity and gained the strength they needed for their daily life at College at this time.

Emma finished her training at Christmas 1860 and returned to her island home – and right back to the parish of Trinity. She was appointed as schoolmistress to Trinity Parish School. The school had been open for six years and had about 70 children, but their attendance was still variable. Funds were needed to keep the school going and parishioners were frequently asked to dig deep in their pockets. In June 1861 it was recorded in the local newspaper that the proceeds from a 'tea meeting' on Midsummer Day were donated to the school. The tea was held at the Jardin d'Olivet and entertainment included a band and 'other amusements'.

The Headmaster was opposed to the growing use of English in the classroom and Emma was expected to teach her lessons in French. Perhaps she disliked this, or maybe her two years in Salisbury had convinced her that the mainland had more to offer. Whatever the reason, by the 1871 Census she was a 'certificated school mistress' aged 32 and working in Totnes, Devon. Maybe she then married and settled down in England. Did she miss Jersey? One visitor in the 1860s, struck by the beauty of the island, commented:

'No scene in nature can be more charming than this earthly paradise'.

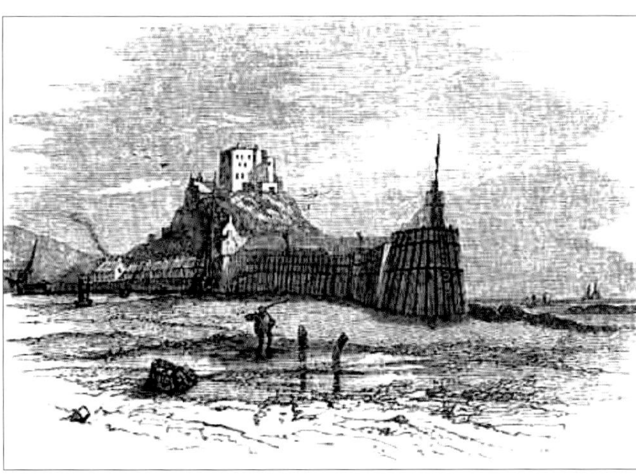

Fig. 3.15 Gorey Pier from a guide book dated 1856

1860–1861 Who was Virginia Butterell?

Virginia was born in St Peter's, Jersey in 1841. Her father was a gardener and her mother a schoolmistress. By 1851 her father had died and Virginia was living with her mother and four siblings in St Helier, Jersey. Her mother Elizabeth, was still working as a school mistress. Virginia was privately educated at a Dame School in St Helier. Could this have been a school run by her mother? Virginia was recommended to the College by the Dean of Jersey and her fees were paid by the government. She entered College in January 1860 and left at Christmas 1861.

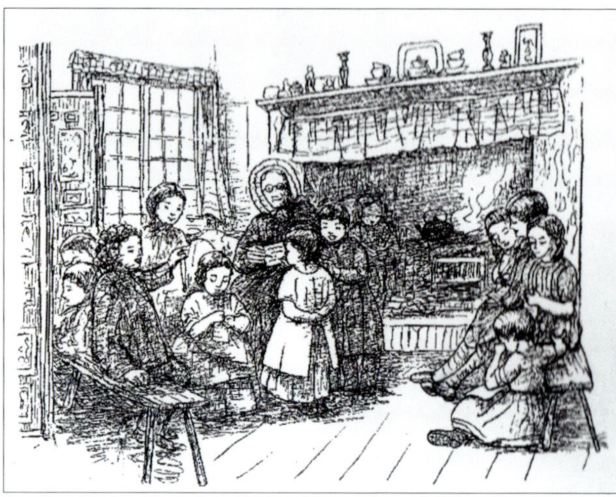

Fig. 3.16 A typical Dame School

On leaving College, Virginia taught for a while in Southampton at Marchwood School. The 1871 England Census shows that she was living as a boarder in Saltash, Cornwall, aged twenty five and working as a governess. The 'Red Book' compiled by Edward Steward, College Principal, indicates that by 1891 Virginia had returned to live in Jersey.

In the 'Red Book', there are 34 students listed for the year 1860 when Virginia was at College. One of her fellow students at this time was Mary Hardy, the sister of the famous Dorset poet and novelist, Thomas Hardy.

It is thought that Thomas Hardy visited Salisbury in 1860, possibly to accompany Mary to College. He visited Mary whilst she was at College and used her experiences when he wrote the novel *Jude the Obscure*. Kate Hardy, Mary's younger sister, also attended the College in 1877. Both students found College life tough, as Virginia would also have done. Students were often hungry, as was Sue Bridehead in *Jude the Obscure*:

> 'She confessed with something of shame, that she was dreadfully hungry. They were kept on very short allowances in the College. She told him about the school as it was at that date, and the rough living, and the mixed character of her fellow-students, gathered together from all parts of the diocese, and how she had to get up and work by gas light in the early morning, with all the bitterness of a young person to whom restraint was new'.

There was little food and rules were strict. Students were well behaved and adhered to the rules.

Rules to be observed in the Dormitories

1. Students to rise at six o'clock and be in the school-room at quarter to seven for Prayers.
2. To turn down the bedding and to open the windows before they leave their bedroom.
3. Not to enter each other's room without permission.
4. Not to take anything to the sick without leave.
5. Hats, Books Jackets etc not to be kept in the Dormitory cupboards.
6. No eatables of any kind, save biscuits, to be kept in boxes and no tea, cocoa to be made in bedrooms.
7. Dresses for Sunday use to be fetched from the Dress Cupboard before dark on Saturday afternoons and to be taken back before nine on Monday morning.
8. Students not to be in bedrooms during the day except Saturday afternoon.
9. Gas not to be lighted without permission.
10. At quarter to ten H S to see that silence is enforced for prayers.

11. Any case of sickness or things for repair to be reported to the Lady Superintendent.
12. No books except books of Devotion to be read in the Dormitories.
13. Cleanliness and tidiness to be observed and care taken of furniture etc.
14. The Head Student to be held responsible for observance of rules.

Canon Steward wrote:

> '1861 – The accommodation was increased, and 67 students were in residence, all but one being Queen's Scholars. HMI Cook drew the attention of the committee to the inadequacy of the staff and the need for a Museum. To the latter various gifts, including an owl, mole and iguana were received. At Christmas 36 students left, 29 after two, seven after one year's residence'.

What would Virginia have thought about the iguana?

In 1860 the new Practising Schools at St Edmunds were opened, and Mary Hardy, Virginia and the other students started to attend them regularly. The Model School, which was attached to the College, was also still in regular use.

Students appear to have enjoyed working in the Model School.

> 'Such a gem of a school where we sat and watched the work in order to report the lessons we heard, and to pick up methods that were to guide us in our own teaching'.

Reading out loud to Mrs Duncan was a regular requirement. One student reminisced in 1862, which was the last year of Mrs Duncan's reign as 'Matron'.

Mrs Duncan was known to say, "Now, my dear, open your teeth and speak distinctly". This had the disastrous effect of locking the teeth, so that the lips even refused to open'.

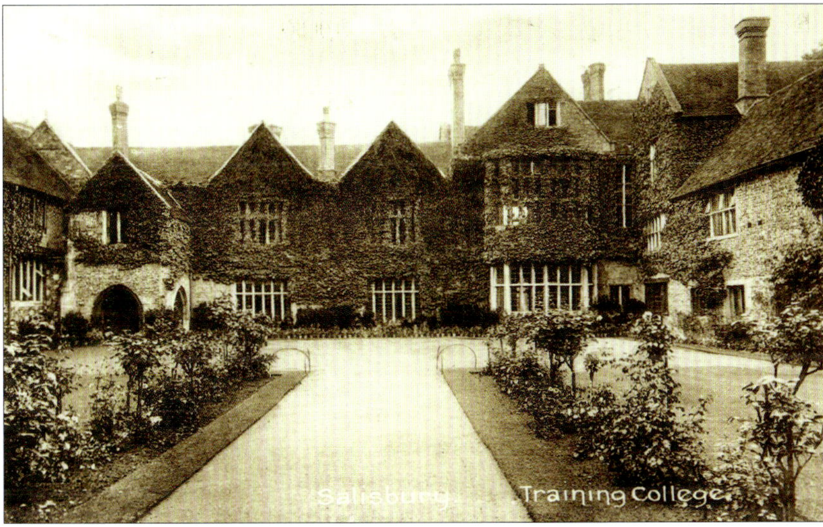

Fig. 3.17 Salisbury Training College

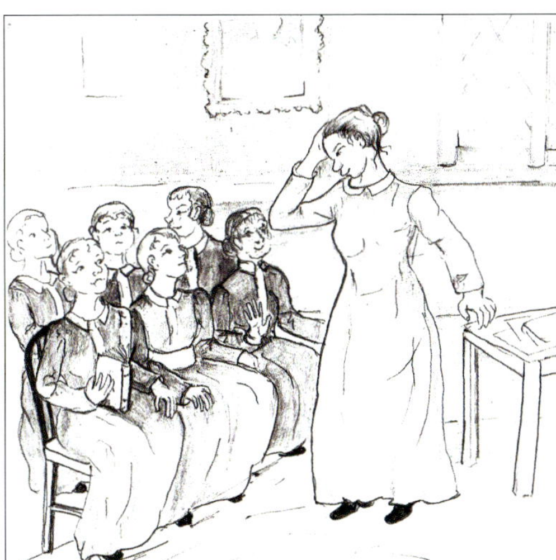

Fig. 3.18 'Whose turn is it to speak next'?

Students, including Virginia and Mary, were expected to help with some chores before breakfast, for example, in the pantry. There were fires to light, washing up and scrubbing and cleaning to be done. A happy memory was the Saturday dinner which was chosen and cooked by the students. There was a Cookery School in place at the College at this time, where the students and children from local schools learnt to cook wholesome food. Needlework featured high in the curriculum and in free time such as during the Easter week holiday, when students made 'wonderful specimen shirts'.

In *Jude the Obscure*, Thomas Hardy described Melchester (Salisbury) and the Cathedral:

> 'Melchester was a quiet and soothing place, almost entirely ecclesiastical in its tone…Standing under the walls of the most graceful architectural pile in England he paused and looked up. The lofty building was visible as far as the roof-ridge; above, the dwindling spire rose more and more remotely, till its apex was quite lost in the mist drifting across it'.

With only 34 students in the 1860 College year group, Virginia Butterell and Mary Hardy would have worked and spent their time together. Did Virginia ever meet the famous poet and novelist on one of his visits to his sister in Salisbury? We will never know, but what is certain is that Thomas Hardy was very much aware of the conditions under which the Salisbury students were trained at this time.

1862 – 1863 Emily Hitchings
She spread her wings and travelled far

Emily Hitchings was born in Jersey in 1843 and joined Salisbury Training College in 1862. Her father was described on the registration form as 'a Classical Professor'. Emily was, like Emma Jane de Gruchy three years earlier, 'recommended' to the College by the Revd Christopher Heath who can be found in the 1861 Census as 'the curate of St Mark's Church.'

St Mark's, which opened in 1844, was built with English immigrants in mind as they found that the services in French at the Town Church were unintelligible. Emily's parents were both born in England. They probably moved to the island in the late 1830s and are likely to have joined this well-to-do congregation with their children. Houses were springing up and there were many new residents.

When Queen Victoria visited the island in 1846, a triumphal arch of welcome was built across David Place in front of St Mark's. Emily would only have been three years old, but perhaps she heard as 'the bells pealed forth a joyous sound as the Sovereign passed' and children sang the National Anthem. It was a day of joy and celebration.

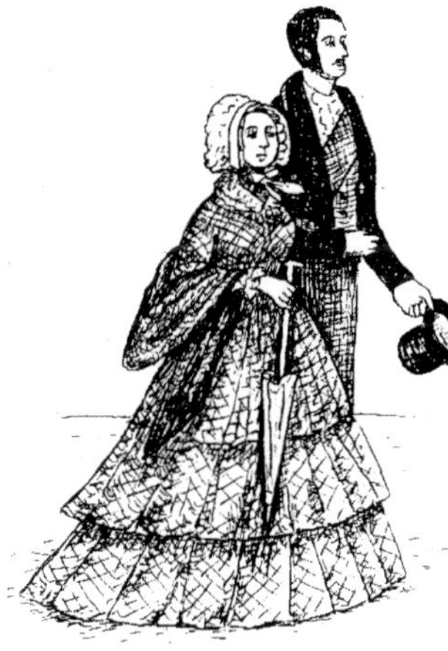

Fig. 3.19 Visit of Queen Victoria & Prince Albert

The congregation gave generously to worthwhile causes and it was through their efforts that St Mark's School was built. Emily attended the school and we can imagine her life as she grew up in St Helier.

St Helier in 1860 was quite a metropolis. It was a thriving, expanding town where tailors, sailors, dressmakers, carpenters, drapers, blacksmiths and cobblers rubbed shoulders with painters, glaziers, fishermen, milliners, printers, grocers, shipbuilders, artists, bakers and merchants – to name but a few. Trade was growing as a result of improving links with the outside world. Roads were being widened so that trucks with exports including potatoes, tomatoes and flowers could reach the harbours more easily. St Helier, like Salisbury, suffered from cholera epidemics from the 1830s, but by the 1860s pollution in the town was under control, sewers were being laid and fresh water was being supplied. Emily, whose home was first in Colomberie, then in Great Union Road and then in Duhamel Place would have seen old buildings being swept away to make room for the new houses needed for the increasing population. Tourism was developing as a local industry and visitors enjoyed using bathing machines and beach huts and going on boat trips and excursions. Life was opening up.

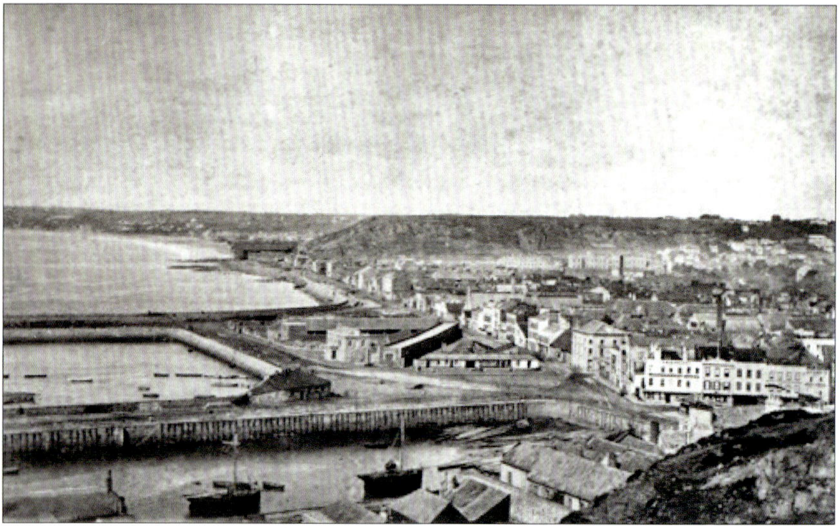

Fig. 3.20 St Helier 1866 by George Bashford

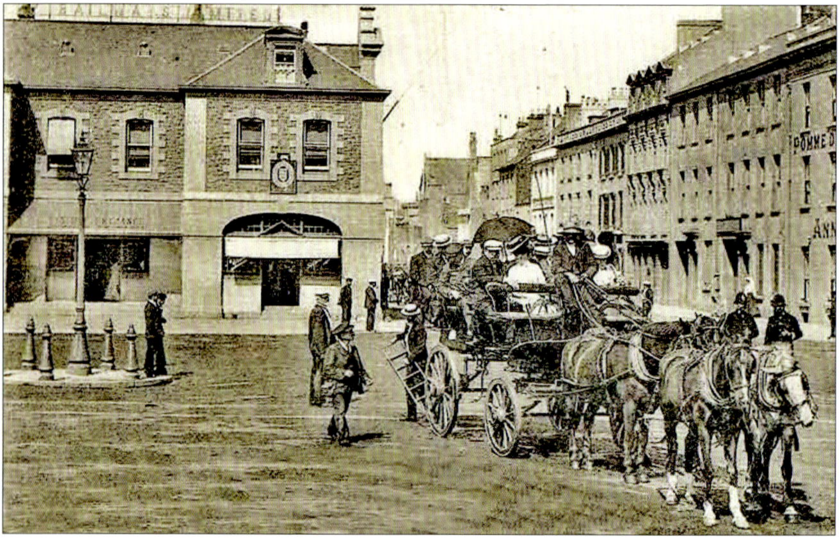

Fig. 3.21 An excursion leaves the Weighbridge

The Public Library had opened in 1811 and Emily, whose father was an academic, would have been encouraged to read books at home. She may have attended concerts given by The Musical Society of Jersey and sales of work organised by ladies from the church. The occasion when the 500 pupils from St Mark's School were entertained by parishioners for tea and games would have been a real highlight.

> 'THE CHILDREN OF ST MARK'S SCHOOL were given a holiday on Thursday afternoon. Under the guidance of their Masters and Mistresses, the children, numbering about 500, proceeded to the residence of Gifford Le Quesne Esq, Fonthill, where they were regaled with tea and cake. The fete was attended by a large number of the members of St Mark's congregation; and numerous play-games enlivened the evening. After the tea and cake had been partaken of, the Rev Christopher Heath, Minister of St Mark's, and others, assisted in adding to the happiness of the juvenile meeting. The children returned to their homes about seven o'clock.
>
> *Jersey Independent and Daily Telegraph,* 25 Sept 1858

Emily and her family probably also went on horse-drawn omnibuses for outings and picnics along the coast. She would have played on the beaches and paddled, but may not have learnt to swim. Despite the dangerous seas around the island and the many wrecks and drownings, most islanders, including sailors and fishermen, did not learn to swim.

The Jersey Swimming Club was founded in 1865 following the tragic deaths of two young boys who drowned in front of onlookers who could not swim.

Emily's parents would have paid one or two pence a week for her education at St Mark's. Her elementary schooling was based on religious instruction, reading, writing and arithmetic. Susan and Caroline Dowland attended the school at the same time as Emily and they too went on to train in Salisbury in the 1860s. St Mark's was one of a number of elementary schools in St Helier, along with many small private schools.

> 'Comparatively speaking, St Helier was better off as regards Educational Schools than most large English towns.'
>
> *Jersey Independent and Daily Telegraph,* 21 March 1860

The instruction at St Mark's was in English. A letter in the newspaper in 1860 pointed out that most of the island education was in English and the acquisition of French was increasingly seen as an extra accomplishment.

> 'In Churches and Chapels English shares with French, in schools the English has the mastery. Why then should the monopoly which maintains French as the exclusive language of The Royal Court and the States be longer tolerated'
>
> *Jersey Independent and Daily Telegraph*, 1860

The British Government had responsibility for education in Jersey and the unwelcome arrival of the Revised Code of 1862 had an enormous impact, as it did in England. Grants to schools were to be based on pupil attendance and on the success of pupils examined in basic skills. This became known as 'Payment by Results' and was extremely unpopular with teachers. A further requirement for Jersey was that French had to be re-introduced into the curriculum. This requirement was so severe that schools had to teach French for up to four hours every day in order to get the results that would guarantee their grants.

> 'The English Code, with all its unfairness, mysticism and severity is likewise the Code for the Jersey Public Elementary schools, about twenty in number. Teachers and children must needs be troubled with 'Code requirements' which turn education into mere 'cram'.
>
> The *Star*, March 1888

Before going to college, Emily worked as a pupil-teacher at a boarding school in St Helier. This was one of the seventy or more small private schools that had arisen in response to the demand from newly arrived English immigrants for schools that provided something better than the dame schools.

> 'The dame schools are in the primitive style and are intended more to take care of children and leave their mothers at liberty, than for any educational purposes.'
>
> *Jersey Independent and Daily Telegraph,* 21March 1860

Emily's 'state of acquirement' when she entered college in 1862 was 'fair', suggesting that she had received a good foundation in education.

She was awarded a Queen's Scholarship. Her health was described as 'very good'. (When Susan Dowland arrived in 1863 her health was described as 'pretty good but rather weak in hot weather.' Perhaps Susan's work had not been up to the mark during a hot island summer!)

1862 was marked by the resignation of Mrs Duncan, who had been the Lady Superintendent of the College since it started in 1841. Students remembered Mrs Duncan with affection and respect as is shown by reminiscences from this last year of her 'reign'.

> 'It was small wonder that as soon as we entered her presence we felt that training had begun in earnest. From henceforth as long as we were inmates of the King's House all must be governed as to studies, sleeping, eating, walking, and dressing'.

Canon Edward Steward, who became Principal of the College in 1890, wrote in the 'Red Book' that Mrs Duncan's work had been greatly appreciated and that she was highly regarded. He mentions her ability, her sound judgement and her practical good sense.

> 'She had watched over the Institution and moulded the character of its inmates since its formation, nearly 22 years before, more than 500 students having been under her care'.

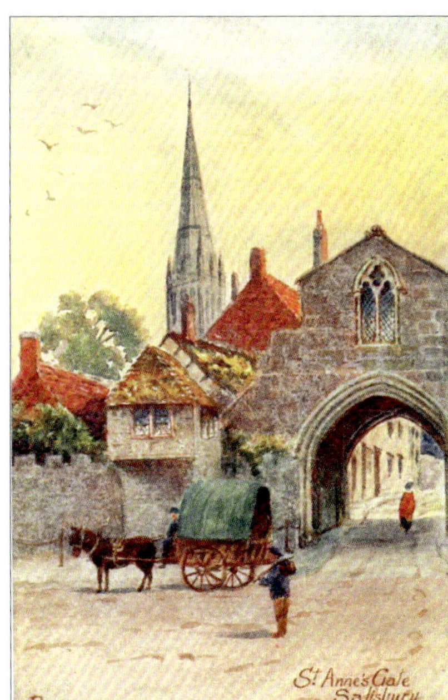

Fig. 3.22 St Ann's Gate, Salisbury

Even in these early days, the students were in great demand and were highly esteemed by schools. The Revd William Butler, wrote in 1861 to ask for another teacher in his school. He already had a teacher who had trained at the College and his letter said that she 'has done us great good, and gives me the highest opinion of the Salisbury Training School'.

Emily's progress at college was consistently 'good' – she was a keen student who made the most of her time at Salisbury. She was ready for the next challenge. Where would it be? Would her island home draw her back?

In fact, Emily remained on the mainland for several years. Her first appointment in 1863 was to be the Mistress of Wilton Infants School, just outside Salisbury. Wiltshire Community History records that Emily was the sole certificated teacher and was responsible for about 180 infants with the help of two pupil teachers. This must have been a demanding start to her long career!

By 1871, when she was 28 years old, Emily was living with her family in Duhamel Place, a short walk from the centre of St Helier. She was teaching at a local school. Emily is likely to have returned home in order to support her parents. Her father was unwell and died in 1877.

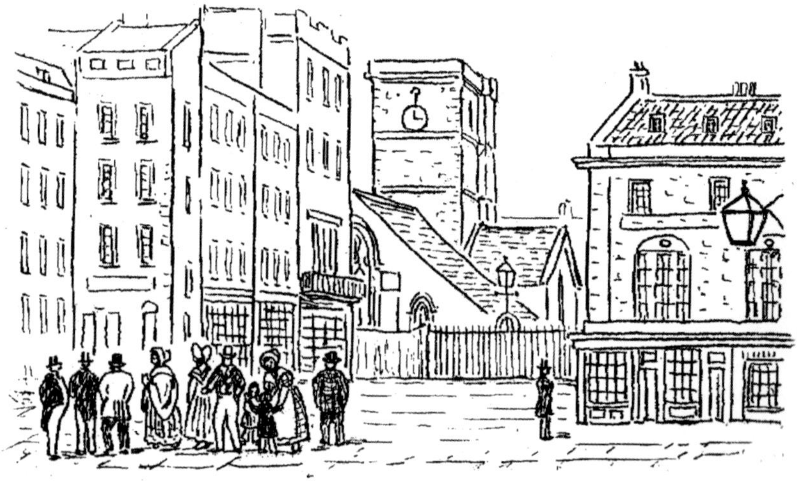

Fig. 3.23 St Helier in the late 19th century

Emily's story suggests that the mainland was really where she wanted to be. By the time of the 1881 Census she and her mother were living in Colwich, a village in the Lichfield diocese in the north Midlands, close to the river Trent. Emily was a schoolmistress here and she and her mother may have lived in the schoolhouse which dates from 1841 and is close to the parish church of St Michael and All Angels. The Grand Trunk Canal was nearby and there would have been plenty to see as the canal was widely used to transport raw materials to the potteries in Stoke-on-Trent and to distribute fragile finished goods. Emily's mother died whilst they were in Colwich and Emily decided to move again. We can imagine her waiting at Colwich Railway Station and wondering what the future would bring.

The 1891 Census finds Emily as the schoolmistress in Claverton, a village in an agricultural area just outside Bath in Somerset. It was rather like Colwich in that the River Avon and the Kennet and Avon Canal were nearby and, once again, the village was served by a railway line. Communications were improving and farm production was growing, but many of Emily's pupils would have come from impoverished rural homes. Amenities such as mains water and sewerage were reaching larger towns, but villages had to wait longer.

Emily was clearly keen to see as much of the country as possible! Her next move was to Stocking Pelham, a small village near Bishops Stortford in Hertfordshire. She was the village schoolmistress and the 1901 Census records her as a 'boarder' in a local house. At this time it was usual for spinster schoolmistresses to live in lodgings with other people. Single women did not live by themselves.

When she retired, Emily moved to Leighton Buzzard and the 1911 Census finds her living at 2, Church Street with her sister, Louisa Rose (a schoolmistress), and Louisa's husband Edward, who was an assistant schoolmaster. Emily died in 1912 when she was 69 years old. During her teaching career she had travelled far, getting to know different parts of England and seeing many changes as the narrow Victorian curriculum expanded and education became both compulsory and free.

1864 – 1865 Annie Alicia Reynolds
To the heart of Dorset

The story of Annie Alicia Reynolds who was born in Jersey in about 1846, suggests that her father died when she was very young. Annie's mother was 'formerly a servant' and her father may have been a sailor who lost his life at sea. Perhaps he worked on one of the ships that crossed the North Atlantic to support the Jersey cod fishing industry on the Gaspé Coast of East Canada. The somewhat startling, 'bald' comment on Annie's college registration form in January 1864 reads: 'Her father is dead. Her mother does nothing'.

Annie was a pupil-teacher at a 'school for girls' in St Helier before going to College in 1864. She was 'recommended' by the Revd P.A. Le Feuvre, a clergyman in St Helier and was 'in very good health'. This was certainly a good thing! She was confronted with the strict regime and spartan living conditions that Kate Hardy, at College in the 1870s, found so difficult to endure. The frugality of the meals, the disciplined environment, frequent examinations and excessive work required strength, health and fortitude. Leisure was still relatively unknown.

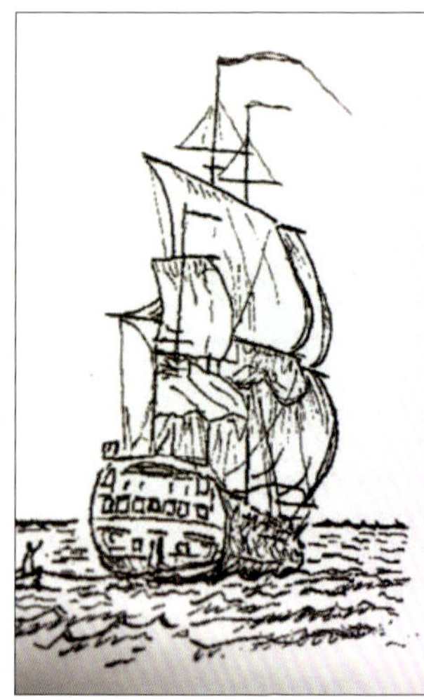

Fig. 24
Sailing to the Gaspé Coast

The new Practising Schools at St Edmunds had been opened in 1860, and Annie would have attended them regularly, as well as the Model School attached to the College.

> 'St Edmund's School was then comparatively new, and many were the trials that fell to our lot there in spite of the help we received from Mrs Wheaton, the head teacher. How well the children behaved when she was present, how badly when she was absent!'

The Chaplain, the Revd E.C. Collard, was a popular man and students enjoyed his lectures in Arithmetic, Grammar, Mental Science and Physical Geography. He seems to have been a supportive listener with regard to teaching practice. 'His sympathy smoothed over all the troubles in our work in the practising schools'.

Miss Greenlaw became the Lady Superintendent in autumn 1865, a few months after Annie arrived at the College. There were approximately 27 students in her year group. Annie and her fellow students attended services at the Cathedral every day. They were often tired and hungry but the worship supported and uplifted them.

'Among the memories none are more refreshing than the daily service in the choir of our Cathedral, our early Communions in the Lady Chapel'.

The only time that they went beyond the walls of The Close was when they went for walks in crocodile formation (two by two), escorted by governesses. The College authorities were responsible for the students and their parents had not allowed them to go to College to risk the dangers of the city.

In 1865 Annie was appointed Mistress of the Stinsford and Bockhampton National School in Dorset, a few miles outside Dorchester. This was where Thomas Hardy received his early education. The Admission Registers for 1866 to 1871 show that Annie's pupils at this church school were aged between 2 and 14 years, which must have been a demanding challenge. The children were mainly the sons and daughters of dairymen, shepherds, carters, coachmen, gamekeepers, gardeners, blacksmiths, labourers and grooms. Many of these parents would have been tenants of the local landowners. Attendance was voluntary but parents were charged a penny a week, which would have been a struggle for some, as would the cost of buying leather shoes for their offspring.

> 'Some shepherds skimped and saved to send their children to school, often because the church taught the 'learning fitted for their station' and left them religious and wanting their child to read scripture'.
>
> Dr Ed Dutton, *Dorset Life,* 2010

On 27 December 1870 Annie Reynolds, a certificated school-mistress aged 25, married Edgar Teague, a railway clerk aged 20 at St Michael's Church, Stinsford. Thomas Hardy had been baptised here in 1840 and his sister Mary in 1842.

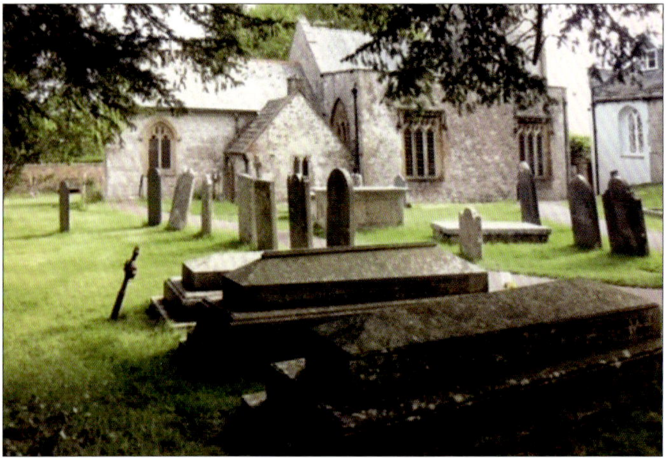

Fig. 3.25 St Michael's Church, Stinsford

Edgar had a reliable job as a railway clerk with the Great Western Railway. He presumably worked at the nearby station in Dorchester, which had opened in 1847.

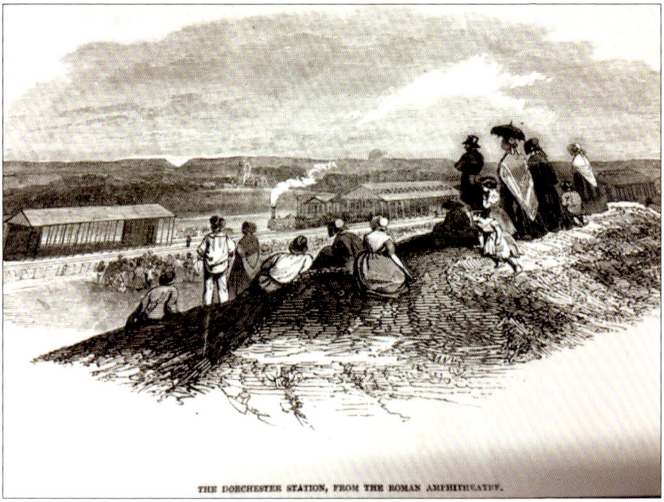

Fig. 3.26 Dorchester station from the Roman amphitheatre, 1847

The 1871 Census for Stinsford shows that Annie, contrary to the custom of the time, continued to teach after she had married and she and Edgar lived in the School House at Stinsford. A few years later Edgar and

Annie's first son was born and by 1881 they had moved to Box, near Chippenham, where Edgar was the Station Master. The records show that the family then moved to Merthyr Tydfil in Wales, where Edgar was again the Station Master. Sadly, Annie died in 1890 when she was just 45 years old, leaving Edgar to bring up their four children.

1868–1869 Mary Ann Guillard
Wool n' Guernsey

Mary Ann Guillard arrived at College in 1868. She was born in Castel, Guernsey in 1850 and lived with her parents Henry and Betsey, and her three older siblings. Her father is recorded as a labourer. By 1861, when Mary Ann was twelve, her father had died and her mother was working as a charwoman to support Mary Ann and her younger sister Rachel. Many rural families lived a frugal existence with just about enough money to provide food and clothing. Wages were low and Betsey must have worked extremely hard to ensure that the family would survive and not be admitted to the Country Hospital (the workhouse for the country parishes).

Mary Ann had a thorough foundation for her teaching, having been a pupil-teacher at Castel Parish School for several years before being admitted to College in 1867. What kind of education did pupils receive at Castel School? Education in Guernsey was increasingly seen as important. Many early school buildings were too small and dark and over time the buildings were replaced or extended and improved. Castel School was originally housed in a small 'Chapelle de St George', but in 1735 a generous gift from Marie de Saumarez was accepted for a new school. Marie de Saumarez was particularly keen that in return, the pupils should receive a thorough grounding in good manners, morals and also learn the fundamentals of Christian religion. In 'Education in Guernsey' included in the 1977 Report of La Société Guernesiaise, Peter Girard explains:

'The gift was to be used to pay the school master, the said appointment to be made not only from persons best qualified to teach reading and writing but from persons of good report, probity, moral integrity and having the qualifications necessary for the instruction of the young'.

The Master was also required to teach, without extra payment, the children of poorer inhabitants. 'Dame Marie finally laid down that she wishes the Master to encourage the children to learn by heart the Apostles' Creed, the Lord's Prayer and the Ten Commandments'.

The school day was to be from seven in the morning until midday and from one in the afternoon until four o'clock. Tests were a regular occurrence and pupils were tested in Church four times a year. The majority of pupils left school as soon as they had mastered the curriculum.

Castel School was further enlarged, close to La Route de St Germain.

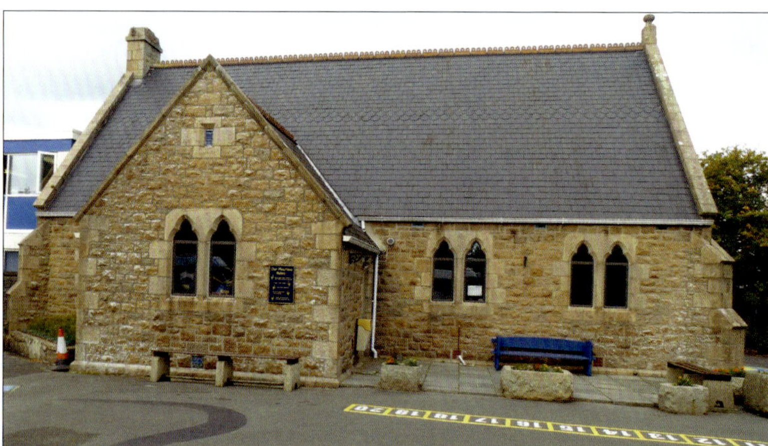

Fig. 3.27 Castel School

It was a long and narrow building which was poorly heated. A report in 1857 stated that the building could not be improved and a new school should be built. It had insufficient foundations and the whole building was too low. Peter Girard concludes that the school which Mary Ann attended was deemed to be 'badly built, insanitary and unhealthy'. It is surprising that this did not put Mary Ann off teaching for ever! Attendance was very poor. In 1852, although there were 188 boys registered, the average daily attendance was only 80. Plans for a new school were accepted and it was formally opened in 1871, by the Rev. Fred C. Carey, Rector of Castel. A fete was held to celebrate the occasion with tea served by the ladies of the parish. The band of the North Regiment played music to add to the merriment.

The building consisted of one large room for boys and one for the girls with a sliding partition in between them. The Headmaster and Headmistress sat on platforms higher than the children, so that they could easily observe what was going on.

Mary Ann was recommended to College by the Revd Osmond Carey who was the incumbent of St Matthew's church in Cobo, Guernsey. Life was tough but Mary Ann enjoyed occasional walks around beautiful Cobo Bay.

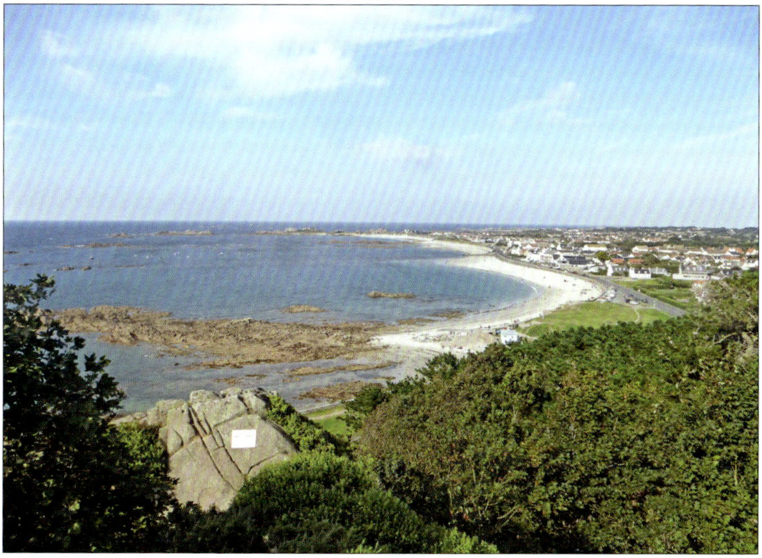

Fig. 3.28 Cobo Bay, Guernsey

She would have appreciated the harsh cliffs of Guernsey but also the 'gentleness inside' described by Victor Hugo.

Just a few years before Mary Ann set sail from Guernsey, the foundation stone of St Matthew's Church was laid, with the church finally completed in 1854. This beautiful Romanesque style church is built in local Guernsey granite with a Welsh blue slate roof.

A young girl named Marianne Carey was on holiday. Whilst out walking she rested close to this area. She felt sorry for the fishermen who had to walk such a long way to get to church and it was through her tireless efforts that the church was built. The London architect John Johnson, was himself a keen fisherman, which is reflected in the interior, particularly the wooden roofs of the nave and chancel, which are similar to an upturned hull of a boat. One can imagine Mary Ann attending the church and enjoying the story of how the church came to be there.

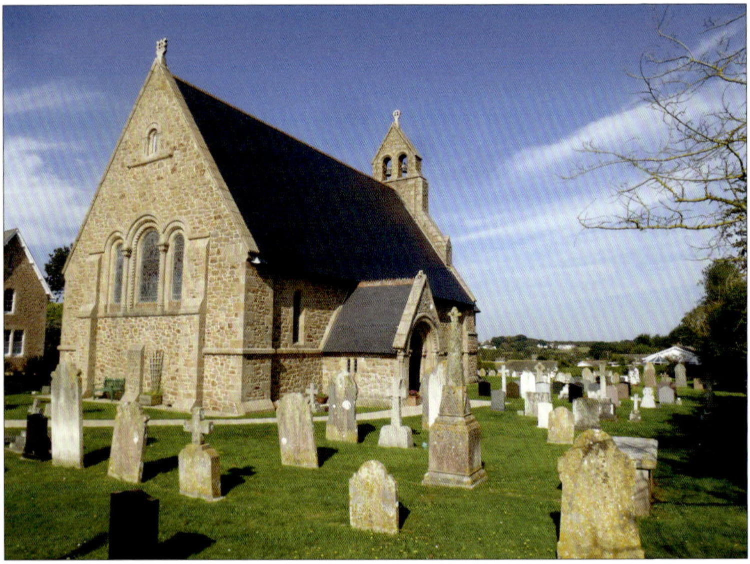

Fig. 3.29 St Matthew's Church, Cobo

When Mary Ann arrived at College she found conditions and life much the same as in previous years – rigorous and demanding. The Revised Code had a negative impact on the number of students entering the teaching profession. The city of Salisbury was expanding; in 1860 The Salisbury Museum was opened and the Theological College was founded.

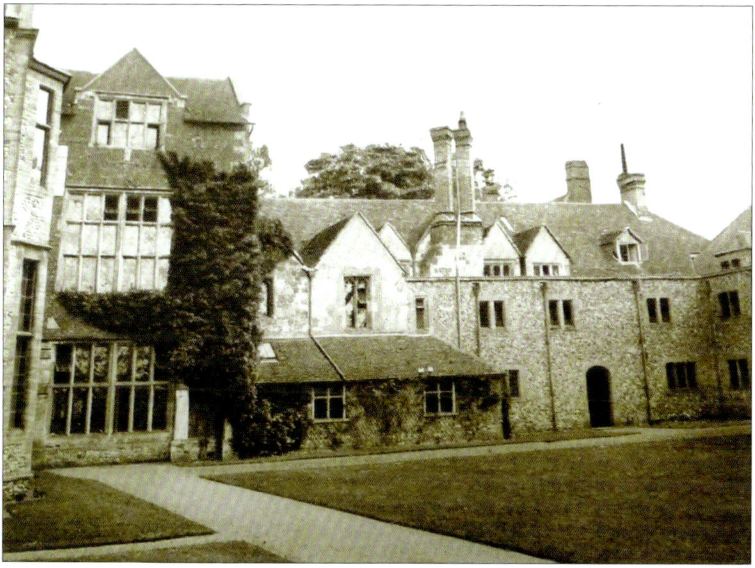

Fig. 3.30 King's House

The College record shows that Mary Ann's health remained good throughout her College days. Initially she was deemed to be idle as a student but this improved to 'very fair'. With regard to the laborious industrial work such as cleaning and washing, Mary Ann was described as 'very good' by the time she left.

Mary Ann Guillard left College at Christmas 1869 at the age of 21 and became the mistress of the school at Wool, near Wareham in Dorset. This was a convenient place for any visits which Mary Ann wanted to make back home to Guernsey. The LSWR had a station at Wool on the line to Weymouth from where she caught the ferry.

Mary Ann lodged within the High Street with the Runyards family. It can't have been very peaceful for her after her busy days at school, as the family had six children with the youngest being less than a year old. The school was situated on the west side of the High Street and described as having rubble and brick walls rendered in stucco. The schoolhouse was of two storeys with a single schoolroom. In 1894, the *Comprehensive Gazetteer* described Wool as:

'A parish with three hamlets in Dorsetshire, on the River Frome, with a station on the LSWR, 125 miles from London and five and a half from Wareham. It has a post, money order and telegraph office in Wareham'.

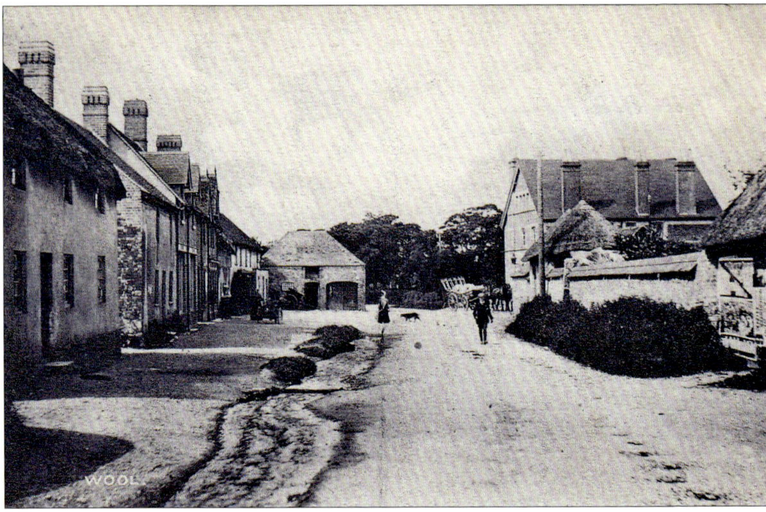

Fig. 3.31 Mary Ann's first teaching post was in Wool, Dorset

Mary Ann returned to Guernsey where she married a Guernseyman, Peter William De Beaucamp Corbet. In the Census of 1881, Peter was not living at home with Mary Ann and their son Robert William. At this time he worked as an official storekeeper at the Town Hospital and Lunatic Asylum in St Peter Port. This was a grim place and, unsurprisingly, ten years later he had changed his occupation and had become a fruit grower. He ran his own business and lived with his wife and four children in St Peter Port. The 1911 Census indicates that when Mary Ann was sixty-one and William fifty four, they were still running their fruit growing business. Mary Ann had witnessed many changes during her life. After her College days and teaching in Dorset, she made the important decision to return to Guernsey, where she lived her later life amongst her family and friends.

4 A True Calling

Salisbury – a good place to live

As the 19th century advanced, Salisbury continued to expand and to prosper. The city was seen as a good place to live. It was certainly becoming a popular place for women to train as teachers. We can picture a young woman alighting from the train at the station in Salisbury, tired after a long sea voyage but full of excited anticipation. It is January and bitterly cold. She is somewhat impeded by her long skirt and heavy suitcase, but nevertheless climbs nimbly up into the horse drawn cab that will deliver her to the College.

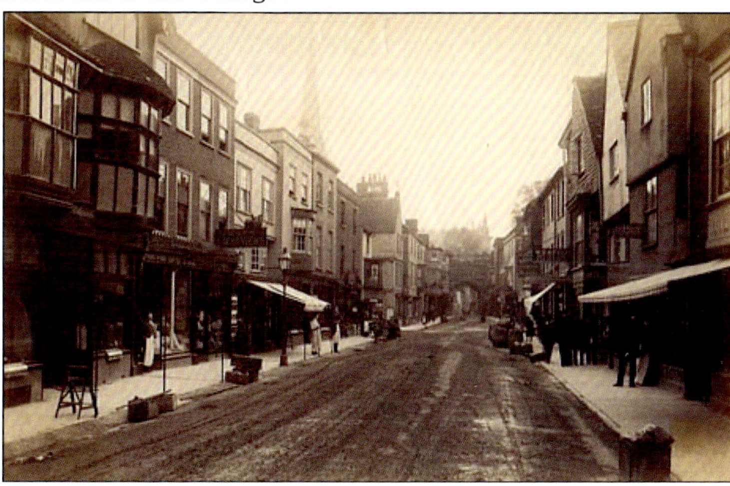

Fig. 4.1 The High Street in the late 19th century

As the cab travels along rutted roads through the market city, the new student spots shops, banks, a theatre, a hotel, breweries and inns. Entering The Close through the High Street gate, she catches her first sight of the towering Cathedral. On a bitter winter's day such as this, the only people to be seen are some children, escorted by a governess and a few tradesmen making deliveries to houses. The cab goes round a bend and she glimpses tranquil water meadows beyond the river. Never has she lived so far from the sea before and she wonders for a moment whether she will miss the beaches, the bustling harbour and the narrow, rambling lanes of home. But there is little time to ponder because now the cab is pulling up at King's House. Her great adventure has begun.

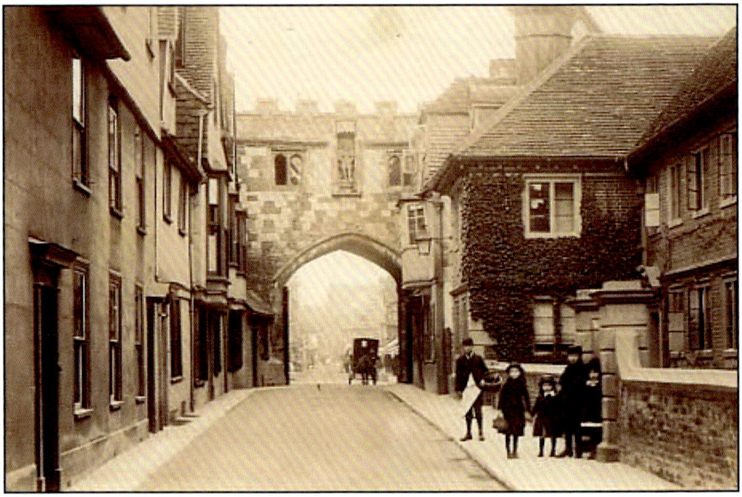

Fig. 4.2 Into The Close

Salisbury in the late 19th century was a larger and healthier city than it had been fifty years earlier. In 1851 the population was 9,455 but by 1900 it would be over 17,000. The construction industry was booming and houses were going up rapidly. A sewerage system was being dug and many residents had piped water supplies. Lighting in houses and streets was provided by candles and oil or gas lamps, but by 1900 electric lights were being widely used. Students who arrived at King's House in 1899 were fortunate as they found that electric lights and hot water pipes and radiators had been installed in the building.. The police force was expanding, the Fire Brigade was supplemented by volunteers and the Infirmary reflected improvements in health care.

During the late 1880s the Bishop of Salisbury, John Wordsworth, led a successful campaign to maintain Church of England control over schools in the city. He was ably supported by Canon Edward Steward, the Principal of Salisbury Training College. The result was the building of three new church schools for elementary pupils, as well as Bishop Wordsworth's School in The Close. These schools all opened in 1890.

Maria Vibert, Rachel Gillard, Florence Frampton and Ethel Anley were just four of the many Channel Island students who arrived at the College in the late 19th century. The young women came from diverse backgrounds as is shown in the old registers that record the 'station of life' and 'residence of parents' for each student.

Maria Verner was the daughter of a 'superannuated coastguard' and Amelia Daniel's father was a boot and shoe maker. Mary Wheller Bryant's father was an accountant and her mother was the Matron of the Jersey Dispensary. Nellie Couch's father was a hosier and shirt maker and Elizabeth Jane Saxby's was a gardener. Elizabeth Hunt's father was a coach builder, Caroline Dowland's father a grocer and Harriet Jerry's was a Captain in the Merchant Service. Louisa and Elsie Cudlipp came from a farming family. Gertrude Le Feuvre's father was a silk merchant and her mother was a dressmaker.

These occupations are reminders of Thomas Hardy's description of the students in the Training School at Melchester in Jude the Obscure, which was published in 1895. Hardy's Melchester is known to be Salisbury and the Training School, which was attended by his sisters Mary and Kate, is Salisbury Training College.

> 'The seventy young women, of ages varying in the main from nineteen to one-and-twenty, though several were older, who at this date filled the species of nunnery known as the Training-School at Melchester, formed a very mixed community, which included the daughters of mechanics, curates, surgeons, shopkeepers, farmers, dairy-men, soldiers, sailors, and villagers.'

Hardy's comments in Jude the Obscure reflect the difficult experiences that his sisters had as students. Nevertheless, the College was making its mark and starting to develop a fine reputation. On 22nd September 1894, the *Jersey Independent* and *Daily Telegraph* was pleased to learn that Miss Ellen De La Mare has just been appointed as Mistress of the Hilgrove School, Gorey. Formerly a scholar and then pupil-teacher at St Luke's, Miss De La Mare spent two years at the Salisbury Training College, where she much distinguished herself, after which she filled the position of first assistant at the Northam Board School (Southampton) in such a manner as to win the regard of all about her, who greatly regret her departure'.

Despite their cloistered lives at the College, students may have experienced something of Salisbury's great celebrations for Queen Victoria's Golden Jubilee in 1887. This was an occasion when the city made merry with the 'ringing of merry peals, great feasting in the Market Place, torch light processions and fireworks'. The newly formed Salvation Army band was invited to play at the celebrations. Those who lived in The Close would have seen Union Jacks floating from the spire of the Cathedral and large bonfires on Harnham Hill.

Whilst the students were still not allowed into Salisbury on their own, times were changing and the city was becoming less rowdy. The economy was diversifying, more people were employed and more children were at school. Perhaps the College staff, who were in 'loco parentis', might even have considered relaxing the rules regarding students going into the city. Whilst this is mere conjecture, an event in 1897 would certainly have put paid to any such thoughts. The government bought land on Salisbury Plain. The Army had arrived!

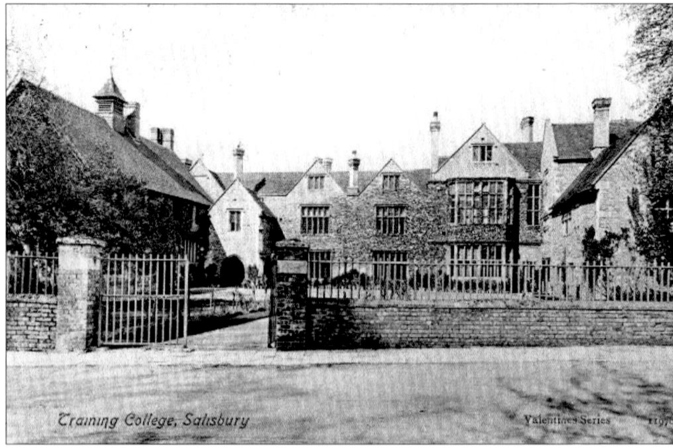

Fig. 4.3 The Training College in the late 19th century

1873 – 1874 Florence Frampton
Town and Country

Florence's father, William, was born in 1829 and was an agricultural labourer in Dorset, as his father had been before him. Times were extremely hard for those working on the land. Real wages had risen a very little since 1700 and many families lived in dire poverty. William grew up during the time of the Swing Riots, when workers rebelled against their conditions and loss of work as a result of the introduction of threshing machines. It was in Dorset in 1834 that the Tolpuddle Martyrs were arrested, tried and transported, after trying to set up a Friendly Society or Trade Union to improve their conditions. Many folk were dispirited and desperate at this time. In 1850 a labourer on a Dorset farm earned about six shillings a week. Children as young as six often worked to help out their meagre existence, doing jobs such as bird scaring.

> 'The boy stood under the rick, and every few seconds used his clacker or rattle briskly. At each clack the rooks left off pecking, and rose and went away on their leisurely wings.'
>
> Thomas Hardy: *Jude the Obscure*, 1895

William, and his wife Emily, decided to start a new life with better prospects. Evershot, a village featured in Thomas Hardy's novel, *Tess of the D'Urbervilles*, is situated about nine miles from Dorchester. There was a GWR station at Holywell, a few miles from Evershot. William and Emily would have caught the train to Weymouth from here and then taken the 'Packet' over to Guernsey to begin their new life.

They settled in St Martin and it was here that Florence was born in 1849. The 1861 Census shows that at this time they had six children, the youngest being only one year old. Ten years later they were still at the same address. Life remained tough for the family, as there were five children to feed. Florence or Flora, as she was known at this time, was doing her bit to help by working as a pupil-teacher at Castel Infant School. It appears that her father's wish to improve himself had paid off, because when Florence entered college he was working as a coachman.

Perhaps he worked at nearby Sausmarez Manor, which was the beautiful home of the Sausmarez family, owned by them for centuries.

During Florence's childhood there would have been trips into busy St Peter Port, which was rapidly expanding. The narrow cobbled streets were busy with the hustle and bustle of the island capital. Commercial trade had increased following the widening of the quay and building of the new harbour. In her rare free time Florence enjoyed cliff top walks and may even have visited the Bathing Pools at La Valette, south of Castle Cornet.

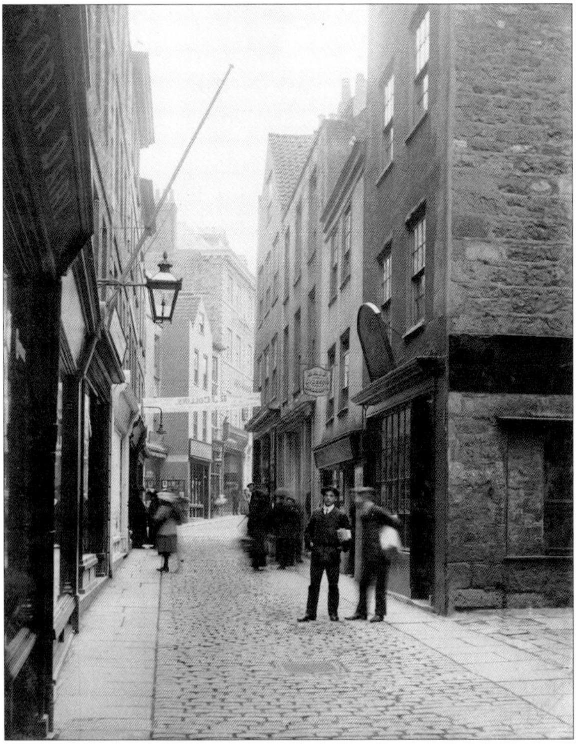

Fig. 4.4 Pollet Street, St Peter Port, would have been well known to Florence. *(The Star)*

During Florence's school years there was again much debate about the teaching of French, which had lapsed. In spring 1867, The Star editorial noted that 'the systematic and powerful effort which is now being made by an association of enlightened men to bring about a revival of the study and use of French on this island'.

Following the 1870 Education Act, the managers of Channel Island Schools queried whether they would still receive grants. The English Education Department suggested a special arrangement could be made where the islands would still bear the full cost of education, but could benefit from HMI if they agreed to abide by English educational codes. They would also be able to obtain trained teachers from English colleges – such as Salisbury. Although Jersey agreed, Guernsey did not. It was in 1872 that Guernsey declared it would retain sole supervision of its schools. Discussions and arguments rumbled on over several years. In her monograph, Rose-Marie Crossan explains that inadequate funding and a basic lack of professionalism meant that Guernsey's schools had failed to keep up with the increasing sophistication and systematisation of education taking place in Britain and France between 1850 and 1900.

It was during this difficult climate of educational change that Florence set sail for Salisbury in February 1873. By now there were regular steamers between Guernsey and Weymouth, which meant a shorter crossing. From Weymouth, Florence took the train to Salisbury to start on her College career.

What was happening at College at this time?

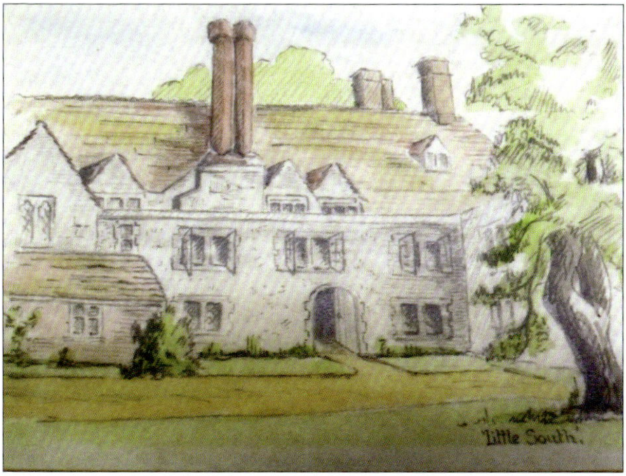

Fig. 4.5 King's House painted by a College student

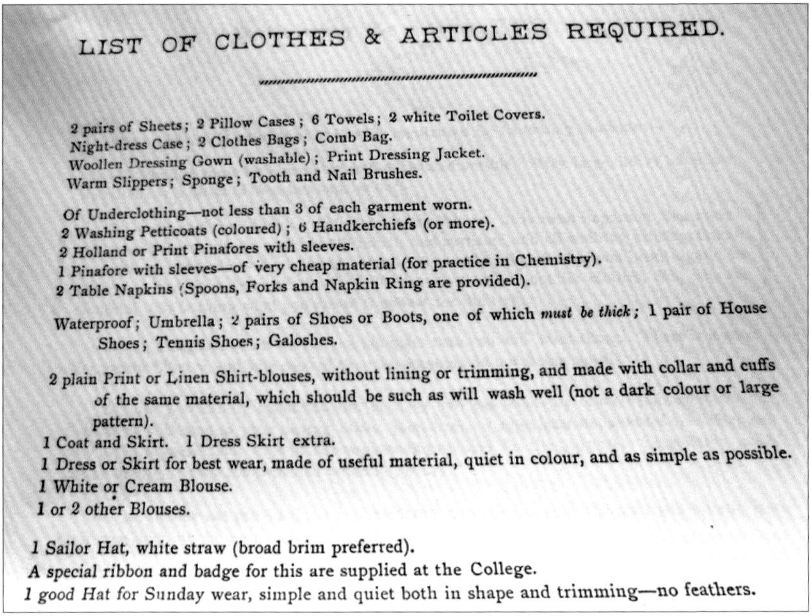
LIST OF CLOTHES & ARTICLES REQUIRED.

2 pairs of Sheets; 2 Pillow Cases; 6 Towels; 2 white Toilet Covers.
Night-dress Case; 2 Clothes Bags; Comb Bag.
Woollen Dressing Gown (washable); Print Dressing Jacket.
Warm Slippers; Sponge; Tooth and Nail Brushes.

Of Underclothing—not less than 3 of each garment worn.
2 Washing Petticoats (coloured); 6 Handkerchiefs (or more).
2 Holland or Print Pinafores with sleeves.
1 Pinafore with sleeves—of very cheap material (for practice in Chemistry).
2 Table Napkins (Spoons, Forks and Napkin Ring are provided).

Waterproof; Umbrella; 2 pairs of Shoes or Boots, one of which *must be thick*; 1 pair of House Shoes; Tennis Shoes; Galoshes.

2 plain Print or Linen Shirt-blouses, without lining or trimming, and made with collar and cuffs of the same material, which should be such as will wash well (not a dark colour or large pattern).
1 Coat and Skirt. 1 Dress Skirt extra.
1 Dress or Skirt for best wear, made of useful material, quiet in colour, and as simple as possible.
1 White or Cream Blouse.
1 or 2 other Blouses.

1 Sailor Hat, white straw (broad brim preferred).
A special ribbon and badge for this are supplied at the College.
1 good Hat for Sunday wear, simple and quiet both in shape and trimming—no feathers.

Fig. 4.6 College list provided for new students

In 1891 Canon Steward published the first edition of 'The Red Book' containing invaluable College Annals and the reminiscences of students from 1841 to 1908:

> '1872 was a year of much anxiety. Two students left in ill-health, and one died of pleurisy while in College. There was, however, an excellent Class List, 18 out of 31 seniors being placed in the first division and none in the third. The great scarcity of teachers brought a further increase in the salaries obtained by outgoing students'.

The committee decided to add accommodation for twenty more students by building a dormitory over the Model School and fitting up a covered space under the principal dormitory originally intended for recreation.

Florence's College record shows that she was strong and in good health when she arrived. Conditions for students remained very hard indeed. In 1877 Kate Hardy, who was Thomas Hardy's sister, enrolled as a student at College. Thomas described the difficult conditions in his novel *Jude the Obscure*. Kate was very unhappy during her years at College as the workload was heavy, food was poor and there were many restrictions.

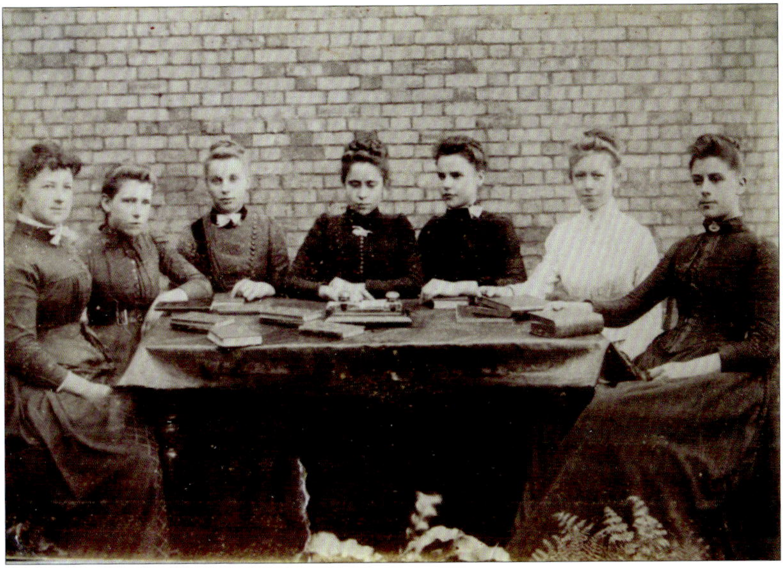

Fig. 4.7 Kate Hardy (far left) with fellow college students a few years after Florence had left.

Students had to rise at six o'clock and be ready for prayers in the school room by quarter to seven: they were not allowed in their bedrooms during the day, except on Sundays; students were not allowed to enter each other's rooms without permission; silence was enforced at a quarter to ten; no reading was allowed in the dormitories except books of Devotion. College life was very demanding!

By the time Florence left College at Christmas 1874, the College had 80 students. Her record states that her conduct was good and she was judged to be 'very fair' in all departments. Florence obtained a post at the village school at Pitton near Salisbury, where there were 50 pupils on roll.

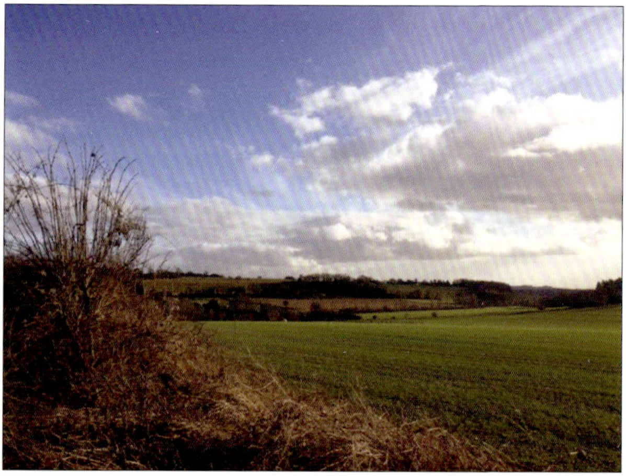

Fig. 4.8 A sunny winter day at Pitton

The log books vividly portray the life in a country school at that time, with a clear focus on reading, writing and arithmetic, with plenty of needlework for the girls. They show that Florence had a positive impact on standards. Children were often absent due to the need for them to help out on the land with beating for 'shoots' and in various jobs at harvest time. The weather was much harsher than today with plenty of snow, which made it essential to keep the school fires burning. On December 20th Florence recorded:

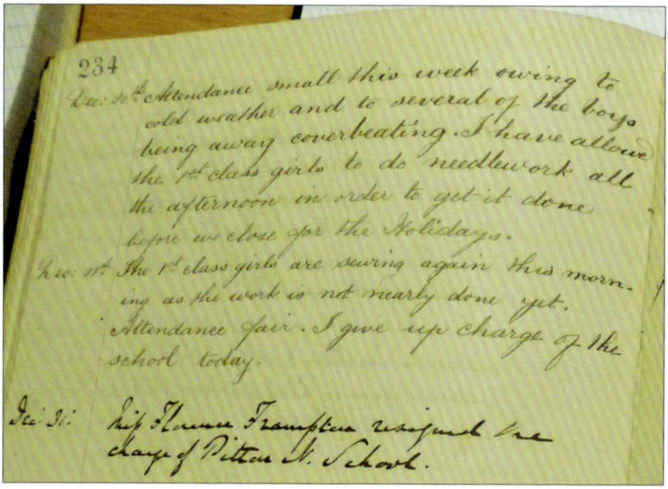

234

Dec: 19th Attendance small this week owing to cold weather and to several of the boys being away coverbeating. I have allowed the 1st class girls to do needlework all the afternoon in order to get it done before we close for the Holidays.

Dec: 20th The 1st class girls are sewing again this morning as the work is not nearly done yet. Attendance fair. I give up charge of the school today.

Dec: 31: Miss Florence Frampton resigned the charge of Pitton N. School.

Fig. 4.9 Pitton School Log Book 1879

Florence left Pitton School in December 1879, having brought about much improvement during her time there.

Where did Florence go next? The 1881 Census shows that she moved from a country village to the city of Bristol. Her hard work and the good results at Pitton paid off and she was promoted to St John's Parochial School, founded in 1851 in Whiteladies Road, Bristol. Her younger sister Ellen, who was a milliner, lived with her in the school house. Teaching children in the heart of a large city would have been so different from teaching the country children of Pitton. Bristol was booming and the port and dock areas rapidly expanding. By the time Florence came to Bristol, rail connections were well established. Horse-drawn trams ran through the city; the first electric trams arrived in 1895. The chocolate industry thrived, as did the tobacco and soap industries. Bristol, like many major cities had numerous people who were poor and lived in unsanitary conditions, although the conditions gradually improved. Florence lived in the middle of the noisy city, but would have been relatively comfortable living in the school with her sister.

By 1891, Florence had met and married her husband William Hunt. William was a railway clerk who worked in Bristol for the Midland Railway. How they met we will never know but William was transferred to Derby, which is where Florence remained for the rest of her life. On the 2nd July 1887 Florence and William were married at St Chad's church in Derby – now demolished.

During the 19th century life in Derby gradually improved. Perhaps Florence, William and their children would have enjoyed swimming in the pool opened in 1873. A School of Art opened in 1878 and a public library and museum in 1879. Horse-drawn trams ran through the streets from 1880 and the first electric lights were switched on in 1894. As in every big city there were many slums and much poverty. However, William and Florence would have been comfortably off, particularly with the expansion of the Midland Railway Company, which made engines in Derby. There were also many iron foundries along with other industries such as brewing and paint making. In the early 20th century Rolls Royce opened a factory where cars and aircraft engines were made. The family may have ventured to the cinema, which opened in 1910 and they would have enjoyed walks in the parks in their free time.

The 1901 Census shows that they had four children and were still living at the same address in Derby. There is no mention of daughter Florence, who was one year old in 1891. Florence Hunt was now aged 46 and her children ranged from eight to two years, her son William being the youngest. In 1911 the family had moved to Porter Road, Derby. Florence died in Derby in March 1937. During her long life she had moved from the island of Guernsey to College life in Salisbury and then made a positive influence in a small Wiltshire village school. She worked in a school in the centre of the city of Bristol and moved finally to Derby where after a full life, she ended her days.

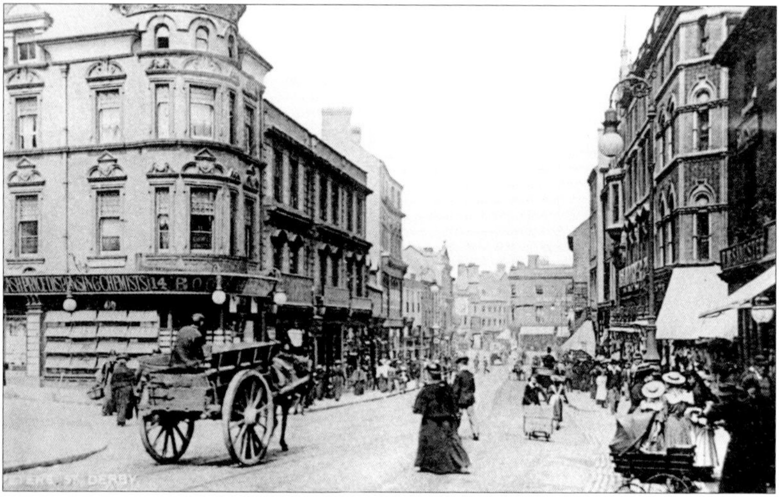

Fig. 4.10 St Peter's Street, Derby c 1900

1876 – 1877 Rachel Gillard
St Ouennais through and through!

Many of the early students from Jersey lived in St Helier. This is not surprising as it was the most populated part of the island. By the mid nineteenth century the population was growing rapidly, the town was expanding and most of those who came to live in Jersey settled in and around St Helier. Many of the island students were not 'Jersey born' .This was not, however, always the case. St Ouen, the largest and most traditional of the parishes, produced several 'home-grown' students for Salisbury Training College during the mid and late nineteenth century.

St Ouen was and still is a distant corner of Jersey. Island roads at this time were plentiful, but they were narrow and often treacherous in bad weather. A trip from St Ouen into St Helier probably took several hours.

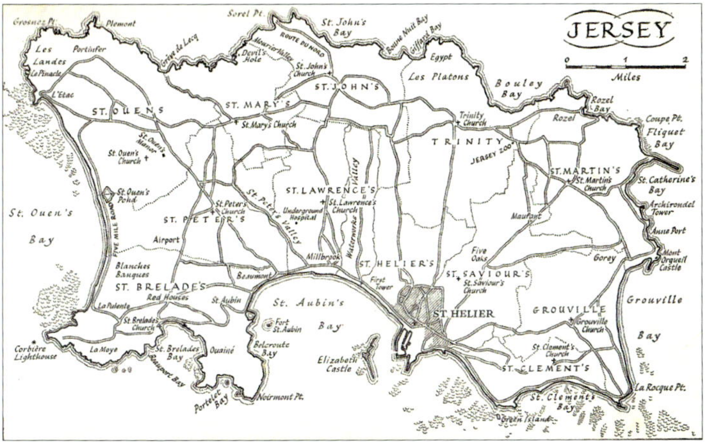

Fig. 4.11 Location of St Ouen in Jersey

Many of the St Ouennais were farmers who had smallholdings. They grew fruit, vegetables and corn for themselves and kept chickens and perhaps a few pigs as well.

Cider apple trees would have been a cash crop, but as this export trade declined, the pedigree Jersey cow became a good earner. By 1875 there were fewer apple trees and more of the highly prized cows.

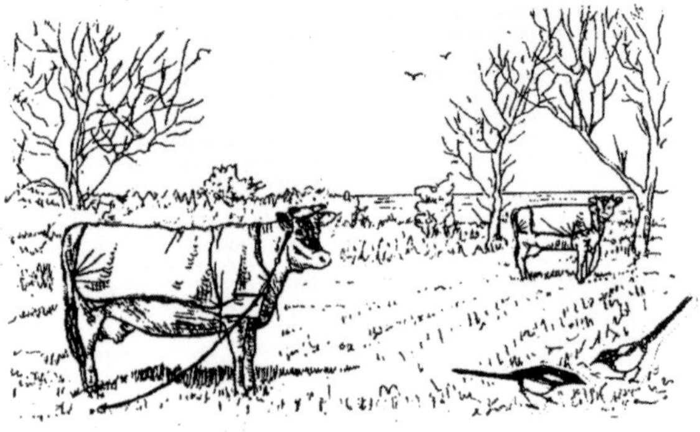

Fig. 4.12 Jersey cows

The big new cash crop was that of the early potato and it was a St Ouen farmer who was one of the pioneers of the industry that became Jersey's most profitable export.

It was so important that the crop was lifted quickly when it was ready that schools used to close for part of the season so that children could help with the planting, the spreading of the vraic (seaweed) and the harvest on the steeply sloping cotils (hillsides) where machinery could not be used.

It is likely that Rachel Gillard grew up on one of these small farms. Her father, George, had moved with his parents to the island in about 1840 when he was 11 years old. George married a Jersey girl (Rachel Perree) and settled down to a farming life in St Ouen's. It was here that they raised their family and their eldest daughter, Rachel Elizabeth, was born in 1859.

Rachel had four younger siblings and the children all attended St Ouen's Parochial School, which was built in the early 1860s, next door to the Parish Hall in the centre of the village. Jerriais (Jersey-French) would have still been the native language in the neighbourhood of St Ouen but at school the children would have learnt English.

Children in the rural areas who spoke Jerriais at home were at a disadvantage at school where the language that they were taught was quite different from Jersey Norman-French. In some schools, so much time was spent on French that little progress was made in English. School log books include inspectors' reports (written in French) and it is possible to identify the areas that were predominantly French – or English – speaking. The parish and town of Saint Helier was an English-speaking area, and the parishes of St Ouen, Trinity, St Martin and Grouville were mainly French-speaking.

A visiting Inspector in 1877 commented:

> 'I am glad to find the infants have received much more attention than last year, but they are still backward for their ages. It must be remembered that their want of the knowledge of English is very much against them'.

The Headmaster, George Cooper, frustrated by the absences of pupils during the vraiking season and potato planting in March, tried to make allowances: 'I have begun school half an hour before two with the consent of the Rector, in order that children may assist their parents who, I regret to say, cannot dispense with them'.

Rachel was a pupil-teacher at the school by the time she was 13. The school log book reveals some of the day to day problems at the school:

> 'June 6 1872: very bad attendance owing to incessant rain. John Vibert readmitted after long absence. Has been reprimanded by the Rector for his very bad conduct, was punished for insulting the pupil teacher Rachel Gillard and calling her names'.

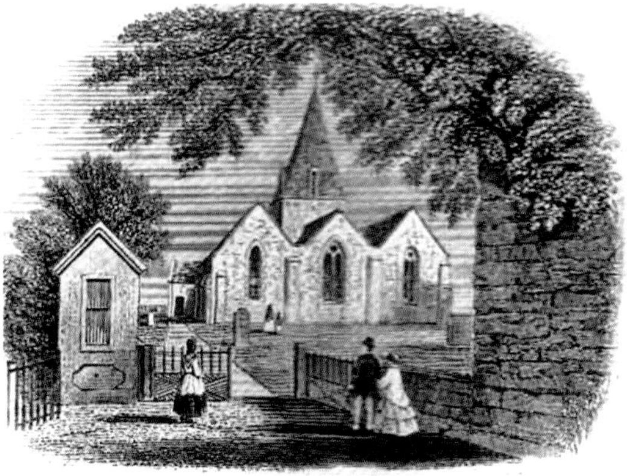

Fig. 4.13 St Ouen's Parish Church 1870

There were, however, worse problems to come. The school Log Books reveal an uncomfortable time in October 1872 when George Cooper and his wife Eliza were still in charge. There were approximately 100 children in the school. Eliza was unable to help her husband much as she was often ill and had a baby to look after. Rachel Gillard was the pupil-teacher who assisted George with the older children whilst two other pupil-teachers worked with the 'lower sections'. The children entered the school speaking only Jerriais and George, who only spoke English, was at an immediate disadvantage! He must have relied enormously on Rachel and the other pupil-teachers to communicate with the children. The curriculum was by now widening and included Reading, Writing, Arithmetic, Music, Poetry, French, Geography and Scripture.

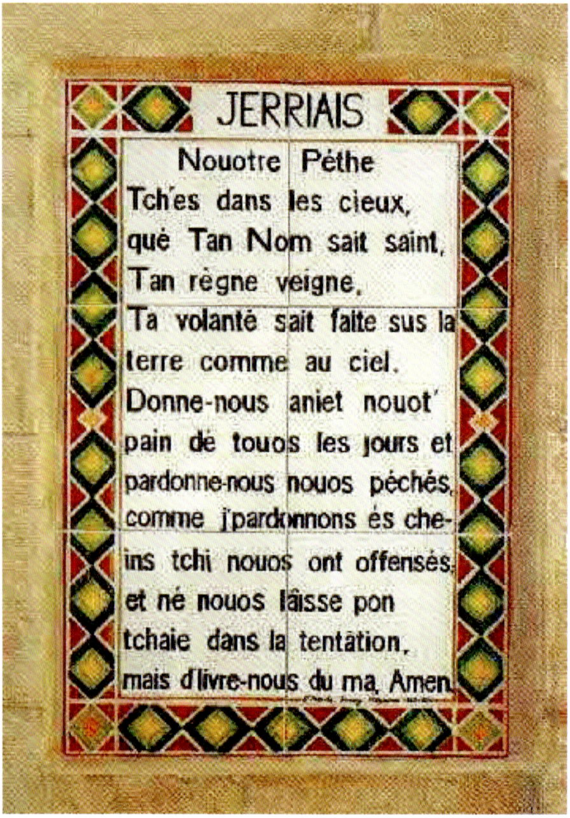

Fig. 4.14 The Lord's Prayer in Jerriais

George Cooper was young and inexperienced, but he was a caring teacher and the log book show how he encouraged parents to educate their children, was kind when pupils were unwell and used his cane sparingly. It seems unfair that his work was badly undermined by malicious gossip that spread through the community. Parents passed on scandalous stories of how George boxed children's ears and caned boys every day. George's wife (Eliza) 'wept bitterly' when she heard these reports. In October 1872 the log book records the discovery that it was one of the pupil-teachers who had carried these stories out of school. George writes that 'pupil-teachers in particular ought to uphold the Master and Mistress'.

Who was the culprit?

Unfortunately, the finger points at Rachel Gillard. There had already been a problem when George had kept children in, but had then found that they had persuaded Rachel to do their homework for them. She had divided loyalties and at the tender age of thirteen or fourteen could not work out whose side she was on, that of the teacher or of the children. One's sympathy is for the Coopers, who resigned at the end of term, feeling extremely indignant at the Rector's accusation that they had allowed the discipline of the school to lapse.

Maria Vibert, another St Ouennais who went on to train at Salisbury followed Rachel as a pupil-teacher. Maria Prigg, a Jersey student who trained at Salisbury, started teaching at this school in 1875 and may have taught Rachel before she became a pupil-teacher.

Rachel Gillard was not deterred by the whole experience. She was still determined to teach and entered Salisbury Training College in January 1876. She was 18 years old and 'strong and in good health'.

Whilst at College, Rachel and her fellow students led secluded lives. They were sheltered from what was going on in the outside world and their lives were strictly ordered. One student remembered their 'complete segregation and lack of free time'. One particularly irksome rule was, however, relaxed whilst Rachel was at College. The students were given permission to wear hats rather than bonnets on their daily walks. Great was their rejoicing, but it was not until ten years later that they were allowed to relinquish the 'round saucer-like white caps' that were worn inside.

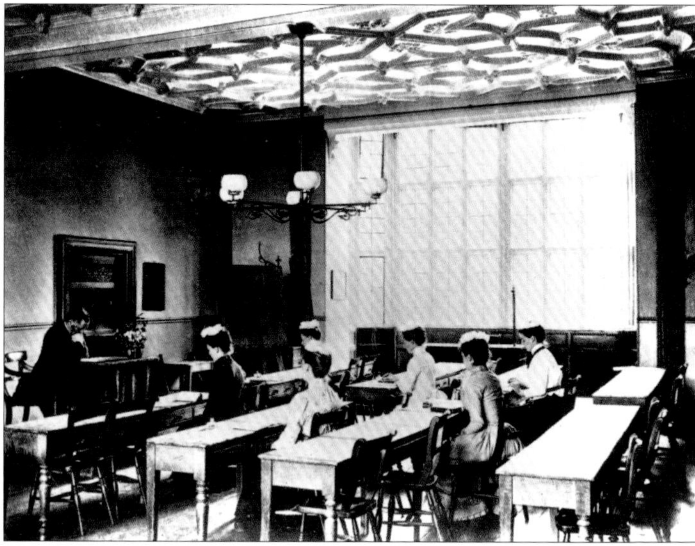

Fig. 4.15 Students working in King's House in the 1870s

Academic work filled Rachel's days, much of it being monotonous and repetitive. Rote learning was in vogue. In addition the students spent many hours at long services in the Cathedral. They were told to do work in their own time but that was in very short supply. A student would have had to be highly motivated to rise in the early hours in King's House, light a small fire and huddle in front of it to read with the light of a candle.

Another change that took place whilst Rachel was at College involved exercise. In 1876 Mlle Simonon of Godolphin Ladies School was engaged to teach Drill. This took the place of Callisthenics, which were exercises to improve gracefulness and strength of movement. It would be interesting to know whether the students viewed these physical exercises as pleasure or torture!

At least it sounds as though the food was improving. Rhubarb, beans, raspberries and cabbages were grown in the garden. The kitchen accounts show that turkey, fish, poultry, rabbits, corned beef, sausages, jelly and cream cheeses were all purchased. Beer, wine, and brandy also appear. It is likely that the staff fared somewhat better than the students!

Rachel was a hardworking student and comments on her registration form were consistently good. When her training had finished she taught for a short time in Chetnole near Sherborne before returning to Jersey and marrying Francis Du Heaume, another St Ouennais, in 1883. After raising her family Rachel returned to teach at St Ouen's Parochial School in 1895. She was one of two 'certificated teachers' at the school. Had she opened the incriminating log book on her first day, it would surely have brought back painful memories, but she settled down to work and from all accounts the school, which was fortunate to have two qualified teachers, did well.

> 'A careful and very efficiently conducted country school. But new furniture is desirable'
>
> Inspection Report, 1905

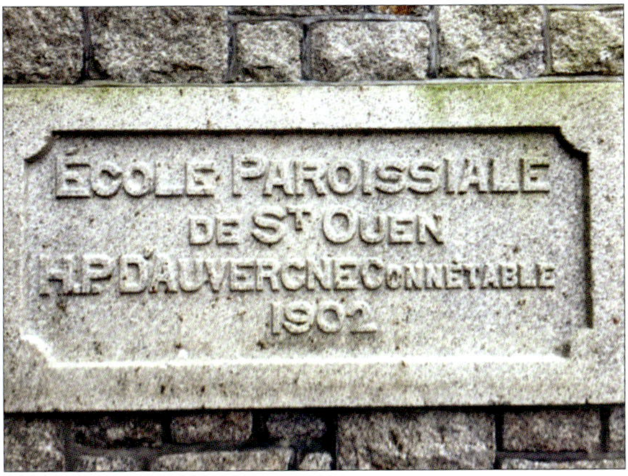

Fig. 4.16 Foundation Stone of St Ouen's Parochial School

Nine years later, in 1904, 'Rachel du Heaume, Certificated Teacher' appears at the head of the staff list. Two of her children also appear on the list, one as a pupil teacher and the other as a monitress. Rachel would appear to be the Headteacher, although this is not acknowledged. She was certainly employing two members of her own family. It is unusual that Rachel continued to teach after her marriage. Marriage was regarded as a full-time commitment and when a woman teacher married, she was expected to relinquish her career.

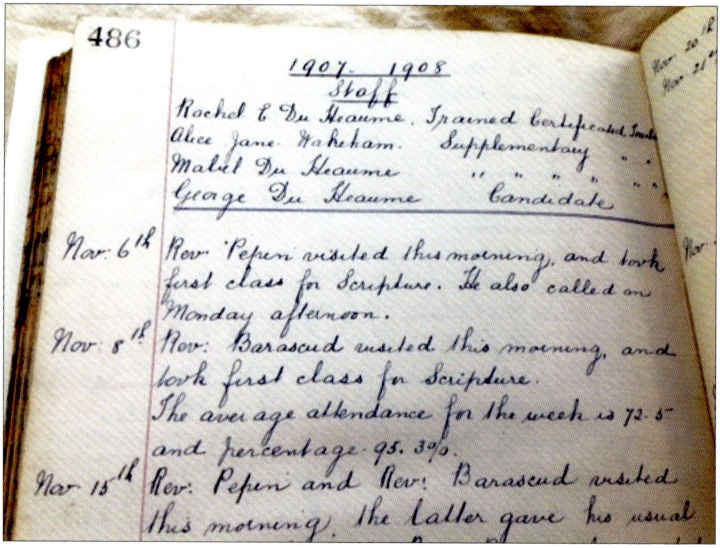
486

1907. 1908

Staff

Rachel E Du Heaume. Trained Certificated

Alice Jane Wakeham. Supplementary

Mabel Du Heaume " " "

George Du Heaume Candidate

Nov. 6th Rev. Pepin visited this morning, and took first class for Scripture. He also called on Monday afternoon.

Nov: 8th Rev: Barascud visited this morning, and took first class for Scripture.

The average attendance for the week is 72.5 and percentage 95.3%.

Nov 15th Rev: Pepin and Rev: Barascud visited this morning, the latter gave his usual

Fig. 4.17 Extract from St Ouen's Parochial School Log Book 1907–1908

The school had 75 pupils in 1906.

The Religious Instruction Report in May 1906 commented: 'The children are evidently taught with great care, and are interested in their lessons. There is a capital tone about the school'.

The entry for December 11th 1908 states that 'the Head Teacher will be absent from the school for the Distribution of States Prizes'. This annual occasion was held in the Town Hall in St Helier. Pupils were given awards for proficiency in French. The Bailiff, speaking in French, explained that teachers in town schools had difficulty teaching children for whom French was not their mother tongue, whilst the ' rural children who came of the old Jersey stock had first to lay aside the local idiom to which they were accustomed'. He pointed out that French had to be taught in Jersey if they were to preserve their old tongue and also because of their 'bi-lingual frontier position'.

The 1911 Channel Island Census shows Rachel and Francis living in the School House, St Ouen with their four children, two of whom were teaching in the school. Their son, Reginald was a gardener and another was a carpenter like his father. Rachel, aged 52, is described as the Headteacher of the Public Elementary School.

The Log Book for 1915–1916 shows that Rachel was by then Headteacher at Les Landes School, St Ouen. This school had opened in 1902.

In 1916 Rachel and her husband received tragic news about the death of their son, Reginald

> 'The list of brave Jerseymen who have given up their lives for King and Country grows daily, the latest addition is the name of Sergeant R du Heaume of D Company Royal Irish Rifles, son of Mrs du Heaume of the School House, Les Landes, St Ouen's, who is believed to have been killed on 6 September'.
>
> *Jersey Evening Post,* 20 September, 1916

Reginald was twenty-seven years old when he died at the Battle of the Somme. He had worked as a gardener before joining up and he and two other young Jerseymen had all been loyal members of the St Ouen's Troop of Boy Scouts.

> 'A brief but most impressive In Memoriam service was that held at St Ouen's Church yesterday afternoon for three gallant lads from the Western District who loyally volunteered when they saw their Country's need and who have now been called upon to make the supreme sacrifice'.
>
> Commonwealth War Graves Commission Record

Rachel continued as Headteacher of Les Landes after the First World War. The Log Books abound with references to epidemics of measles and diphtheria and the lack of pupils due to the planting of potatoes. Some of the staff too were frequently absent with illness. Learning English continued to be a struggle for children in this country school:

> 'Only a few of the children of the first class can employ themselves in English with any freedom or accuracy'.
>
> Inspector's Report, 1922

Rachel 'hung up her coat' and retired on August 31st 1923 after teaching for twenty-eight years in the parish. Her short, graceful and somewhat poignant message is recorded in the Log Book.

> 'This afternoon having reached the age limit (65) I sever my connection with the school. I wish to thank my assistants for their co-operation in the work of the school, also for their kindness to me, during the seven years and three months I have been Headteacher. I wish all success to my successor'.

1882 – 1883 Maria Vibert
'An Excellent Mistress'

Maria Vibert was, like Rachel Gillard, another St Ouennais. She was born in 1861 and her 42 year old father's occupation was that of Master Mariner, or in other words the Captain of a ship. Perhaps this was one of the passenger boats, or maybe it was a cargo ship or a fishing vessel. He might have been the Captain of one of the many island ships that crossed the Atlantic to fish for cod off Newfoundland, although the heyday of this trade had already passed.

Maria was educated at St Ouen's Parochial School. In the 1881 Census her mother is registered as 'annuitant' meaning that she was receiving money, probably from her husband who was away at sea. When Maria entered college in January 1882, the register records: 'Father a sea captain.' She was 21 years old and was a confirmed member of the Church of England. She had been a pupil-teacher at St James's Girls and Infant Schools in St Helier.

Ellen Ireland, also from Jersey, started her training at the same time as Maria. Conditions at the College were still hard, but times were changing and life was opening up. The city of Salisbury was 'out of bounds' to the young trainee schoolmistresses, but Maria and Ellen enjoyed the excitement of an outing in a horse-drawn vehicle to the New Forest in July 1882 and to Stonehenge the following year.. Copies of the *Illustrated London News* started to appear in the College, tennis and croquet equipment was purchased and there were two pianos.

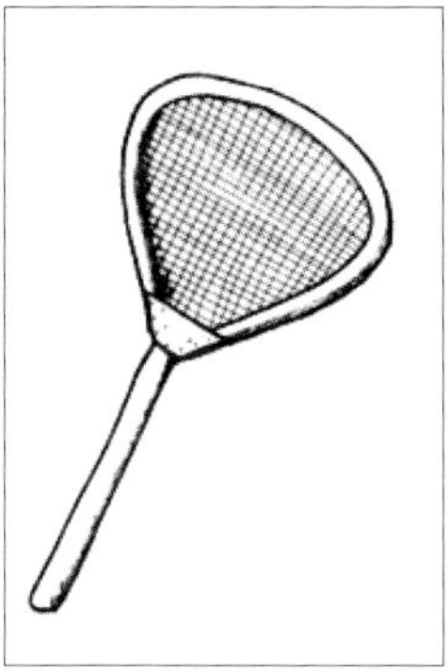

Fig. 4.18 Battledore rackets were purchased by Christmas 1883

Discipline was still very strict and Clara Grant, also a student in the 1880s, recorded an incident when she was 'caught' reading Dickens at College, when she should have been reading books on the syllabus:

> 'Fortunately, Canon Edward Steward, being a man and an Oxford man, proved more tolerant than the mistress who reported me'.
>
> Clara Grant: *Farthing Bundles*

Industrial work was much in evidence. As there were only four servants, Maria and Ellen took their turn in sweeping, dusting and helping in the kitchen and the laundry. Students also resented the academic work, finding it unacceptably narrow, heavy and monotonous. The timetable was packed full and one student mentioned that she could 'only find pleasure in her own thoughts when she was concentrating on her needlework'. They did, however, have 'excellent lectures in School Management'. This sound teaching must have guided the subsequent careers of many students.

Ellen and Maria both returned to Jersey after their training. According to Canon Steward's Red Book, Ellen went to teach at St Luke's whilst Maria first taught at St Matthew's. St Matthew's Church, then a 'nondescript chapel' had been built in 1840 to serve the growing community at Millbrook in the heart of St Aubin's Bay. A mixed school was attached to the church and it was here that Maria taught. The Headmaster's Log Book does not begin until 1894, but the following evocative description helps one to imagine the challenging place where Maria started her teaching career:

> 'A scrappy, struggling school, clinging to the skirts of its mother church, striving to educate generations in this harsh land where the sand dunes met the potato fields'.
>
> Paul Darroch, author of *Jersey: The Hidden Histories*

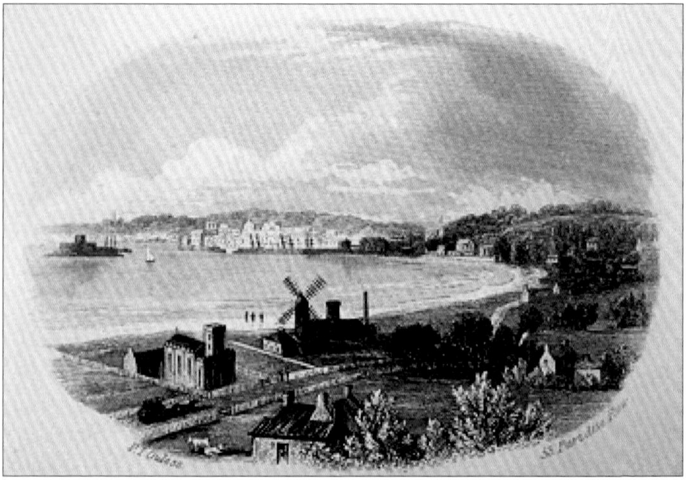

Fig. 4.19 St Matthew's Church

By the 1891 Census Maria was the Headteacher of St Luke's Girls' School. She was sharing the School House with her mother and her younger sister Anna, who was an assistant teacher at the school. Her father is not mentioned in the Census return and her mother is described as 'living on her own means'. Maybe the fact that her mother was now alone had influenced Maria's decision to return home after college. Perhaps her father had drowned in one of the many accidents at sea. Maria stayed at St Luke's until 1903 when she embarked on her second headship:

The parish is on the outskirts of St Helier. St Luke's Church was built in the 1850s to support the growing population. The school followed some years later.

> 'Miss Vibert, the popular headmistress of St Luke's School, severed her connection with St Luke's and commenced her duties as Headmistress of St Lawrence's new Parochial School. Miss Vibert has been connected with St Luke's for sixteen years. She has raised the school to the highest level of efficiency, earning unstinted praise. St Lawrence is to be congratulated on procuring the services of such an excellent mistress.'
>
> *Jersey Independent and Daily Telegraph*, Nov 7, 1903

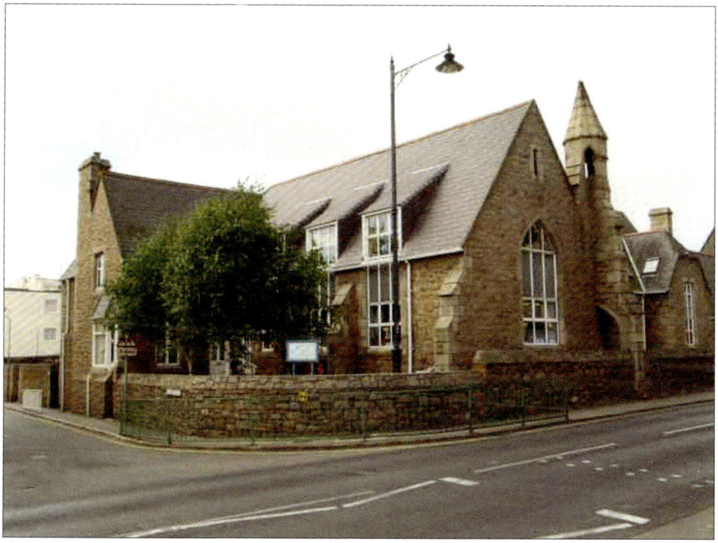

Fig. 4.20 St Luke's School, 1897

Mrs du Heaume (née Rachel Gillard) and Miss Vibert had much in common. They were both born and bred in St Ouen, both attended college and both returned to give long years of service to island schools. We can imagine these two dedicated head teachers occasionally meeting up at school events and perhaps reminiscing about their earlier years, both in Jersey and in Salisbury. They were of course just two of the growing number of young women who crossed the sea from both Jersey and Guernsey to train as teachers. Many of them chose to go to Salisbury.

The question of language …

Rachel Gillard and Maria Vibert both worked at a time when the teaching of French in elementary schools in Jersey became a significant challenge. By the mid-19th century, French was largely seen as an optional 'extra' in schools. There was a growing English influence in the island, with extensive use of the English language in St Helier. What happened to 'rock the boat'?

The Revised Code, which had been introduced by the British

government in 1862, continued to be deeply unpopular. Schools struggled to fit four hours of French tuition into the curriculum in order to obtain the results needed for a grant. There was a great outcry about the unjust system. In 1872 control of the elementary schools passed from the British government to the States of Jersey. French became even more important with the issue of additional 'Reglements' (guidelines) in the 1880s. French and English were to be taught on a comparable basis, an equal amount of time being devoted to each language. Grants would still be based on results. Maria Vibert, teaching at St Matthew's School, joined other teachers in a letter of complaint:

> 'The additions and alterations made by The Committee on Education greatly increase the excessive demands made already on the teachers and will be productive of no lasting good to the children'
>
> *Jersey Independent and Daily Telegraph*, 11 October 1884

Her Majesty's Inspectors of Schools visited Jersey at the expense of the States. French inspections and examinations revealed variable standards and from 1886 a school only received the French grant if the person teaching the language had gained a qualification called a 'Brevet de Capacite'. The inclusion of French as a compulsory subject was, however, applauded by some:

> 'It is necessary that all Jersey children should become proficient in French ... 'it increases their intellectual powers to be able to think and speak in two languages'.
>
> *Jersey Independent and Daily Telegraph*, 2 October 1880

Many Jersey people also held a conviction that because their way of life had French origins, children should be taught the language from an early age. The following words, expressed by Dr Frank Le Maistre in 1947, would have rung true with many islanders fifty years earlier.

> "... when the old walls in the country no longer echo the pleasant sounds of the Jersey language, when those docile and graceful natives, the Jersey cows, are no longer addressed in the Jerriais they have

understood for so many generations, when the Jersey soil is trampled upon by descendants of her sons uttering a foreign tongue to it, when children are lulled to sleep in English, when the seagulls cry out to the cliffs in English and when the dogs bark in English – then Jersey will no longer be Jersey and we shall have lost irretrievably a very precious possession indeed.

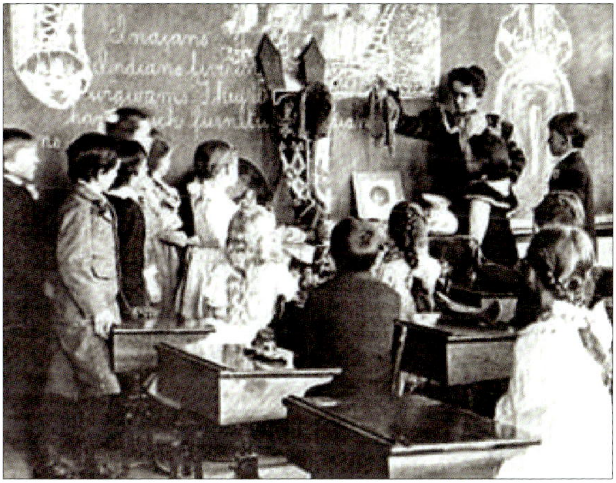

Fig. 4.21 Island school in the 1890s

In 1897 the system of paying grants based on performance ended. In 1899, twenty-nine years after the 1870 Education Act in England, Jersey introduced compulsory education for children up to the age of 12.

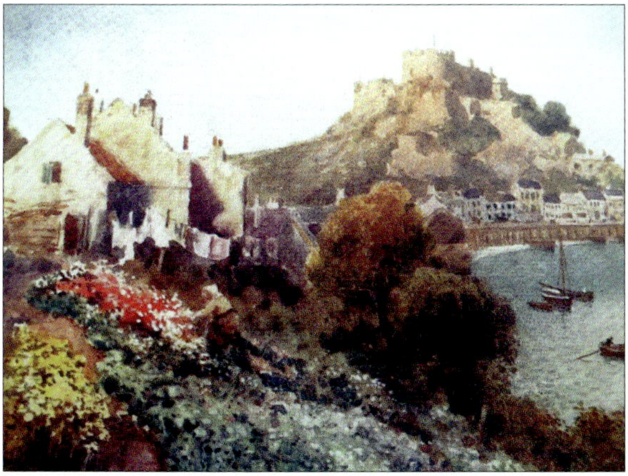

Fig. 4.22 Gorey harbour, 1911

1891 – 1892 Ethel C. Anley
A First Class Student

Ethel was born in 1871 in Halifax, Nova Scotia, Canada. Her mother, Caroline Anley was born in Guernsey but emigrated to Canada. Ethel's 1891 College entry record states that her father was a ship's captain. This referred to her birth father in Canada and may explain why her mother, Caroline, went to live in Canada.

Eventually Caroline, Ethel's mother, returned to Guernsey, where she later married Thomas C. H. Knight. Thomas had been married before and had nine children with Susan, his first wife. Their marriage took place in Minnesota, USA, but the couple settled in St Peter Port, where the children were born. Times were hard especially for a large family and sadly three of their sons died as young babies.

The Census records from 1861 state that Thomas C. Knight, Ethel's stepfather, was a baker. The 1881 Census reveals that his wife, Susan, was a 'baker's wife' and two of his sons, Ernest and Osmond, worked in the shop as assistant bakers. There were plenty of hungry people to feed in St Peter Port. Many French people continued to settle in the town in the hope of improving their situation. The town centre was a maze of crowded buildings and narrow cobbled streets with busy markets and shops. By 1879, many of the old buildings had been demolished and redeveloped. Ethel is likely to have visited the library and Assembly Rooms, with its beautiful entrance hall which welcomed users from 1888.

Ethel worked as a pupil-teacher at St Peter Port Infant School and, in an examination of the Parochial Schools, gained second prize for English and French. Ethel enjoyed her experience at St Peter Port Infant School and decided that teaching was her vocation.

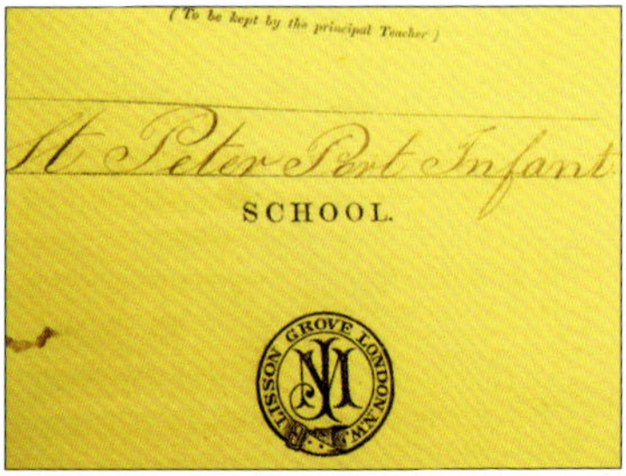

Fig. 4.23 1890 School Log Book

An entry from the log book just before Christmas 1890 states: 'The school was somewhat disarranged this afternoon on account of preparations being made for the children's treat'. The entry for the next day says: 'Same as yesterday'. The children enjoyed their treat on the last day of term and then broke up for the school holidays. A school inspection found it was 'still an excellent school'. Ethel was indeed fortunate to have been a pupil-teacher there.

By the end of the nineteenth century there were fourteen infant schools in Guernsey. Nearly all these were church schools maintained by the Anglican Church until they received aid from the States. During Ethel's years at College a fierce argument and confrontation took place between the local ratepayers and the States Committee, with regard to the schools in St Peter Port. In 1893 a law was passed which stated that the States Committee, with the Parish Committee, should be responsible for the direction of the schools. It would cover half the cost of education including improvement and buildings. Ratepayers and school managers had to bear the cost of the other half. Gradually parishes lost the independent direction of their school and began to resent the intrusion of the States Committee. The conflict became so intense that ratepayers refused to continue to pay their half of the school costs. The result of this argument was that St Peter Port Parish ran out of money and the schools were closed for several weeks. The situation rumbled on until eventually the St Peter Port Parish admitted defeat. Arguments also took place with regard to religion in schools, as non-conformists maintained that religious teaching was too biased in favour of the established church.

The local inspector, The Revd V. J. Pilbeam, produced a report in 1894–95 which showed that there were 2,003 children in the country schools and 1,118 in town schools. He found much accommodation was inadequate, with badly lit classrooms and poor ventilation. The lack of finance and professional training meant that the schools had fallen behind educational standards and provision in England and France.

It was decided to commission two educational specialists to report on Guernsey schools. Mr John A. Munday MA, from the Diocese of Winchester, was appointed to report on the schools. The Revd Edouard Luce, a Rector of Jersey, was to report on the teaching of French. The reports showed that the schools were unsatisfactory and in 1898 Mr

Munday was appointed Superintendent of Schools, initially for three years. He re-categorised subjects into 'core' and 'class' subjects. French was not defined as a core subject and Munday's 1899 Code stated that no more than five hours a week should be given to teaching it. His aim in this was to make more time for the teaching of other subjects where standards were very low. Although the amount of time for French teaching was reduced, Mr Munday placed no restrictions on teachers using French as a medium for instruction. In some isolated western parishes, Guernsey French survived as a means of instruction, particularly with the younger children up until 1912.

During the decade from 1890 to 1900 the LSWR and GWR began to try and outdo each other by achieving the fastest sailing times to the Channel Islands. The newly acquired GWR built three steamships in 1889, and in 1891 the Ibex joined them from Weymouth. Unfortunately the Ibex struck a reef at St Peter Port and sank with the loss of one passenger and one seaman. After this incident the two companies agreed to operate an amalgamated steamer service. Up until this time many passenger vessels also carried cargo such as hundreds of baskets of tomatoes and other produce. The companies realised that separate cargo vessels were needed and so the sea passage across the Channel became more comfortable. More visitors were attracted to the islands on excursions and for holidays.

In 1891 Ethel bid farewell to her family and set sail for England.

Ethel experienced a very rough sea crossing as shown by Miss Hill's entry in The College Log Book:

August 21 1891

Students returned. Weather too rough for Jersey and Guernsey girls until Saturday.

She joined a cohort of 40 other students about to embark on their College careers.

As Ethel entered the Cathedral Close, heading for King's House, she would

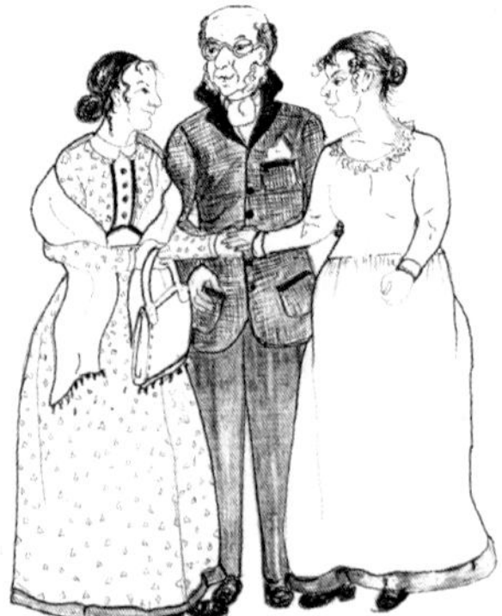

Fig 4.24 *'A fond farewell'*

have felt a heady mixture of apprehension and excitement.

Ethel's College record states that on arrival she was 'strong and in good health'. This was just as well as during the previous year there was much illness at College with numerous cases of influenza amongst staff and students.

Ethel did very well at College: she gained first prize in School Management and French and second prize in history. Her health was good and her conduct consistently excellent. Ethel was certainly a first-class student!

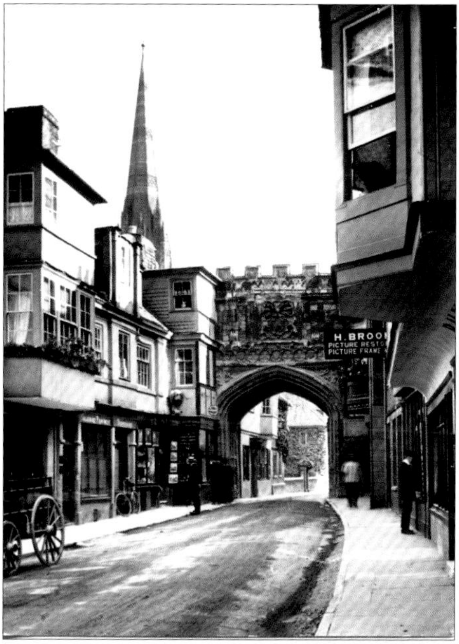

Fig. 4.25 Nearly there!

The 1891 Census shows that Constance Mary Hill, aged 42, was the Lady Superintendent and Matron of the College, Barbara Forth aged 30 was a Governess, along with 4 other Governesses, 73 students 3 laundresses, 2 kitchen maids and 2 housemaids. Canon Steward was the newly appointed College Principal and Chaplain.

The College Jubilee Year in 1891 was celebrated with a remarkable reunion of 200 guests, including the first student, Martha Gibson. It was such a success that a Triennial Reunion was suggested. Following this Miss Mildred Gill who was Head Student of 1893–4 suggested the formation of the 'Salisbury Club'. Miss Gill expressed the hope that Salisbury students could meet to renew old friendships and keep the Salisbury link strong. One hundred and twenty six years later years later hundreds of former Salisbury students continue to meet each year.

In 'The Red Book' Canon Steward recorded:

'Dr Fitch, Sir John Stainer, the Dean of Chester and Miss Harrison (cookery) inspected the College work. The year's expenditure was

£3,470. Miss Hill's "Special Fund" was started and the "Salisbury Diocesan Guild" founded a branch at the College'.

The aim of the Special Fund and The Guild was to give support to students in need after their College years. The fund was still receiving donations in 1968.

In the 1890s there were fierce discussions in the press concerning the standard of work and achievement in Training Colleges being too low. Church Colleges were criticised because of the amount of time given to Religious Knowledge. The results from Salisbury indicate that the students' secular work did not suffer because of their religious studies. In 1892 Salisbury gained 27 'Firsts'. In 1893 it ranked with Brighton, Stockwell and Tottenham, holding first place in needlework and reading, and third in history.

In 1890 Canon Steward purchased Audley House, next door to King's House. It had been the home of Anthony Trollope's mother. This provided extra accommodation and a Cookery School, where students and pupils from local schools were taught to cook healthy and nourishing meals. Extensions were also beginning to be made to King's House. Between 1895 and 1900 many improvements were made, including a new dining room and the conversion of the former Model School into a science laboratory. King's House was a warren of corridors, classrooms and dormitories. The building had great character and students who lived and worked there felt a true sense of history and belonging.

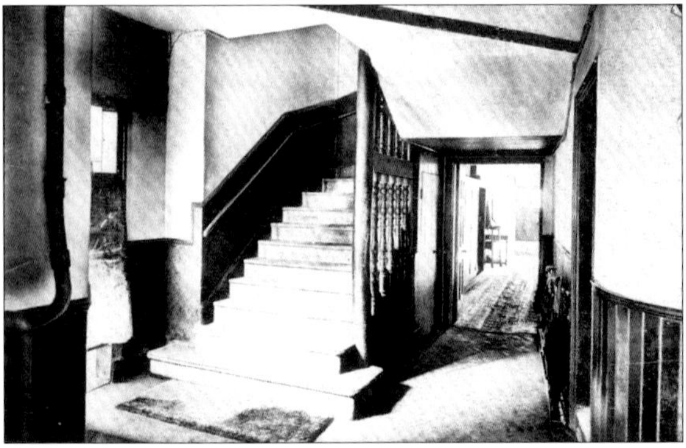

Fig. 4.26 The Great Staircase in King's House

Ethel's days were full with lectures, chores and services in the Cathedral. Subjects studied included English Literature, Grammar, Arithmetic, Drawing, Geography, History, Economy, Cookery, Religious Studies, Botany, Needlework and School Management. French was also reintroduced after an interval of 13 years. How relieved Ethel would have been that she was graded as good!

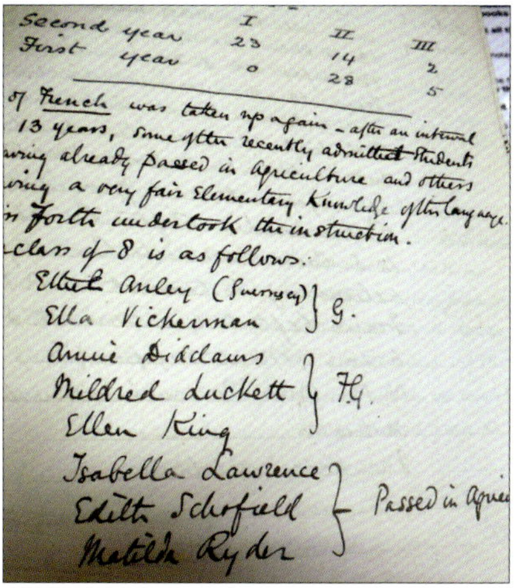

	I	II	III
Second year	23	14	2
First year	0	28	5

of French was taken up again – after an interval
13 years, some of the recently admitted students
...ving already passed in Agriculture and others
...ving a very fair elementary knowledge of the language
...n Forth undertook the instruction.
...class of 8 is as follows:
~~Ethel~~ Anley (Guernsey) } G.
Ella Vickerman
Annie Diddams
Mildred Luckett } F.G.
Ellen King
Isabella Lawrence
Edith Schofield } Passed in Agri...
Matilda Ryder

Fig. 4.27 College Log Book

Students gained strength from the Cathedral services, but at the end of a long day were often exhausted.

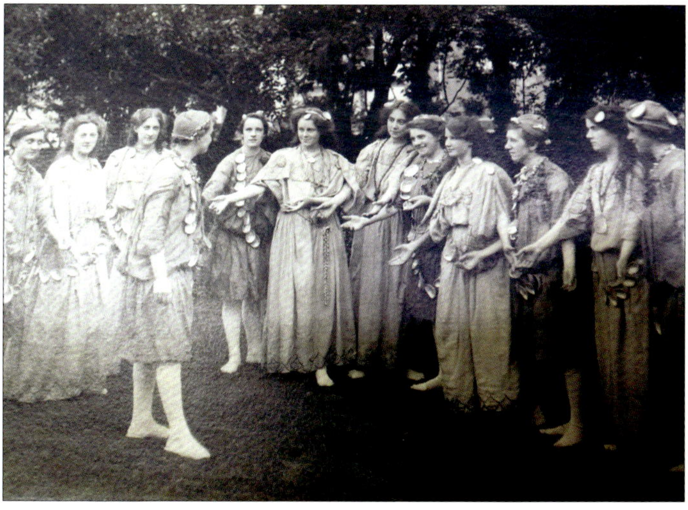

Fig. 4.28 Drama in the College gardens

Any free time was spent on recreation such as lawn tennis. In the evenings students often gave concerts and performed plays – in the gardens if the weather was good.

Ethel decided not to return to Guernsey at this time, perhaps because education in St Peter Port was going through such a difficult period. She secured a post as an assistant teacher at St John the Apostle School in Vassall Road, Kennington, London. This was an infant school with 300 children and her salary was £70 per annum.

What a change this must have been for Ethel! By 1901 she had returned to St Peter Port to live with her mother and stepfather, who had retired from the bakery. Now aged 30, she worked as a school mistress, teaching in her home at 1 St Thomas Place.

In 1914 there was a reunion in Guernsey of former Salisbury students. An account written in the Salisbury Training College Magazine of 1915 mentions that Mrs Cochrane (Ethel Anley) was present for the occasion. The 1911 Census records that in 1910 Ethel, aged 37, had married Harold Cochrane a Guernseyman aged 31 and that they were living at 104 Victoria Road, St Peter Port. Ethel was working as a teacher in a private school and Harold was a grower of greenhouse produce.

There is no doubt that the College Chapel was an important and integral part of Ethel's College life. On the 29th September 1957, the Chapel of the Holy Angels was extended. A plaque in the Chapel reveals that the extension was made possible largely because of a bequest of nearly £3,000 left by Ethel Anley. The College Architect, Mr Christopher Green, drew up plans for the enlargement.

'When the Chapel was first dedicated in 1899, only 120 students could be comfortably seated, but now that the transepts have been added, it is possible to seat 200 persons…In previous years many people have found blessing in the Chapel and now that it has been enlarged and so beautifully decorated, we hope and pray that students will continue to find peace and strength there'. Salisbury Training College Chronicle 1957

Ethel Anley died in 1955. She found inspiration in the College Chapel: through her generous bequest she enabled many others to do so in a beautiful and well equipped Chapel.

5 Training the Island Teachers

1898–1990 Margaret Montgomery, Student and ... 1900–1909 College lecturer

Margaret Montgomery, known as Maggie, was born in Southampton in 1878. Her parents married when her mother Janet, who was born in Scotland, was seventeen years old. The 1881 Census shows that by then her mother had been left with six children. Margaret's father John Peden Montgomery died in 1880 aged 47, when Margaret was only two years old. John, who was born in Ireland, had been a sergeant in the Royal Engineers based at Ordnance House, Southampton. Three of Margaret's siblings were teachers, so it is not surprising that Margaret decided to enter the profession.

During her first year at College Margaret was the Head Student – this was an impressive achievement. In 1898 the College had a visit from Bishop George Francis Popham Blyth, who was the Bishop in Jerusalem. Margaret made such an impression upon him that he presented her with his own Jerusalem cross, which had been laid on the site of the Holy Sepulchre. Margaret worked hard at College and was appointed to the College Staff in Midsummer 1900, when she was aged 22. Whilst working as a member of staff she sat several examinations including English, Chemistry, French and Education. By 1903 she had gained the Lady Literate in Arts (LLA) qualification. The LLA was held by many of the staff at this time, before women were allowed to graduate from university.

Margaret remained on the College staff until she left in 1909. The 1910 College Magazine records how much she was missed:

> 'Much did we miss Miss Montgomery, who had worked for nine

years with us and whom, with deep regret, we felt compelled to spare for the important work of the Headship of the Pupil Teacher Centre in Jersey. We know from our long and happy connection with her that she is bound to be appreciated and highly successful in her new sphere of work'.

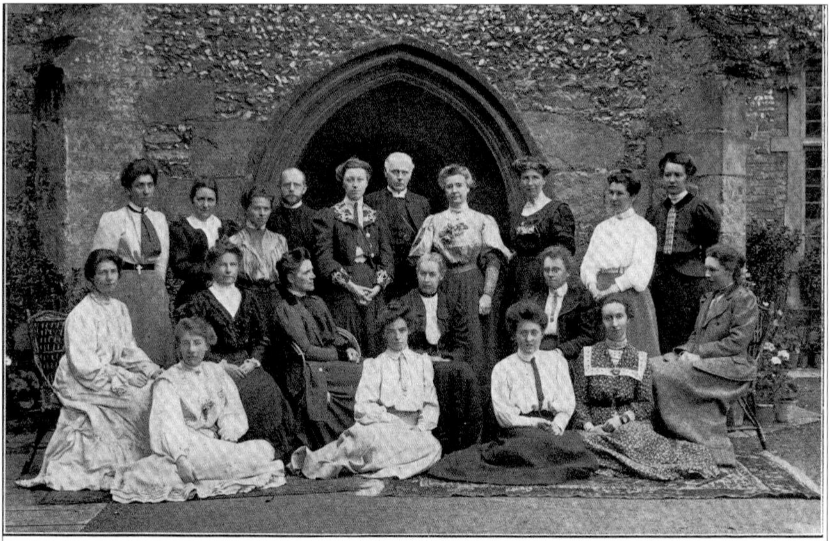

Miss Sewell. Miss Whatley. Dr. Baker. The Principal. Miss Gardiner. Miss Stevenson.
Miss Allen. Miss Street. Miss Forth. Miss Newman.
Miss Montgomery. Miss Thorp. Miss Black. Miss Hill. Miss Ellis. Miss Mitchell.
Miss Thompson. Miss Fildes. Miss Gill. Miss Grist.

Fig. 5.1 Margaret Montgomery with fellow members of staff circa 1908

Presentations were made to Miss Montgomery:

'They will always serve to remind me of the eleven happy years I spent in Salisbury, and of the many friends I found there'.

College Magazine 1910

During Margaret's eleven years at College, student numbers had been increasing. Where would they all be accommodated? The 1910 edition of the College Magazine is full of items connected with Barnard's Cross. Canon Steward, College Principal, realised that due to the growth of secondary education there would be an increase in the number of students wanting to train as teachers. He persuaded the College authorities to acquire Barnard's Cross, in St Ann's Street, which was initially a hostel for non-conformists.

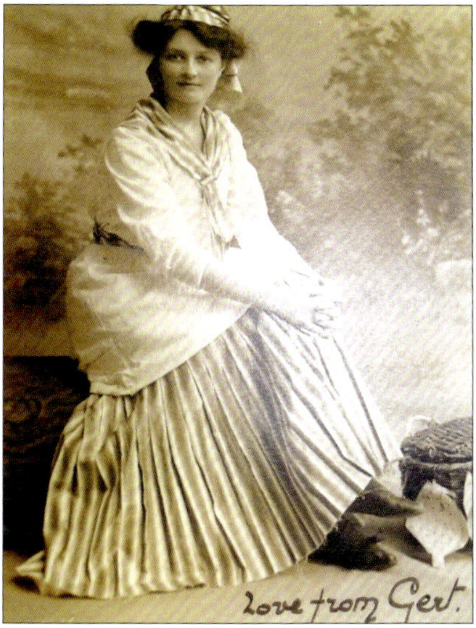

Left: Fig. 5.2 A student from Barnard's Cross in 1911

Below: Fig. 5.3 Barnard's Cross postcard

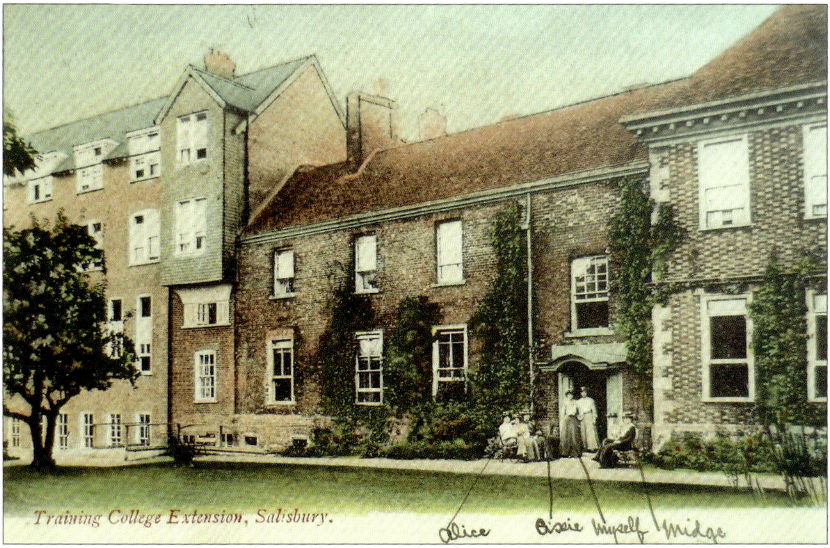

The large house and gardens were purchased in 1903 and accommodated 25 students. After the agreement drawn up between the States of Jersey Education Committee and the College, Barnard's Cross also became home for most Channel Island students during their College years.

Additional building work in 1904 meant that a further 25 students could be housed there.

A grand opening was held in November 1904. The 1910 edition of the College magazine indicates what an energetic and lively bunch of students lived there! The magazine is full of reports of all the many different activities that took place. There was also a great need for a Chapel:

> 'Ever since Barnard's Cross was opened… the need of a Chapel had been felt by Staff and Students alike. It was manifest that there were disadvantages in holding Divine worship for a community in the hall which was associated with their meals and various social entertainments'.
>
> College Magazine, 1910

The Chapel was dedicated on a very 'wet and tempestuous' afternoon in October 1909, but staff and students from both houses heartily joined in, sheltering under a huge awning. As one student commented, 'no weather could dampen our happiness over the completion of the Chapel'.

The many Channel Islanders who lived in Barnard's Cross found it to be a place of warmth, friendship and support. A student remembered her arrival at Barnard's Cross in 1914 and the warm welcome from Miss Rodgers who subsequently became the Head of Barnard's Cross:

> 'In the half light of passage and stairway lurk hesitant students with problems: illness of loved ones, school practice worries, misunderstandings in friendships…but the Miss Rodger's name on the door had come to mean understanding, sharing and halving problems'.

There were so many activities on offer. In 1910, plays including *Antigone, The Cricket on the Hearth, The Rivals* and *Alice through the Looking Glass*, were performed; there was a concert of Morris dancing and folk songs, with proceeds given to form an 'Old Students Sick fund'. Mission Sales were a regular event and, on one occasion, photographs of the Chapel were sold with all stocks running out.

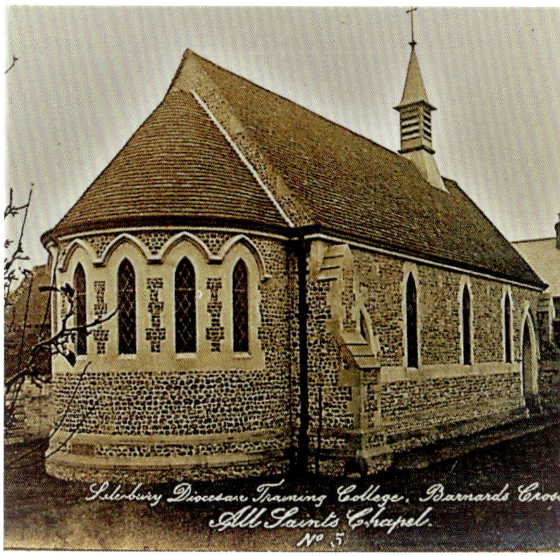

Fig. 5.4

There were outings and expeditions, and debates were always popular. Sport was important and the hockey players excelled:

> 'The half backs were strong, especially M. Stone, who seemed to those who played against her to have found the secret of being in half a dozen places at the same time'.

Physical exercise was increasing at College with the introduction of 'Hygiene and Physical Exercises'. However, students did not enjoy the inspections, which must have been exhausting. A Channel Islander recalled:

> 'Twice this year have Miss Fildes and Miss Holmes brought out their troops of students for inspection. The ordeal lasted a whole day at King's House and half a day at Barnard's Cross'.

A healthy rivalry existed between King's House and Barnard's Cross in sports, debates and examination results. They all shared a warmth and affection for the College and Cathedral and looked back on their years there as being special years of happiness, comradeship and fulfilment.

In 1902 Margaret Montgomery passed her examination in French for the LLA. She made good use of her language skills when she contributed to Lottie Wilkinson's autograph book with a quotation in French by Jean-Jacques Rousseau.

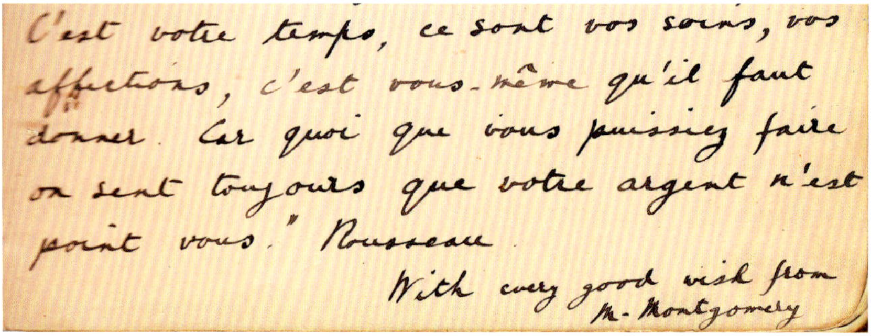

C'est votre temps, ce sont vos soins, vos affections, c'est vous-même qu'il faut donner. Car quoi que vous puissiez faire on sent toujours que votre argent n'est point vous." Rousseau.

With every good wish from
M. Montgomery

Fig. 5.5

Miss Montgomery wished to emphasise that true charity is not in the giving of money but in the giving of yourself: 'It is your time, it is your care, your affection, it is yourself that must be given'.

How useful her command of French would be in Jersey! Since 1900, Margaret had given her time, knowledge and expertise to the College and its students, but now the Channel Islands beckoned and she set sail for pastures new.

1909–1938 Miss Montgomery in Jersey 'The efficient teacher is the keystone of a sound educational system' – H. Harrison

Jersey and Guernsey are only 35 miles apart, but they often do things differently. The development of teacher training was no exception.

When in 1909 the need of teacher training and of preparing students for college life in England was recognized in Jersey, it was to Canon Steward that the Dean of Jersey and the Education Department of the States turned for help.

He recommended Miss Margaret Montgomery, a former much-beloved Head Student, and for several years a member of the Training College staff, to be the first Principal of the Pupil Teacher Centre in St Helier'.

She was hand-picked for the job. The Dean of Jersey and the Education Committee wished to appoint someone from the mainland whose knowledge of the British educational scene would benefit the island. Canon Steward had no hesitation in recommending Miss Montgomery, an ambitious, adventurous and able young woman who would rise to the challenges of this exciting post. Her destiny was sealed.

Six years earlier, the island had taken an important step in the provision of improved training for elementary school pupil-teachers. Central classes were started in Jersey later than in most places in England, but a new Pupil-Teachers' Centre was opened in 1903. It was based in a house in Hill Street. Mr H. J. Carter, the former head of St Ouen's Wesleyan Day School, was appointed as the teacher. His job was to train the pupil-teachers, at the same time as furthering their education. There had been great difficulty in finding a supply of trained teachers and the Education Committee had inaugurated this in the hope that there would always be a supply of Jersey teachers. It was also hoped that pupil-teachers would no longer need to go, at great expense, to colleges in England.

In October 1904 an agreement was drawn up between the States of Jersey and Salisbury Diocesan Training College. A considerable number of island candidates wanted to attend the College and it was intended that they would mostly join Barnard's Cross. The States of Jersey agreed to pay £200 towards the expense of this College extension. The money would allow the Jersey Education Committee to nominate two pupils every year for exhibitions for admission into Barnard's Cross. The agreement was not widely approved and a letter to the newspaper argued that, as the States had already voted £200 towards the training of pupil teachers, it would be better to vote £400 towards improving the new Pupil-Teacher Centre rather than pay £200 for two nominated pupils to attend Salisbury Diocesan Training College.

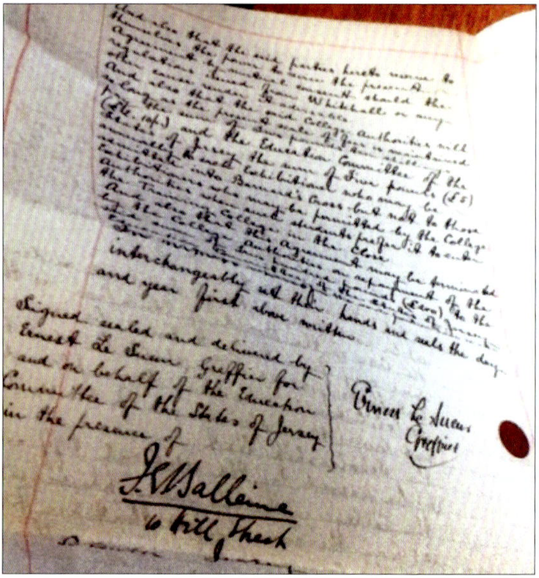
Signed sealed and delivered by Ernest Le Sueur Greffier for and on behalf of the Education Committee of the States of Jersey in the presence of

Fig. 5.6 Agreement between Salisbury Diocean Training College and the States of Jersey

> 'If it will wisely exercise itself to see that our Jersey pupil-teachers are properly educated, and if it can provide the funds for that purpose, the teachers will succeed in finding places for themselves in any of several training colleges by fair competitions, not by nominations'

The writer also pointed out that 'no nominations are suggested for male teachers'. In fact the College received the promised £200 and Jersey was allowed the privilege of nominating two candidates to the College each year. By 1906 the provision at the Pupil-Teacher Centre which had been 'fairly adequate' a few years earlier, had now fallen much behind that in England.

> 'We find that in England all pupil-teachers serve in school only half time and attend class for at least five half days a week, whereas in Jersey they are employed in school for eight school meetings a week and attend class for three half days only. Unless the conditions are equalised, or nearly so, the Jersey pupil teachers must henceforth meet those trained in England at a disadvantage in the competition for admission to training colleges. The efficient teacher is the keystone of a sound educational system and the demand for a trained teacher is steadily growing. The people of Jersey will not be content to be left behind'.
>
> H. Harrison, Jersey States Education Committee

Mr Harrison went on to suggest that pupil-teachers should be made half timers and that they should have a full time preparatory two year course for those whose parents guaranteed their intention to follow the teaching profession. He recommended the employment of specialist subject teachers for the Pupil Teacher Centre and better facilities, such as a library and a laboratory. Mr Carter, the Headteacher, was doing his best, but the Jersey Pupil Teacher Centre had inadequate staffing and facilities.

> 'In these days of specialising, a Pupil Teacher Centre that is worked by one man, however able he may be, and that is forced to keep down expenses within £200 per annum, will never compete with the English centres and will assuredly never secure to the island an efficient teaching personnel'.

In March 1909 Mr Carter resigned. He was appointed as Headmaster of the First Tower Schools. Marjorie Starck, who subsequently trained at Salisbury, presented him, on behalf of the pupil-teachers, with a 'handsome silver rose bowl, suitably inscribed'.

When Miss Montgomery arrived in the island a few months later, she found that education was considerably below the standard of that in England, where fees had not been charged since 1891 and compulsory attendance for children up to the age of 11 had been enforced in 1893.

The principle of compulsory elementary education had been agreed in Jersey in 1894 and had become obligatory in 1899, but parents were still expected to pay a nominal fee. Those who could not afford this were reluctant to ask for parish aid and be seen as paupers. During the next decade the realisation grew that if education was to be compulsory it must be free, as it was in England.

> 'As our children have to be judged by the standards of the Mother Country, it is necessary that we follow the Mother Country in this respect'.
> H. Harrison, March 1905

Elementary education became free in 1908, the year before Miss Montgomery arrived.

During 1909 the new Education Bill was hotly contested in the States of Jersey. By this new law, all grants would cease and the States would take over the management of schools. Some of the rectors of the island churches were reluctant to hand over their parish schools. Jersey watched most carefully what was happening across the water. It was felt that it would be

> 'a decided advantage to adopt the English Code of Education', for that would provide one uniform standard of education across the island, rather than (as now) one standard in each parish'.
> Education debate in the States, 24th July, 1909

Unable to reach a final agreement on a hot summer's day, the States voted for the postponement of the Education Bill until the next session in 1910. Meanwhile, Miss Montgomery had arrived in Jersey.

Jersey Independent & Daily Telegraph, 21 August 1909

> 'Miss M Montgomery, the newly appointed Head of the Jersey Pupil Teacher Centre will take up her duties at the school after the summer vacation. She comes from the Salisbury Diocesan Training College with very high credentials from Canon Steward on whose recommendation the appointment was made'.

During Miss Montgomery's first year, the new law was passed and all public elementary schools were placed under the direct management of the States Education Committee. School attendance was now free, and it was compulsory until the age of fourteen. The Education Committee also agreed that the pupil-teachers required a fuller education. The Pupil Teacher Centre needed to be extended and so did the curriculum.

At the time of the 1911 Census, Miss Montgomery was living at 4, Temple Villas in Stopford Road, St Helier. Substantial town houses had been built in this area in the mid-19th century and she was sharing the house with three other people. It was in a central location and she had an easy walk to the Pupil Teacher Centre, which was now housed in the building that is today Jersey Arts Centre in Phillips Street.

Marjorie Starck who was born in 1892 was a pupil-teacher at St Mark's School in St Helier and one of Miss Montgomery's first students in Phillips Street. In 1914, following her training in Salisbury, Marjorie returned to teach in Jersey at Halkett Place School. Her daughter, Faith Herbert, remembers her description of Miss Montgomery carrying lots of keys on her belt and saying that she felt 'special' in Jersey because she was a foreigner.

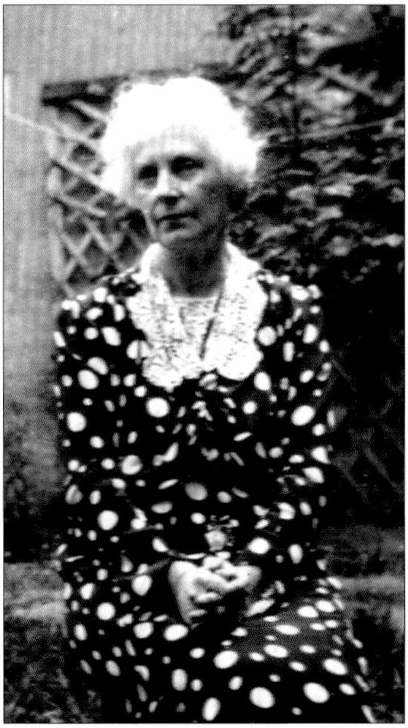

Fig. 5.7 Miss Montgomery

It must have been a shock for Miss Montgomery to find herself marooned on a small island! Having lived in the college community for some years, she would have missed the companionship of friends and colleagues. Perhaps she also missed the Cathedral and its regular patterns of worship. St Helier, however, had quite a lot to offer. It is likely that, as an English person, she attended St Mark's Church and got to know other new incomers. The Opera House offered entertainment and she may even have gone to the Battle of Flowers. There were markets, a busy harbour and two railways, one in the east of the island and one in the west, out to Corbiere.

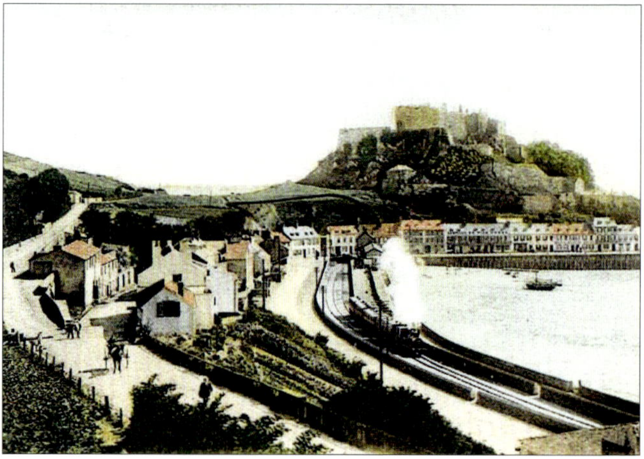

Fig. 5.8 On a summer's evening the return train trip from Snow Hill to Gorey would have been most agreeable.

Electricity arrived in the island much later than in England. Houses in Salisbury Cathedral Close had electric lighting by 1900, but the Jersey Electricity Company did not start to supply consumers until 1925. On the plus side, however, Miss Montgomery had sea breezes, the ever present cry of seagulls and summers that seemed to go on forever. Life was pretty good!

Visiting her pupil-teachers in their schools would have been part of her job. Outside St Helier, the island was still very rural. She travelled in a horse-drawn bus in the early days and saw for herself the potato planting and the vraic gathering – and the many children who were still being kept off school to help their parents. Old habits die hard.

During her years in Jersey Miss Montgomery saw the first sea planes arriving in the island in 1912 and flying boats in 1925. In 1937, the year that she retired, the airport at St Peter's was built. Until then, the wet sands of St Aubin's Bay had served as an aerodrome and the timetable of flights was regulated by the tides. Now London was, unbelievably, just an hour away.

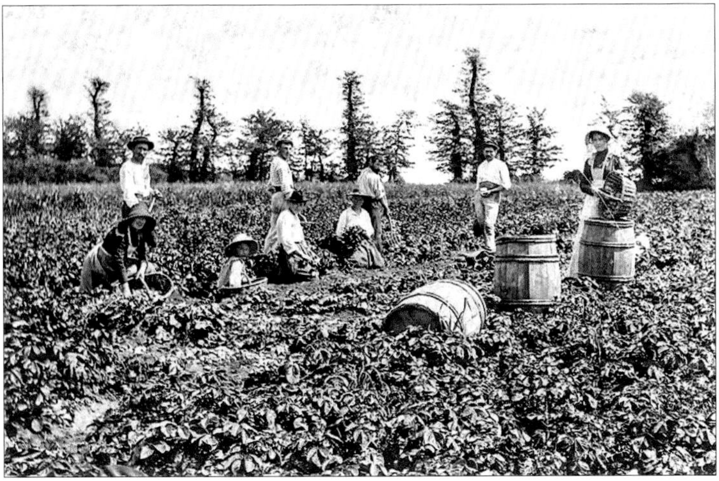

Fig. 5.9 Harvesting the potatoes, 1906

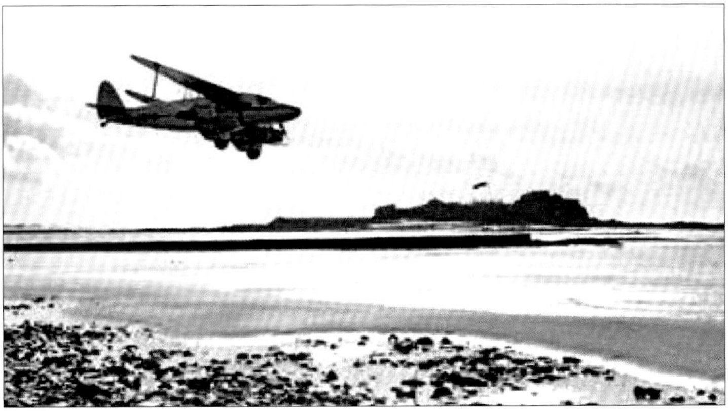

Fig. 5.10 Landing on the beach at West Park, early 1930s

The Log Book for the Jersey Pupil Teacher Centre begins on September 13th 1909:

> 'The classes recommenced after the summer holidays with Miss Margaret Montgomery (formerly Third Mistress at Salisbury Training College) as Head Teacher'.

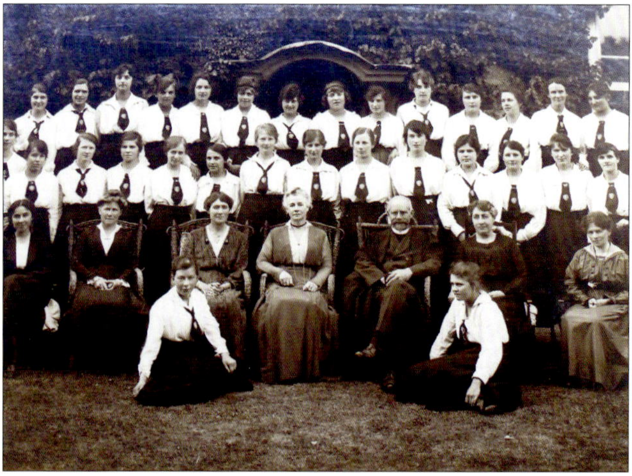

Fig. 5.11 Miss Barbara Forth, Principal of Salisbury Training College from 1913 until 1928, with students. During these years many of Miss Montgomery's pupils in Jersey chose to train in Salisbury.

Miss Montgomery worked in Jersey for the next twenty-nine years. She was instrumental in convincing the Public Instruction Committee that students intending to be teachers should be sent to England for professional training. The Pupil Teacher Centre subsequently moved to Rouge Bouillon, where it shared premises with the Brighton Road Elementary School. It was later called the Teachers' Training Centre and it then became the States Intermediate School in 1929. Miss Montgomery remained the Principal. It was said that she 'accomplished wonders at the Intermediate School on inadequate resources and in cramped conditions. She made the school her life'.

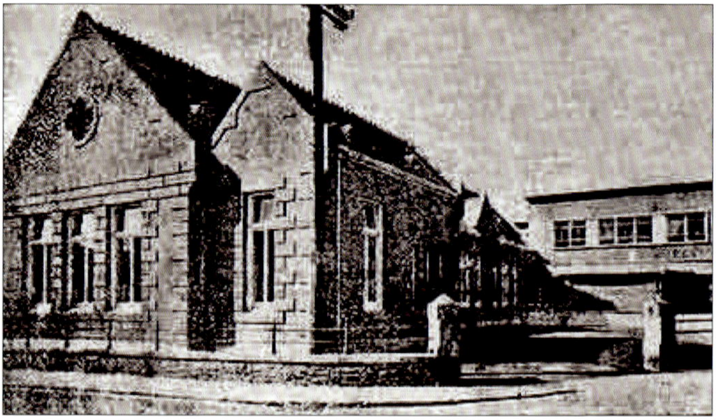

Fig. 5.12 The Pupil Teacher Centre shared premises with Brighton Road Elementary School

The Intermediate School was a co-educational, selective school, with entry at age eleven by examination. As the places were limited, the standard was high but the school had no Sixth Form and pupils finished their education at the age of sixteen with the School Certificate Examination. The few who stayed on were provided with a wider curriculum and a specific course that was aimed at further education. A former pupil described Miss Montgomery as 'something of a pioneer in Jersey educational history and far in advance of her times when she first came here. I know that most of us found ourselves better equipped educationally than other students when we went up to our various Training Colleges'.

Miss Montgomery was an influential person in the lives of numerous young people, many of whom had long teaching careers in the island. They remembered her with gratitude and affection.

Gladys Gruchy was educated at New Street Girls' School from the age of six. She became a pupil-teacher there in 1919 and also received education at the Pupil Teacher Centre. Miss Mellor, the Headmistress at New Street, reported that she had always been a painstaking student, had been punctual and her lessons had been well done. She commended her musical ability and felt that 'she should make a very capable teacher'. Gladys's vicar was the Dean of Jersey, the Revd J. Balleine. He described her as 'a particularly nice minded girl, anxious to be useful and very loyal'

Having passed the Cambridge Senior Examination, Gladys went to College in 1921, living at Barnard's Cross. She returned to Jersey after her training and taught there for 42 years. Gladys's considerable skills in Needlework and Music must have been appreciated in her schools.

Florence Mary Renouf was the daughter of a Jersey farmer. She had been educated at Jersey Ladies College before attending the Pupil-Teachers' Centre for just one term. She lived at Barnard's Cross in Salisbury from 1927 until 1929 and returned to teach in the island for 41 years. She described Miss Montgomery as 'the much loved and respected Head of the Pupil-Teachers' Centre. It may be that she encouraged her girls to train at her college, for in 1927 five of us applied and were accepted. No interviews were held but a good medical report and credits in London General or Cambridge exams were required'.

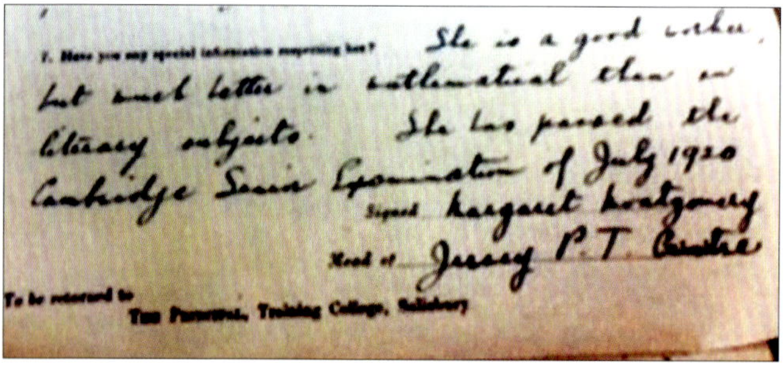
She is a good worker, but much better in mathematical than in literary subjects. She has passed the Cambridge Senior Examination of July 1920

Signed Margaret Montgomery

Head of Jersey P.T. Centre

To be returned to The Principal, Training College, Salisbury

Fig. 5.13 Extract from Miss Montgomery's report on Gladys Gruchy for the Principal at Salisbury Training College

Miss Montgomery kept in close touch with the Principals of Salisbury Training College. Comments about individual pupils included 'lethargic temperament' and 'knowledge of French below the average of Jersey students' but positive comments were also included. One pupil was described as 'a very capable girl with many interests and much initiative'.

Her letters also mentioned more mundane matters: 'Hasn't the weather been dreadful! The crossings have been some of the worst on record. I have been very glad to think that it was not crossing time for me'.

The Intermediate School Log Book for December 12th 1937 marks the end of an era: 'Miss M Montgomery left on retirement after 28 years' service in Jersey, and is succeeded by Miss Coad, Senior Assistant'.

Miss Montgomery was presented with gifts from her old Jersey pupils and an album containing 550 of their signatures. 'Miss Montgomery has, only this Christmas, retired from the Principalship of the Intermediate School into which her Pupil Teacher Centre developed; One of her first pupils, Mr D'Authrean, said:

> 'We have come to say 'Good-bye' to a very dear friend, one whom we all love and respect, and to whom we owe a great deal. No-one can take her place, for both as a woman of charming personality and sterling qualities, and as an educational force, she was – and is unique'.
>
> 'She has given twenty-nine years of inspiration, driving force and complete devotion to secondary education in Jersey and to the building up of a well-trained Teaching Staff for the schools of the island'.

Extracts from speeches on the occasion of her retirement.

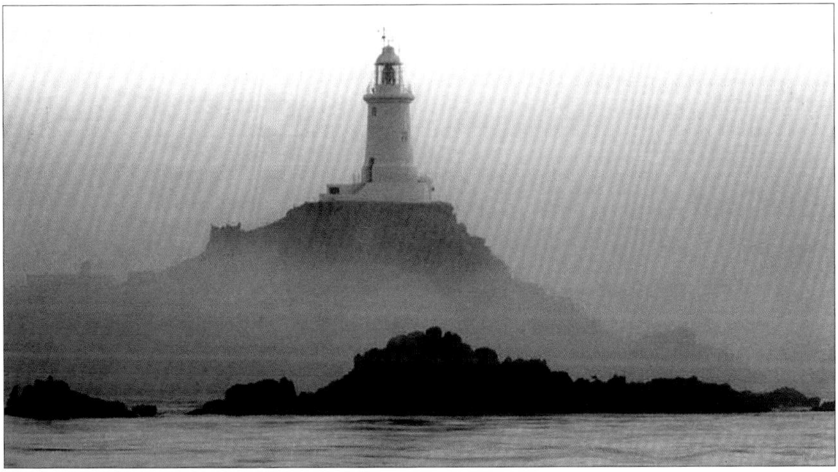

Fig. 5.14 Corbière lighthouse

Miss Montgomery sailed for home, but one year later her contribution to island education was acknowledged when the school was visited by HMIs:

> 'Under devoted and inspired headships the school in 1938 (accommodated in rooms and corridors shared by Brighton Road Elementary School) had 146 students, drawn island-wide by selective examination. The school had fully justified itself and had won an enviable reputation throughout the island'.

The report went on to say that the school's 'undoubted progress was thwarted by lack of space, staff, educational facilities and playing fields'. It was recommended that the Jersey Intermediate School should be closed. In fact, the Intermediate School carried on throughout the Occupation and survived until the mid-1950s.

Miss Montgomery died in 1964 and the Jersey Club, which was made up of former students, arranged a Memorial Service, which was held at St Marks Church in St Helier. She had fulfilled Canon Steward's predictions and had indeed risen to the challenges of the job.

'Pupil Teachers are not Assistant Teachers' – Preliminary Teacher Training in Guernsey

Between the years 1900 and 1910 there was a noticeable gap in the number of students from Guernsey training to teach in Salisbury. Perhaps this was because the education system in Guernsey was heavily reliant upon young pupil-teachers who were given too much responsibility, with inadequate training and supervision. This may have discouraged some students from further training. Inspection reports during this period highlighted their difficult and often exhausting daily grind. There was very little difference in the salary of a College trained teacher and an uncertificated one. This gave very little incentive for pupil-teachers to travel to England for a two-year training course.

Students who trained at Salisbury during this period, including Marion Cumber, Dorothy and Marjorie Falla and Edith Albiges, had attended the Guernsey Pupil Teacher Centre. They also worked as pupil-teachers at schools across the island. Edna Bisson, who started college in 1913, worked for three years as a pupil-teacher at St Peter's in the Wood Boys' School.

What was the Guernsey Pupil Teacher Centre and why was it founded? Insufficient funds and inadequate teaching had led to some poor school reports. In 1898 John Augustus Munday, formerly Organising Master of Winchester Diocese, was appointed by the States to oversee the improvement and re-organisation of Guernsey's primary schools. He remained in this position until 1914.

The fascinating collection of 'Annual Reports on Public Primary Schools in Guernsey 1900–1920', show that it was a time of change for Guernsey schools.

The inspections were sometimes critical of the schools, but the States demonstrated that it wanted a better education for pupils and introduced several positive changes in legislation. Some of the improvements included:

- In 1900 school attendance became compulsory.
- School inspections became more regular; a law in 1903 stated that schools should be visited by an external inspector every three years.
- In 1903 the Education Law stated that each Parish should be responsible for primary education up to the age of thirteen. Pupils should remain in education until this age.
- From 1914 the States Education Committee requested annual HMI inspections.
- English Inspectors had advised more uniformity in educational provision: the setting up of the Education Council in 1916 made this more possible.
- In 1923 the compulsory school age was set at six to fourteen years.

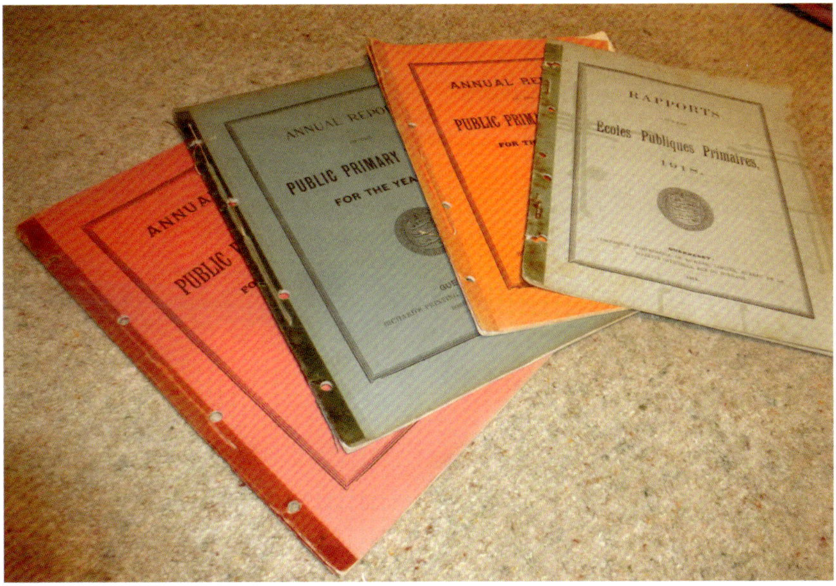

Fig. 5.15 Annual Reports for Public Primary Schools

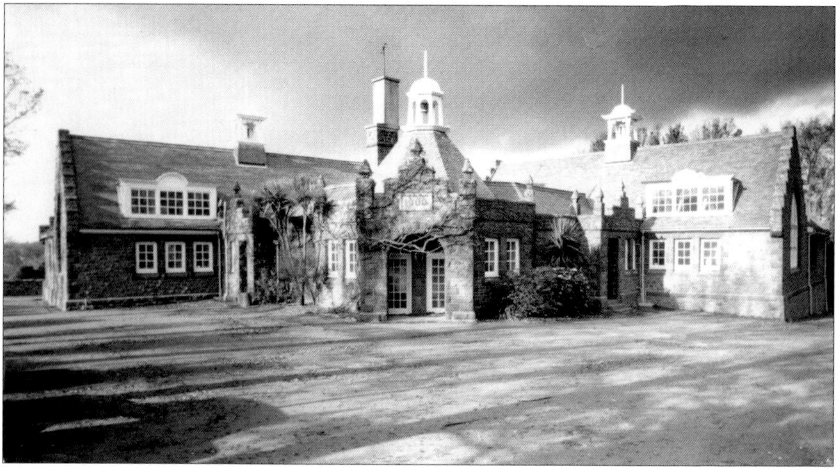

Fig. 5.16 Amherst School St Peter Port, 1901

The 1899 report states clear reasons for setting up a Pupil Teacher Centre:

> 'Twelve months ago the question of the future supply of teachers was a serious one. On one hand, School Committees, seeking in vain for efficient teachers and finding none, appointed anyone, however incompetent, who chose to apply for a vacant post. On the other hand, young teachers were hopeless and discouraged, unable to compete with pupil teachers across the Channel, finding it impossible to attain to the efficiency and status which a Training College career can give, and taught perhaps by seniors, who themselves could not pass their own examinations.'
>
> John Munday Inspection Report, 1899

The aims of the Centre were not only to give instruction but as the report explained:

> 'By means of model and criticism lessons its pupils are trained and exercised in the art of teaching and are taught those principles which guided the professional teacher as distinguished from the inexperienced amateur'.

However, by 1902 the original Pupil Teacher Centre no longer existed as:

> 'It did not go far enough, but considering the staff that was available and the material with which they had to deal, the wonder is that the record is so good'.
>
> Mr E.M. Kenney Herbert, Inspection Report, 1902

In a 1902 inspection he confirmed that there was too much responsibility placed upon untrained school teachers and that some type of apprenticeship was required. He criticised the two grades of Assistant Teachers – qualified and unqualified. The unqualified teachers often had unattractive jobs and low pay. There was no superannuation scheme and a system was used by which teachers received a bonus if examination results were good. He described this as utterly indefensible in principle and based on mistrust of teachers by the Authority.

Although some school buildings were good, others were poorly lit and cloakroom facilities were deemed unhygienic. The lack of continuity and conformity in the system hampered the quality of education. Salaries were inconsistent and there was too much dependence on young pupil-teachers who were sometimes left in charge of whole classes without adequate supervision. Mr Kenney Herbert commented:

> 'Pupil Teachers are not Assistant Teachers. They are apprentices, and apprenticeship places upon the employer the duty of seeing that the apprentice is properly instructed both in his studies and in Practical Teaching'.

It was difficult to recruit qualified teachers, partly because any teachers who came from England had to relinquish their superannuation rights and had no form of pension to look forward to.

In 1909 the typical salary for a newly appointed College trained teacher was around £75 per annum. It was only a few pounds less for a teacher who had not been College trained which gave potential teachers very little incentive to travel to England to train. In 1920 a much fairer salary structure was introduced, which was a significant factor in ensuring an increase in the number of qualified teachers on the island.

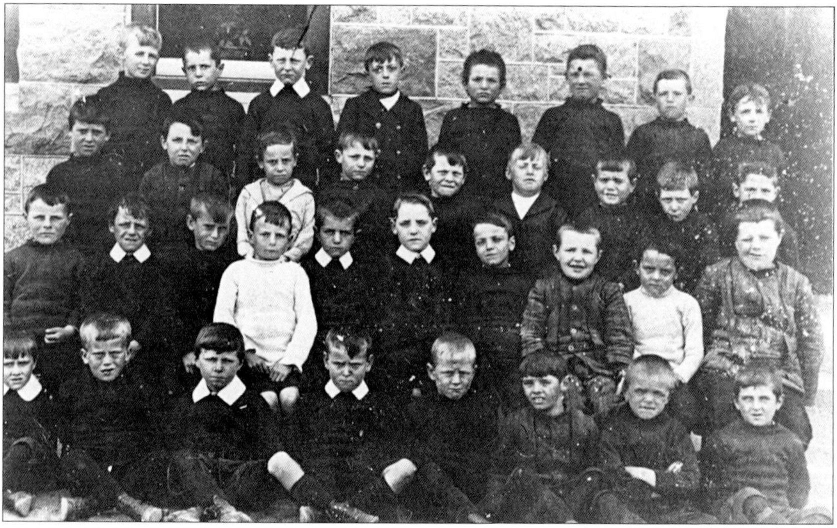

Fig. 5.17 Pupils from Castel School around 1909

Following the closure of the Pupil Teacher Centre, Miss Mellish the Headmistress of Guernsey Ladies College, was asked to organise a special department for the benefit of pupil-teachers. It was held at Myrtle Lodge and was under the supervision of the States Committee for Parochial Education. The curriculum included Scripture, Mathematics, Drawing, French, Botany and Drill. Science and Phonetics were added in 1915. The pupil-teachers received free instruction and a small salary. The students had a demanding load: they were expected to attend the Pupil Teacher Centre for two days per week, and teach in schools for three days per week. They also faced an annual examination.

The 1907 report stated that 187 students had come under the influence of the Pupil Teacher Centre.

> 'Of these, 32 have obtained scholarships and have completed their professional training in English Colleges at the expense of the Imperial Exchequer. Already many have returned to take up appointments on the island, and more will return provided that our educational system

continues to merit and secure the favourable recognition of the Board of Education'.

Mr John Munday, Inspection Report. 1907

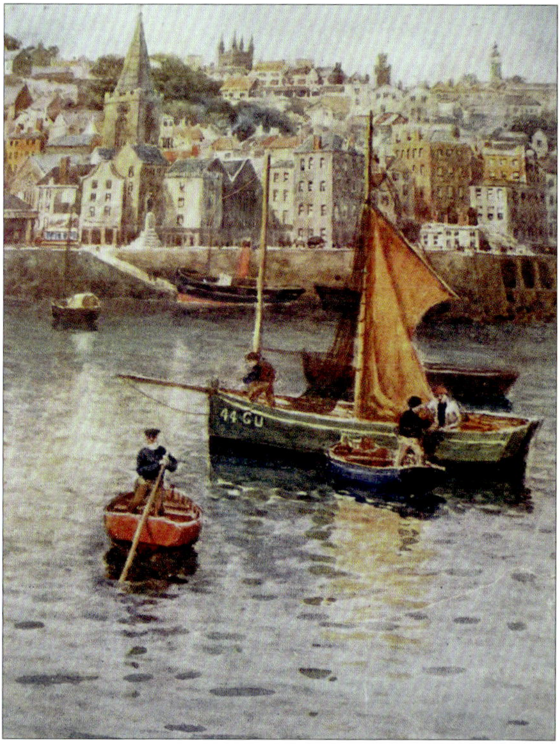

Fig. 5.18 St Peter Port Harbour 1911 – a welcome sight for returning students

Unfortunately the situation regarding pupil-teachers had not improved. The inspector expressed concern for the young people. 'Most of them are growing girls, and I think that their lives are too strenuous'.

By 1909 the central classes for pupil-teachers were held in the Vauvert School buildings in St Peter Port, which hopefully made their lives a little easier. They could now meet for their collective lessons in the same building they attended in the week.

In 1912 several students, including Marjorie Falla, gained admission to Teacher Training Colleges:

> 'The Pupil Teacher Centre continues to give admirable training to its students. The large number of young teachers who gained admission to the English Training Colleges in 1912 caused some embarrassment to local Managers who are accustomed to utilize the services of ex Pupil Teachers as members of the School staff.'
>
> Mr John Munday, Inspection Report, 1912

Widespread use of pupil-teachers remained: in 1914 in three St Peter Port Schools there were 22 pupil-teachers. A recommendation in the report of this year was that school staffing should not depend upon pupil-teachers. It was suggested that some of the girls should be given scholarships to the Guernsey Ladies College and be able to carry on their education there, followed by two years as a pupil-teacher instead of four. By 1914 teaching was provided by staff from three Guernsey schools: Elizabeth College, the Ladies' College and the Intermediate School for Boys:

> 'The work done is of good quality. The teaching heard was excellent. A test examination was given without notice and the students' results were 'highly commendable'.
>
> Mr C.H.B. Elliot, Inspection Report, 1914

Elizabeth College

This prestigious fee-paying and selective school for boys was founded in 1563 by orders of Queen Elizabeth the First to provide education for boys beyond the primary level. The school went from strength to strength, with numerous successful and eminent pupils. When the Pupil Teacher Centre closed the junior male pupil-teachers were transferred to Elizabeth College.

Guernsey Ladies' College

Many Guernsey girls attended private schools in Guernsey or England for their secondary education. In 1872 Guernsey Ladies' College was founded to provide a corresponding education to that provided for boys at Elizabeth College. The school was aimed at upper-middle class parents who wanted their daughters to have a fuller education, including subjects such as French, Latin, German and Music.

The headmistress, Miss Mellish, organised a special department for pupil-teachers at Myrtle Lodge. The association continued until 1917. At this time there were fifteen boys and sixty-one girls at the Centre. Ivy Gillam, who attended Salisbury Training College in 1922, was a former pupil.

Intermediate Schools

By 1872 the States Parochial Education Committee had oversight of all Guernsey Parish Schools. The Committee was keen to establish schools which would provide a thorough education. Some pupils were admitted at eight, others by eleven plus scholarships and others when they reached the top classes of the parochial schools. The school for boys was set up in 1883 and the one for girls in 1895. They were very popular and the number of pupils rapidly increased. Both schools were fee paying except for scholarship pupils. However, the fees were much less than at Elizabeth College and Guernsey Ladies College. Several Salisbury students attended the Girls' Intermediate School, including Marie Brigant, Ethel Hamel, Dorothy and Marjorie Falla, Dorothy Le Huray and Daphne Lacey.

The 1915 Inspection report reflects the impact and some of difficulties brought about by World War I. There were seventy pupil-teachers training at this time, but there was a severe shortage of teachers, which increased as the war went on. One of the pupil-teachers was Edith Albiges, who from 1915–1920 worked at St Andrew's Girls' School.

> 'It takes six years to make a teacher, viz, four years at the Pupil Teacher Centre and two at the Training College.'
>
> Mr A. F. Page HMI 1916 Inspection Report

The 1916 report describes the situation in that year:

> 'No less than 15 women teachers have gone from Guernsey to be trained…it is almost twice as great as at any previous period in

Guernsey, in fact, during 5 years 1910–1914, only 18 women teachers went to be trained'.

Mr A. F. Page HMI

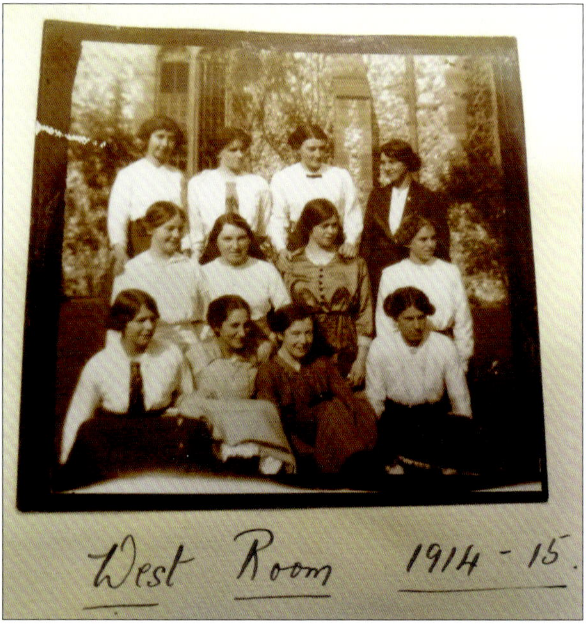

Fig. 5.19 Students in the College garden

It was difficult to secure trained teachers from English colleges, partly due to the huge demand for teachers in England. In his inspection of 1918, Mr Page stated that at the insistence of HMI the Council now recognised another grade of student teachers.

> 'These young people are employed for a year between the ages of 17 and 18, after they have passed a qualifying examination for entry to a Teacher College, to which they proceed at the end of the year's teaching experience'.

The system was changing, but in 1920 securing sufficient suitably qualified teachers remained a problem:

> 'As a good number of young teachers annually return from Training Colleges, it is hoped that the Managers will shortly have a reasonable field for selection and be relieved of the anxieties that have characterised the administration during the past decade'.
>
> Mr A. F. Page HMI

Five out of eight female teachers who completed their teacher training at this time took up posts on Guernsey and several others, after teaching in England for a while, returned to the island.

The pupil-teacher system was still in a state of flux. A letter in 1922 from John David, Secretary of the Education Council of Guernsey to The Principal of Salisbury Training College states:

> 'Guernsey is in a transition stage as regards the preliminary training of young teachers. It has discarded the Pupil Teacher Centre and adopted the Student Teacher System'.

In July 1925 the Pupil Teacher Centre was judged to be no longer needed and it closed.

Channel Island students, who chose to train to teach in Salisbury in the early years of the twentieth century, had an extremely demanding and rigorous start to their teaching careers, and are to be much admired for their determination, fortitude and courage.

6 Blood, Sweat and Tears

Channel Islanders at College during the First World War

Records indicate that in the first decade of the twentieth century Agnes Le Huray may have been the only Guernsey student trained at the College. By now, several other colleges were open for the training of female teachers and some students may have opted to train elsewhere.

However by 1910, Guernsey students were once again crossing the channel in order to attend Salisbury Training College. Dorothy Falla was admitted to the College in 1910, having been educated at The States Intermediate School. She attended the Pupil Teacher Centre before working as a pupil-teacher at St Martin's Primary School, as did her sister Marjorie who trained at the College in 1912. Both sisters were resident at Barnard's Cross. They returned to Guernsey after training and during World War Two, when the Channel Islands were occupied by the Germans, the sisters were evacuated with their schools.

Ethel Hamel and Marion Cumber went to College in 1911. The Census for this year shows that Ethel, aged eighteen, was working as a pupil-teacher before she went to College. We can imagine how pleased Marion would have been to have another Guernsey student living in Barnard's Cross. After her training, Ethel returned to the island where she taught at Amherst Girls School until she married in 1925.

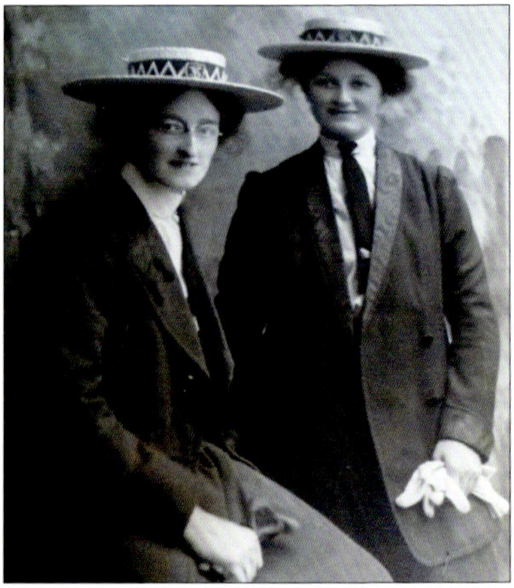

Fig. 6.1 Two Salisbury students *circa* 1914–1916

Edna Amy Bisson arrived at College in 1913. Winifred Florence Le Poidevin attended College in 1916.

Education ran in her family as the 1911 Census records that her two sisters were both headmistresses at 'States Primary Schools' in Guernsey.

Approximately 20 Jersey students arrived between 1900 and 1910 and rather more between 1910 and 1920. One reason for this was the opening of Barnard's Cross in St Ann Street, Salisbury in 1904. In a small island community, the word must have spread and Salisbury became the college of choice. Faith Herbert, whose mother was Marjorie Starck, one of Miss Montgomery's first pupils, remembered her mother saying that 'all the girls went to Salisbury'. Marjorie Starck arrived in 1911 along with Dorothy Ahier and Edith Balleine.

Perhaps the Guernsey students missed their regular swimming sessions at the Bathing Places in St Peter Port. A College Log Book from 1910 records their efforts to have regular swimming lessons. It was not to be!

> 'The Students from Barnard's Cross approached the Principal with a request to be allowed to use Salisbury Swimming Baths on Fridays 2.30–3.30. The Medical Officer was of the opinion that 2.30 was too close to dinner, and that consequently it could incur a change of timetable, and that the students' recreation was so ample that bathing could not be considered necessary. The summer holiday would give ample opportunity for swimming lessons.
>
> The Principal and Miss Hill concluded that it would be an unnecessary and unwise experiment, possibly affecting the studies afterwards for the rest of the day, and requiring the attendance of a member of staff at the Baths'.

In 1914 Gwendoline Bailey, Margaret Cadiou and Alice de la Haye all arrived at Barnard's Cross. The following year they were joined by Mabel Ahier, Ruby Dupre, Ivy Boulanger and Muriel Le Breton. Alice Hambly and Florence Le Poidevin, Edith Smith, Alice Berry and Winifred Le Poidevin followed in 1916 and Edith Le Marquand and Kathleen Maher in 1918. These fourteen students were all at College during the First World War.

During the First World War Miss Edith Rodgers was the loved and respected Head of Barnard's Cross. Ruby Dupre, writing forty-five years later, remembered arriving at the house after her long journey from Jersey:

'A chintzy, decorated sitting-room gay with flowers. Against the fireplace stands a tall, gracious figure with an outstretched hand welcoming a group of very raw recruits to the halls of learning – the Islanders had arrived'.

Salisbury Training College Chronicle, 1959

This must have been an anxious time to be away from home and Ruby's memories of Miss Rodgers, whose 'door would open to the slightest knock' show that she had a good listening ear and that she could provide comfort, reassurance and understanding. Ruby also remembered her visiting Jersey in later years:

'Miss Rodgers on holiday here with her sister, in our lanes and bays, knowing at long last that in our little island we didn't fall off the edge when we had walked a few miles and we had not exaggerated when we lauded its beauty'!

Salisbury Training College Chronicle, 1959

Several of the Jersey students who were at Barnard's Cross during the First World War went on to have long teaching careers in Jersey.

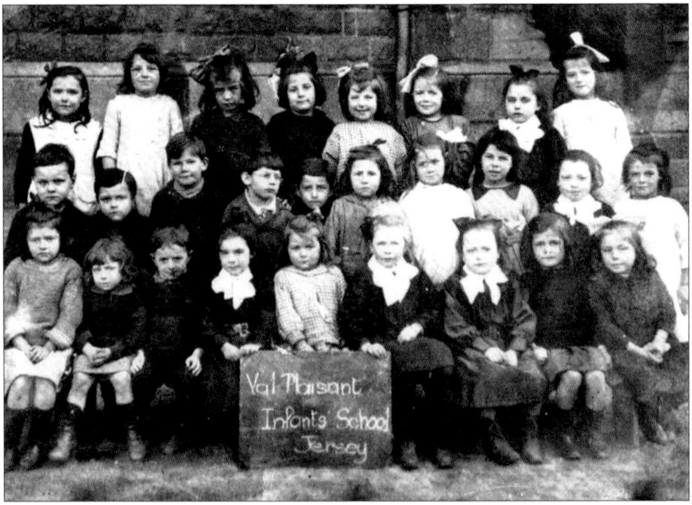

Fig. 6.2 Val Plaisant Infant School in 1922

What was it like for the students at College in the years leading up to and during World War One? Students continued to work hard under difficult conditions. Food was in short supply and the lack of heating was a problem. There was often thin soup and bread for lunch followed by a stodgy pudding. If it was too cold, students wrapped themselves in blankets for lectures. Care was taken to ensure that all lectures took place in daylight hours. Extra bedrooms were rented in the Cathedral Close to enable students to stay within the Close during the winter months. Students shared the tension and sadness of others who may have received news of injured family members or friends.

Students retained their sense of humour as seen in this excerpt from a student's diary. It also indicates that the staff members were viewed with good humour!

What would the Govs say if the Zepps came?

'Miss Hill: Have you all got your umbrellas and galoshes?'
Miss Grist: 'Of what educational value is this raid?'
Miss Hill: 'Bombs! I cannot have this noise!'
Miss Story: 'I'm too busy changing from PE to notice these trifles!'
Miss Ruby: 'What a perfectly sweet boy in that Zepp. A perfectly lovely young officer!'
Miss Newman: Clapping her hands "Oh Dear! Oh Dear!'

There were no air-raids on Salisbury, but on one night all lights were quickly extinguished as a Zeppelin was reported over Southampton. At Barnard's Cross, the students held 'Zeppelin Drill, when by the light of candles and electric torches we find our way down to the cellar'.

Students took part in 'war work' and sent parcels, letters and cards to soldiers on the front, and received some back in return. Lectures and lessons continued with the addition of science.

It was a positive start to a subject which would gain much more prominence in later years. English, including the speaking of English, was deemed extremely important. Students dreaded the spoken English test, and understandably they often dried up or faltered.

Students dreaded 'Major Days' even more. This was when they had to give a practice lesson in front of other students and staff, who then gave a critical assessment of the lesson. What an ordeal! When it was over, students celebrated with a 'Major Cake' which was some consolation. A student in 1916 described the ordeal:

> 'A Major is a test of nerves and not of teaching ability. A student teaches a prepared lesson to some stodgy, stupid children but all the time she see no children, but only the crowd of students and lecturers in the background of the room...hard at work writing down their hard criticisms of the poor nervous students. Majors give rise to a nervous disease called 'Majoritis'.'

During the war, teaching practice continued. In addition to working locally, some students were sent further afield to schools in Eastleigh. The train line ran directly to Eastleigh so perhaps that was one reason for the link. There were so many College rules which students had to abide by and probably Eastleigh provided more freedom and even the chance of meeting some men! Students were banned from going into Salisbury during the war, as the soldiers were thought to pose a threat to them. Miss Forth, the College Principal, had the students' well-being at heart, but this humorous excerpt from a student in 1915–1916 shows that perhaps the students felt it was overdone where the soldiers were concerned:

A vital question asked by Miss Forth (College Principal) to the Mayor of Eastleigh:

> How many soldiers do you have in town?
> Give me the names and addresses of all of them under 89. Tell me definitely where each individual may be found between 8 & 9, 12 & 1 and 4 & 6 each day, so that I may warn my girls against them–or perhaps you could just send all the men away for the week????

Students made their own entertainment. At Barnard's Cross the students performed plays, including 'Morality Plays'.

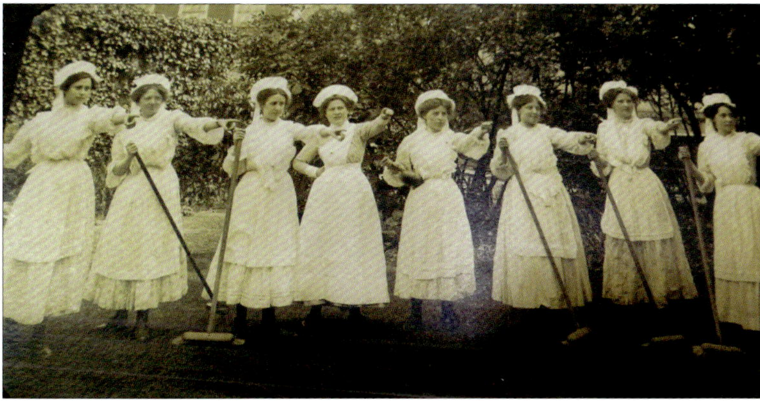

Fig. 6.3 Students performing a play in the garden of Barnard's Cross

At the end of the war Salisbury Cathedral was packed for a special Armistice Day service and enormous relief was felt that the war had ended. Students celebrated 'with a hurriedly arranged but highly successful concert'.

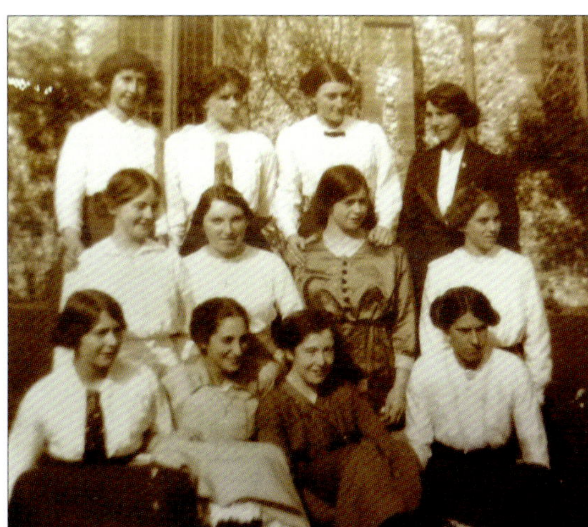

Fig. 6.4
Wartime students

During the war, the students showed courage and stoicism and were strengthened by the calmness and spirituality of the Cathedral and their beloved College chapel. They continued to work hard and prepare themselves in the best way possible for whatever the future held.

1911–1913 Marjorie Sabina Starck – the Lighthouse Keeper's daughter

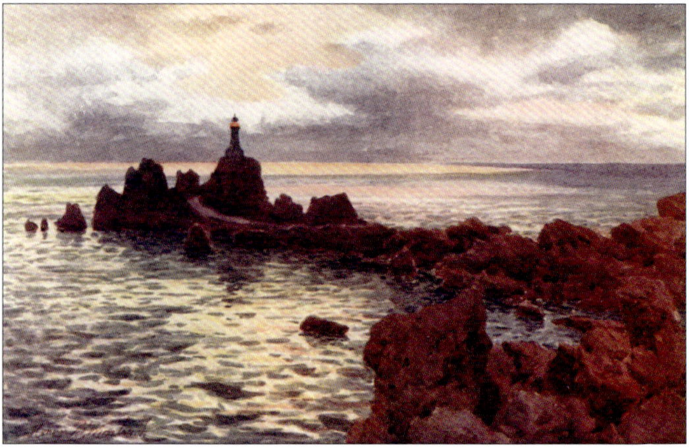

Fig. 6.5 Corbière Lighthouse, 1911

Marjorie Starck, who was one of Miss Montgomery's first pupils in Jersey, was born in the Parish of St Martin on October 16th 1892. Her father, John Starck, was a Master Mariner and had 'a ticket under steam and sail'. An unfortunate accident led to one of his ships going on the rocks in Newfoundland and at this stage he took his family to live in London, where he was in charge of the hand operated steam-driven machinery that opened Tower Bridge. This was an interesting new challenge, but John found that Bermondsey was a rough place. He was homesick for Jersey and missed the sea. He returned to the island with his wife Clara and their children: Clara, Jack, Diana, Blanche, Marjorie and Alfred. They all lived with John's aunt.

By 1909 John (Captain Starck) was one of the keepers of the lighthouse at Corbiére. This lighthouse stands in a spectacular position on the south west tip of the island. The coast around Jersey is treacherous and the island is often shrouded in fog. John, a seafaring man, was well suited to this crucial job. The family lived at Corbière Lodge, St Brelade, a house at the top of the causeway. It was probably divided into separate cottages for the keepers and their families.

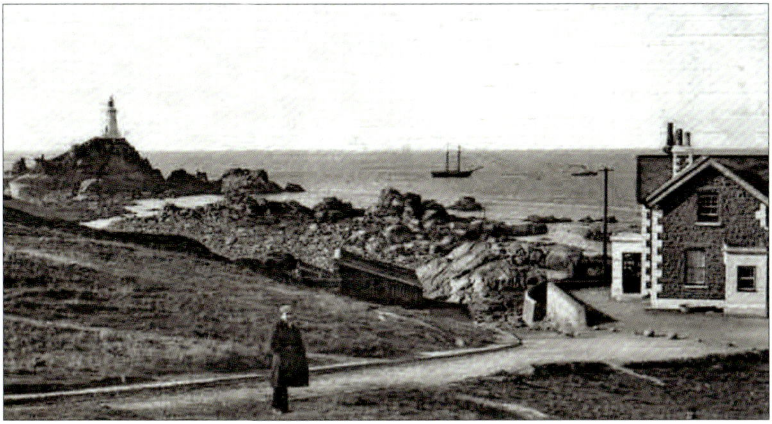

Fig. 6.6 Corbière Lodge at the top of the causeway

Marjorie, who had been a pupil at Keetons Road School in Bermondsey, became a pupil-teacher at St Paul's National School in St Helier, which had opened in the 1840s. A new school building, which is today St Paul's Centre, was completed in 1871, just across the road from the church. It was considered to be the most substantial and best built school in town. The staff consisted of a master for the boys, two mistresses for the girls and infants and three pupil-teachers. Approximately 300 children attended the school, although attendance fluctuated considerably.

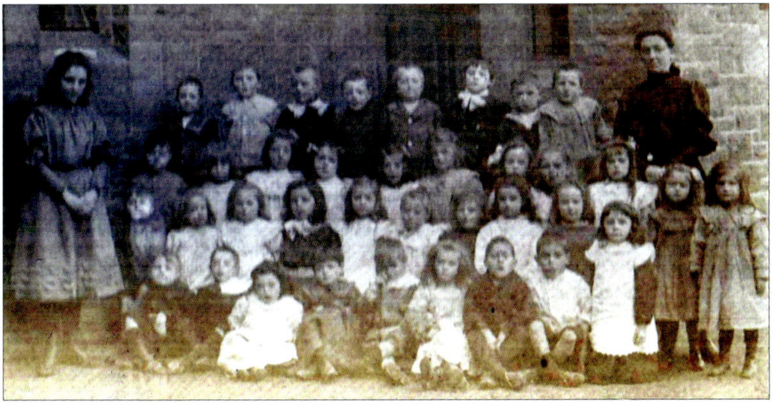

Fig. 6.7 Marjorie Starck (left) as a pupil-teacher at St Paul's National School, St Helier

By 1912 the total size of the school was probably still about the same size. The building operated as three schools and there were separate entrances for the boys, girls and infants, but inside the building the classrooms were cramped. The playground had limited space and the schools took it in turns to let their children out to play.

There were 100 infants and the States Public Instruction Committee threatened to withdraw its heavily relied upon grant due to the attendance of too many infants – ten above the States-imposed limit of 90. The issue was, however, quickly sorted out when the incumbent of St Paul's Church, the Revd A Poynder, replied to the effect that one of the pupil-teachers had turned eighteen and the number could in fact be increased to 110!

Marjorie encountered considerable challenges as a pupil-teacher in a large school with a small number of staff.

In 1913 the States took over the management of the St Paul's Schools and renamed them St Helier's (New Street) Boys', Girls' and Infants' Schools. In 1924 all the girls were transferred to the Halkett Place Girls and Infants School and the boys remained at New Street.

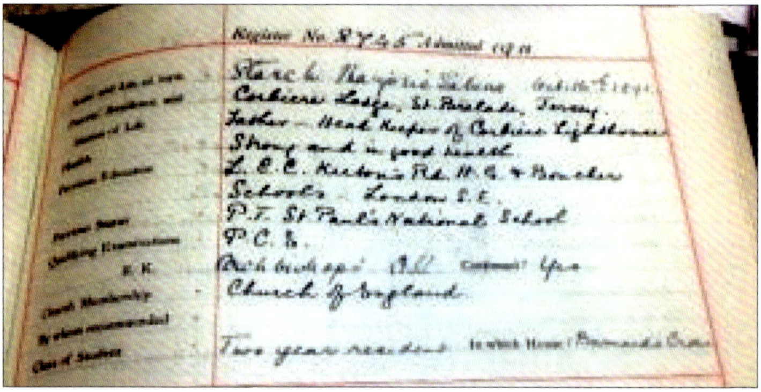

Fig. 6.8 Marjorie's entry in the College Register

Marjorie arrived at Salisbury Training College in 1911. She was resident at Barnard's Cross for two years. Her registration form declared that she was 'strong and in good health'. Marjorie had passed the Archbishop's Certificate, and she was a confirmed member of the Church of England.

Whilst she was at College, Marjorie's father died. It is thought that he may have suffered a heart attack whilst walking back along the causeway from the lighthouse. His funeral was on May 9th 1912.

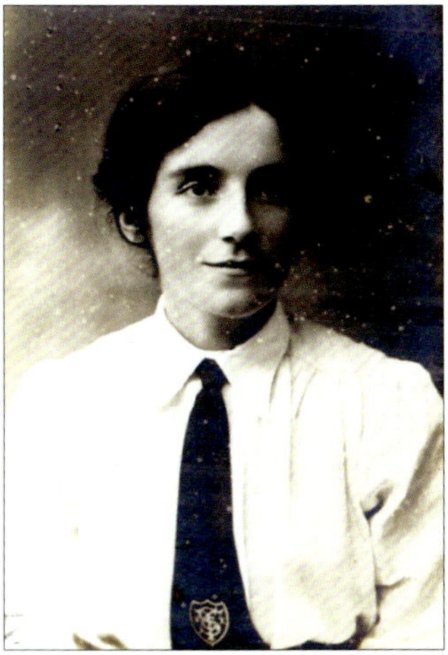

Fig. 6.9 Marjorie as a student

When Marjorie finished at College in 1913, she returned to Jersey and taught at Halkett Place School. This elementary school was located in St Helier on the site now occupied by the Public Library. Marjorie worked at the school for the next 10 years and was there during the First World War.

The outbreak of war in August 1914 took Jersey largely by surprise. The island's tourism and agricultural industries felt an immediate effect as German hotel staff and over 2000 French farm workers left to join their respective national armies. British reservists also left for the front and the atmosphere in the island changed. Concerns over enemy spies grew and there were numerous reports of suspicious behaviour with 'foreign nationals' singled out as being potential German spies. In one incident a local farmer denounced one of his workers as being a German spy, despite having employed the man for 30 years. In the countryside, farmers appealed against conscription orders so that their sons could remain and help them in the fields. This led to bad feeling between families in the town whose sons left to fight.

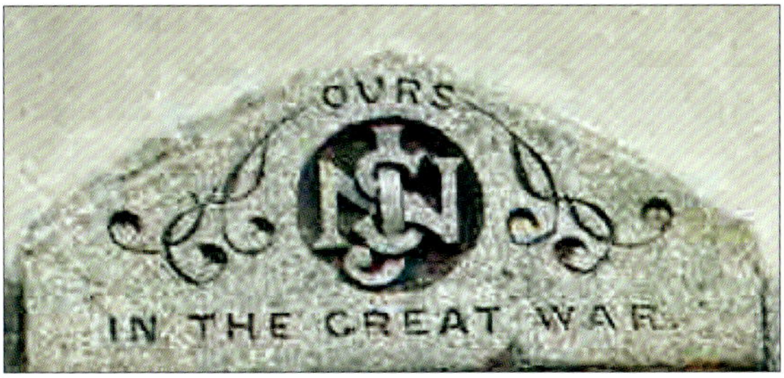

Fig. 6.10 Halkett Place Primary School Memorial is the roll of honour of past pupils who died in World War 1. The school closed in 1982.

The threat of enemy air attack also caused concern and the sound of an aircraft caused considerable anxiety. Jersey's trained militia was mobilised to stand guard over the coast as fears of attack and even possible invasion spread through the community. St Helier might be attacked from the sea, spies could slip into the island, enemy aliens might be anywhere – the rumours abounded. The war led to the 'Alien Restriction Order 1914' which required Jersey residents who were not of British origin to write their personal details in registers. Travel Permits were also introduced and were completed by each passenger before embarking, listing the reason for their travel and where they were going.

In fact, life went on much as usual and the island was peaceful. Newspapers and mail arrived daily from England throughout the war and only sugar and petrol were rationed, but some goods were in short supply. Islanders, however, lived with emotions running high and suspicion, anxiety, loneliness and grief were part of everyday life. Whose turn would it be next to receive that telegram notifying them of the death or injury of a son or brother or father?

As the British army reservists left to join their units, families watched their men leave the island with a mixture of sadness and pride. By the end of 1914 Jersey, watching recruitment on the mainland, had started to raise its own 'Pals' unit. By March 1915, there were 230 volunteers who were later joined by a further 96 men. The Jersey Company, as it was called, first became part of the 7th Battalion of the Royal Irish Rifles and later joined the Hampshire Regiment.

The departure of so many men to fight in the war led to an increasing number of women joining the workforce to replace them. In addition, women worked for the Red Cross, collecting items and making up parcels of clothes and food to send to prisoners of war and medical items to hospitals.

Women were sometimes employed as auxiliary teachers. Edith Le Marquand, who was born in 1895 and lived in St Ouen, was employed to 'fill in' at St Ouen's Parish School. The experience must have convinced Edith that she wanted to teach, for she arrived at Salisbury Training College in 1918. She was still attending Salisbury Club meetings for old students in 1980.

John Le Marquand, a prominent Jersey politician and President of the

Education Committee wrote positively about the reaction of schools to the loss of so many male teachers who left to fight 'for King and Country':

> 'Despite the call-up of male teachers to the colours, schools were tackling their job with increased vigour and confidence, because of the States' progressive policy of increasing the numbers of qualified staff since the nationalisation of elementary education. At the end of 1916 the proportion of trained certificated teachers to the total staff had almost doubled'. John Le Marquand: *Education in Jersey*

Although Jersey escaped any direct fighting or occupation, the First World War had a traumatic and long lasting impact on the small island community. It is now believed that about 1500 Jerseymen lost their lives. Of the 266 members of the Jersey Company who left the island in 1915, 80 were killed and a similar number were seriously wounded.

In 1923 Miss Mellor, the Mistress of Halkett Place Girls School, received a circular from the Public Instruction Committee advising her that the States would not retain women teachers on the staff of Public Elementary Schools after their marriage. Co-incidentally, Marjorie Starck married Harold Stephens, a farmer, on August 2nd 1923.

It seems likely that Marjorie did not consider the possibility of continuing her teaching career. Despite women having had the opportunity to work outside their homes during the war, nothing had really changed and the expectation that a woman would relinquish her job when she married was still there. The circular that Miss Mellor received was probably sent to reinforce that point. Marjorie and Harold lived in St Helier and Marjorie worked for a short time at the Barnardo's Home before settling into the busy life of a farmer's wife. When Harold subsequently took over the running of the Jersey Animals' Shelter, she was, to quote their grandson, Tim Herbert, his 'right hand'. Running the house, looking after the family and catering for the staff was a demanding, full- time job. The Occupation years were undoubtedly tough, but they kept going and Harold retired in 1960.

Marjorie died in 1967 Her two years spent in Salisbury had been influential ones and, like so many students, she made good friends. Auntie Edith (Edith Balleine), Auntie Gwen (Gwendoline Mundy) and Auntie Bea (Beatrice Le Huquet) were all part of her daughter Faith's childhood.

1913–1915 Marion Cumber

Education and Medicine – A Perfect Mixture!

Marion was born in St Peter Port on 27 July 1895 to a large and well-known family of Guernsey chemists. *The Star,* September 1894, announced the marriage of Perry Cumber to Bertha Langlois Bienvenu.

Fig. 6.11

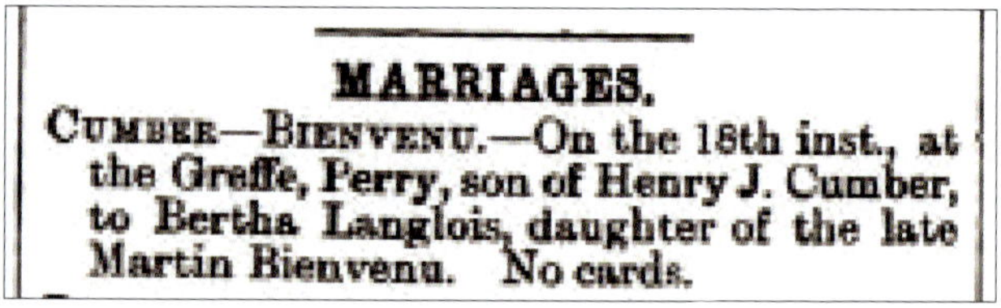

MARRIAGES.

CUMBER—BIENVENU.—On the 18th inst., at the Greffe, Perry, son of Henry J. Cumber, to Bertha Langlois, daughter of the late Martin Bienvenu. No cards.

Sadly, the 1901 Census shows that Marion's father, Perry Cumber, was by now a widower with three young children, employing a full time housekeeper and servant to care for the family. The family lived at 28, Cambridge Park, St Peter Port, and they still resided in the area in 1911, by which time they had moved to L' Hyvreuse Terrace. Cambridge Park is a very attractive area of St Peter Port, with rows of old trees. Duels used to take place there and it was where Militia and other parades were held.

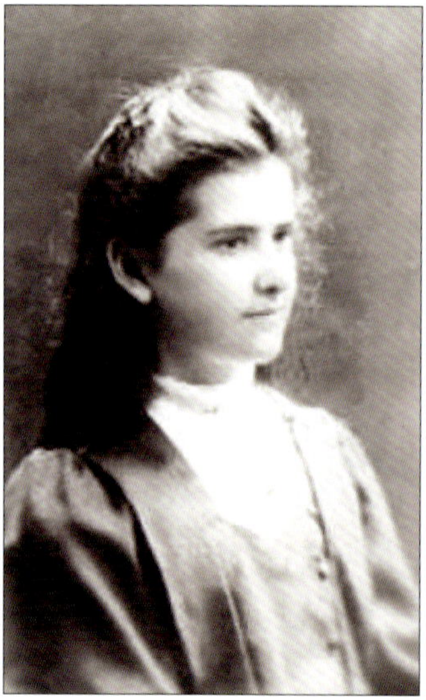

Fig. 6.12 Marion at around the age she entered Salisbury Training College

Marion attended Grove House School, Elmhurst, and later, the States Intermediate School. She completed six months as a pupil-teacher at Amherst School for Girls in Guernsey. When Marion was seventeen she was accepted for Salisbury Training College.

Marion wrote fascinating notes of her family history, which describe how her ancestors were involved in setting up and establishing the chemist's shop in The Pollet, Guernsey in 1818. This shop was an extremely important institution in Guernsey, providing cures and remedies of all types.

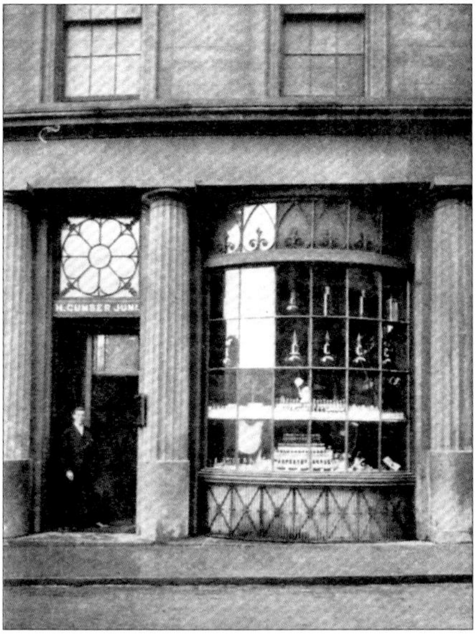

Fig. 6.13 Cumbers Chemist Shop

A Descriptive Account of Guernsey Illustrated published around 1896 includes a full and colourful description of the chemist's shop:

> 'As a thorough high class pharmacy "Cumbers" in Fountain Street has no superior. The dispensing department particularly recommends itself to both residents and visitors'.

At this time and after, there was much concern about health issues such as influenza, as described in *The Star* in 1893, just two years before Marion was born:

> 'Winter is almost upon us, and in its coming I regret to see that is has brought that mysterious disease "the Russian Influenza" along with it. It seems to me that this dangerous sickness has discovered a happy hunting ground in the British islands and holds high revel there with its usual attendants of chest and lung complaints'.

As part of the St Peter Port business community, members of the Cumber family served on the House Committee of the Town Hospital and had an important role in its running.

In 1913, seventeen year old Marion took the ferry to Weymouth and then the train via Westbury to Salisbury. Finally, after a long journey, she arrived at the welcome sight of Barnard's Cross, her home for the next two years.

On leaving College in 1915, Marion went to teach at Bramley Mixed Parochial School in Hampshire, situated between Reading and

Basingstoke. Bramley was on the GWR railway line which made travelling to Weymouth or Southampton to catch the Channel Island ferry much easier. It was a small village set amongst beautiful countryside. In 1917, an army camp was opened there, which was used as an ammunitions depot and later, a POW camp.

In 1915, Marion returned to Guernsey for a Barnard's Cross reunion. Seven former students met with Dr and Mrs Baker during a visit which they made to Guernsey. Dr Baker was a much loved College lecturer and chaplain.

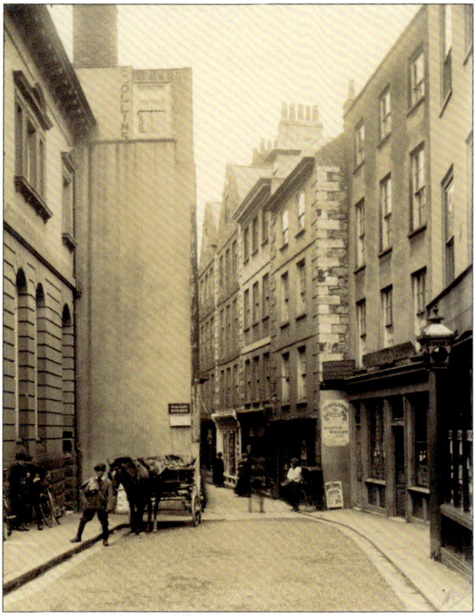

Fig. 6.14 Pollet Street, Guernsey before it was widened.

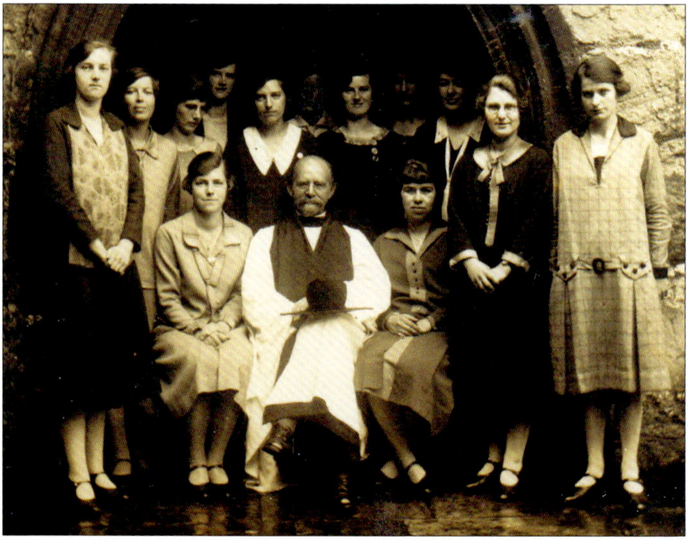

Fig. 6.15 Dr Baker with students at College *circa* 1912

'We invited Dr and Mrs Baker and Dorothea to L'Ancresse Common – our Salisbury Plain. We all met at a pre-arranged meeting place and took a tram to the Common, which has a good stretch of beach. Arriving there, we settled ourselves amongst the rocks and fell at once, as is usual at Club meetings to talking over old times'.

The group enjoyed a special tea 'with a kettle and stove'. They talked, walked and sang. Later they retreated to Candie Gardens, where photographs were taken. 'So now we have, beside many happy memories, a lasting memento of our first Re-union in Guernsey'.

The family remained close and whilst living in England Marion met up with her cousins. Charles Davis Cumber was Marion's uncle and a practising chemist working in Bournemouth. In 1911, just before Marion arrived at College, his son Percival, aged seventeen, was working as a chemist apprentice.

In 1934, Percival and Marion, who was then aged 39, were married in Bournemouth. By now Percival Cumber had qualified as a surgeon at Guy's Hospital, London. He had a practice in Wimborne Road, Bournemouth, which was a road lined with terraces of shops of every kind – some of which were quite grand. Moordown and Winton were growing areas of Bournemouth with a mixed and lively population.

Bournemouth was renowned for its health-giving air; many people suffering with tuberculosis and other ailments came to the area. Doctors and pharmacists would have been in great demand. We can imagine Marion contentedly entering into the lifestyle. It would have been a full and busy life, but Marion and Percival also enjoyed lighter moments; in her notes she mentions regular croquet parties. Marion's father may have been living with his daughter, as he died in Bournemouth in 1940, aged 81.

Percival died in 1973 and Marion died in Christchurch one year later aged 74. Marion had witnessed many changes, not only in education, but also in the rapidly developing field of medicine.

1917–19 Mabel Annie Ahier – a loyal and devoted teacher

Mabel Annie Ahier's story begins on June 25th 1899, when she was born in St Peter Port, Guernsey. At the time of the 1901 Census Mabel, aged two years, was living with her parents and May, her nine year old sister, at 3 Well Road.

Mabel's father, Philippe, is recorded in the 1901 Census as being a clergyman, but also an author and a professor of French. He was in fact a Jerseyman, having been born in St Helier in 1849. He was the eldest son of Philippe Ahier, a solicitor, and the young Philippe was educated in Paris and intended for the Jersey Bar, where the legal language was French. When he was fifteen he saved a man from drowning in the sea at St Helier and his courage was rewarded with a gold medal from the Royal Humane Society.

Philippe decided to take Holy Orders in the Church of England, rather than follow a legal career and in 1870 he attended St Bees Theological College in Cumberland. After a curacy at Skelton in Cleveland, he became the vicar of St Thomas's Church in Glaisdale, North Yorkshire in 1876. According to subsequent newspaper reports, he was a kind and conscientious priest who worked hard and endeared himself to his parishioners by taking an interest in their spiritual and social welfare. Sadly, however, there were problems and his marriage to Eleanor Elizabeth Ahier failed. Following an acrimonious and high profile clerical court case, the couple finally divorced in 1895.

In the meantime Philippe moved to London, where he met Annie Hellier, whose home was in Wandsworth. The 1891 Census records Philippe, a 'professor of French and an author' living in Battersea with Annie, who was a dressmaker. Philippe was 'deposed' by the Archbishop and could no longer work as a priest. Annie and Philippe were married at the Wandsworth Registry Office on 6th January 1896. By 1899 they had moved to Well Road, Guernsey with their elder daughter, May. Their younger daughter Mabel was born there. Well Road was a pleasant location, being high up the hill, with views over the roof tops of St Peter Port. The family would have seen the busy harbour, with the island of

Herm just across the water. As Mabel grew older and started school, we can imagine her running up and down the many stone steps and along the cobbled streets. This was the time of the Boer War and in July 1900 the 2nd Wilts Regiment was on the island and recruitment took place. Mabel's mother joined the war effort, as was recorded in the *Star* on June 23rd 1900: 'Mrs Ahier of Well Road is collecting tobacco and eau-de-cologne for the men of the 2nd Wilts Regiment in South Africa'.

During the Boer War, 39 men from Guernsey and 12 men from Alderney lost their lives.

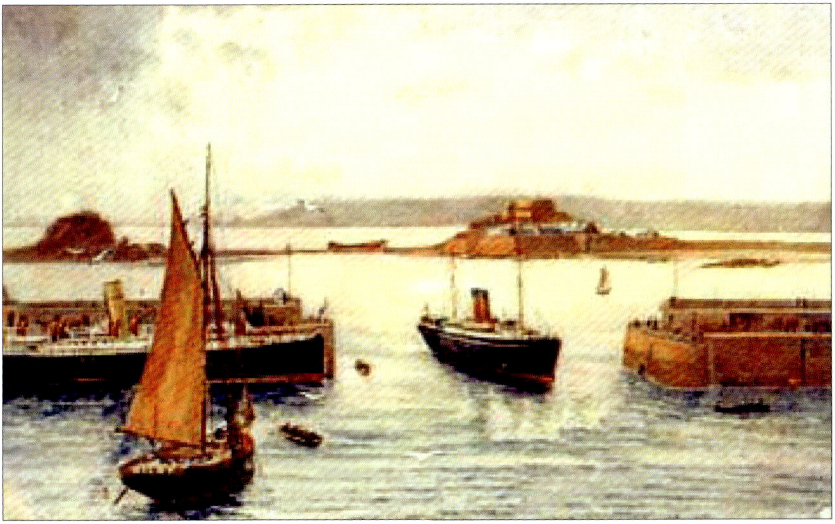

Fig. 6.16 St Helier Harbour, 1905

Within a few years the family was on the move again, this time to Jersey, where Philippe was born. Were family connections and a yearning for home the reasons that drew him back?

By the 1900s new residents as well as tourists were flocking to Jersey, lured by the advertisements in the newspapers:

> JERSEY for PLEASURE, COOL BREEZES. GOLFING, HOLIDAYS, FISHING. CYCLING. SANDS. SEA BATHING. YACHTING
>
> Saturday, 23 August, 1902: *London Daily News*

Another compelling advertisement at this time claimed that Jersey was 'the sunniest spot in the British Isles for health, pleasure and the brightest weather.'

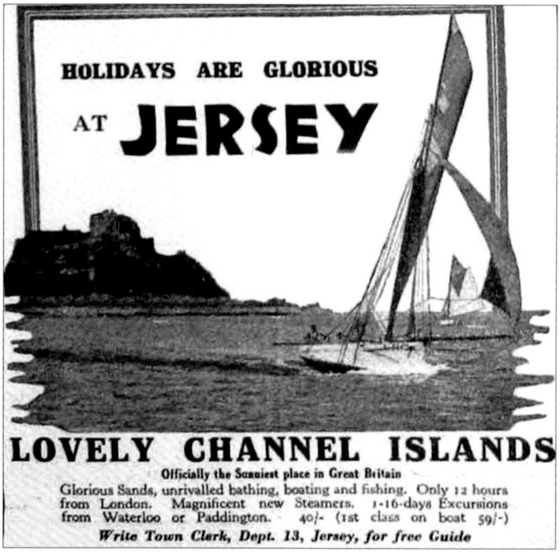

Fig. 6.17

The family lived in the house in St Helier in which Philippe had been born. This may have been in New Street where his father, who had died in 1893, had been living. May started work as a music teacher and Mabel attended a school in the town. Despite the extravagant claims of the advertisements, it was probably not the happiest of times for the family as Philippe's health was failing and he died in 1908.

Less than a year later the *Jersey Independent* and *Daily Telegraph* reported that May Hellier Ahier had been presented with a farewell gift for her work as an organist. The family was on the move again and this time Annie returned to the mainland with her daughters. They settled back into life in Wandsworth and the 1911 Census records Annie as a widow who was working as a dressmaker. May was seventeen and a music teacher and Mabel was a twelve year old schoolgirl.

Mabel arrived at Salisbury Training College in 1917. She was a student at Barnard's Cross and was excited to meet a student in King's House who had been born in Jersey. She wrote a postcard to her mother:

> Dear Mother
> I am sending you the record of Housecraft. I met a Junior of King's House who said she was born in Jersey. Her name is Edith Neat. We got quite friendly, but I have not seen her to speak to since. We had to

get an apron, cap and half sleeves for Housecraft. It was cheaper to buy them over here. Lilian and I went and bought them – three shillings and tuppence half-penny in all.

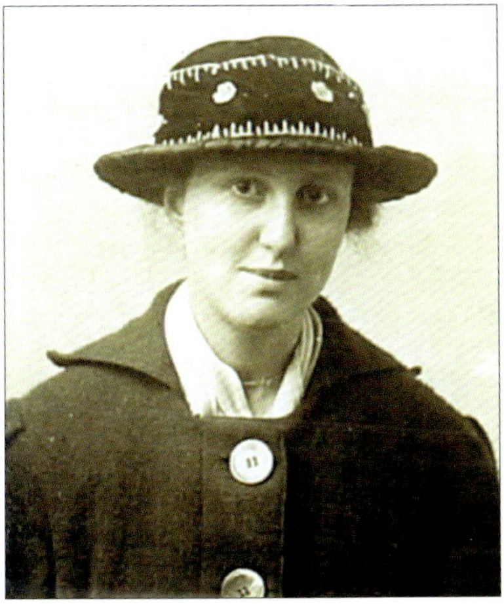

Fig. 6.18 Mabel Ahier

The words on the postcard 'cheaper to buy them over here' suggest that by the time she went to college, Mabel's home was once again in Jersey. Another indication is the fact that she lived at Barnard's Cross, where most of the Channel Islanders were housed. During the First World War there were at least ten other girls from Jersey and one from Guernsey.

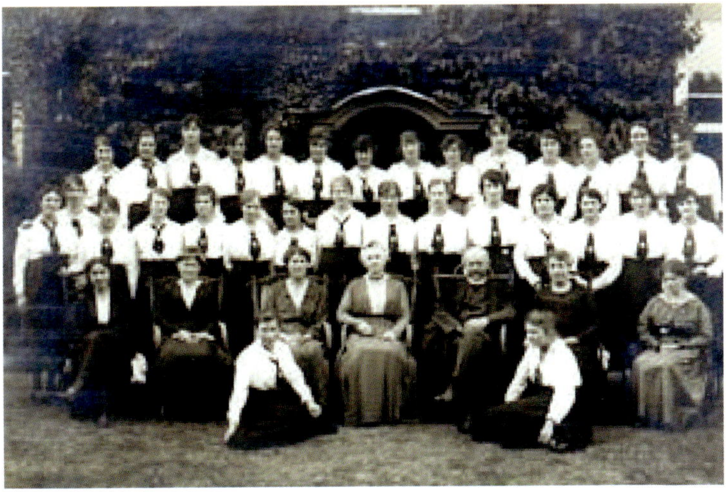

Fig. 6.19 Miss Barbara Forth (Principal) with staff and students at Salisbury Diocesan Training College

By 1917 Salisbury was the centre of a vast area of camps on the Plain and had, in the words of Edith Olivier, a local author, become 'a sea of brown khaki'. The streets were crowded with troops from every part of the British Empire, as well as lorries carrying war material. Planes buzzed overhead.

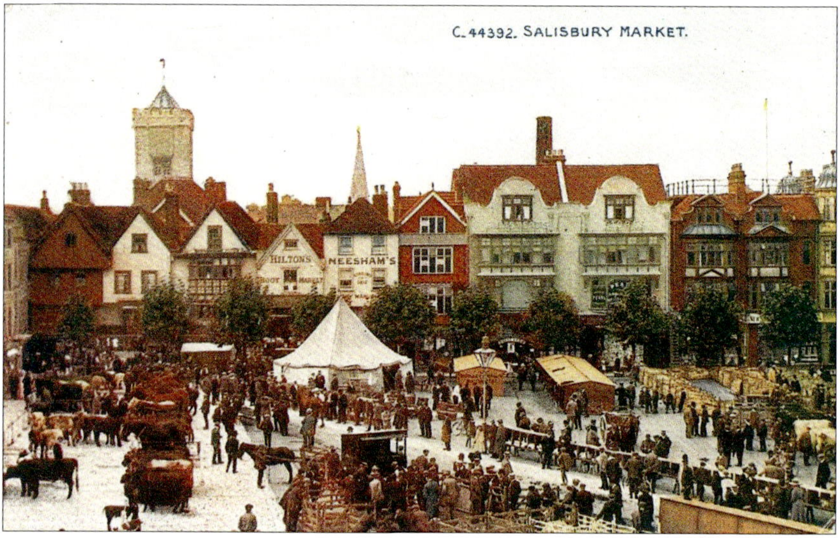

Fig. 6.20 Salisbury Market Square, 1914

Disorderly behaviour in the city worried the College staff, and students were consequently kept in close confinement. This loss of independence must have been particularly trying for the islanders who would have been accustomed to walking in and around St Helier.

Salisbury was a hive of activity. Many soldiers were nursed at the Infirmary, a voluntary Fire Service was set up and a branch of Queen Mary's Needlework Guild was started in order to supply clothing to the troops. Wiltshire was also at the forefront of the Women's Land Army, which supplied voluntary labour to farms. Concerts, plays and patriotic meetings took place in the city.

On Sundays the Cathedral was packed from the choir to the west door with soldiers in uniform. Volunteers in Salisbury organised a guest house for soldiers, providing a place where they could relax and enjoy meals. Students and staff from the College contributed to the city war work in different ways, in addition to setting up a successful scheme whereby parcels of food and clothing were sent to prisoners of war. The resources of the country were stretched, prices rose and housewives learnt to economise. Hens and rabbits were kept and gardens were given over to the cultivation of fruit and vegetables. Panic buying of food such as bread, meat, butter and sugar led to the food shortages that were frequently mentioned by students. In 1918, rationing was introduced to guarantee the supply.

The Close, in contrast to the city, remained very quiet and must have seemed like another world to Mabel and her friends, who lived at Barnard's Cross.

> 'We still heard only the clock which chimed the hours, various bells rolling for the services, and the floods of music which twice a day gushed out through the open windows of the Cathedral. This unaltered peace was the chief gift which Salisbury had to give to the soldiers who passed through the city on their way to and from the Front. All through the war they continued to come through the Close gates to drink in this miracle of celestial quietude'.
>
> Edith Olivier: *Without Knowing Mr Walkley*

Mabel left College in 1919 and returned to Jersey to start her career. The island, which had a population of about 50,000, was a sad, depressed place and the legacy of the First World War would linger for years to come. Victory had come with a heavy price and the sacrifice made by so many was felt throughout the community.

Mabel's teaching career in Jersey spanned 43 years. In 1937 she was working at Halkett Place Girls' School with Alice Hambly, another former Salisbury student. She remained in the island during the Occupation and her identity card shows that in 1941 she was living in Midvale Road, St Helier.

Marooned in their island and cut off from communication with the outside world, islanders could occasionally send and receive postal messages through the Red Cross. Mabel received a birthday message in 1944 from her college friend Margaret Howe, who was teaching in Hampshire. The messages were restricted in length, censored and could only refer to family matters.

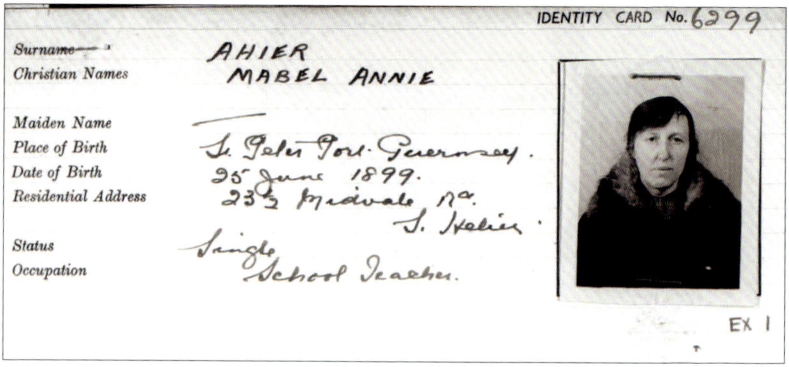

IDENTITY CARD No. 6299

Surname AHIER
Christian Names MABEL ANNIE
Maiden Name —
Place of Birth St. Peter Port. Guernsey.
Date of Birth 25 June 1899.
Residential Address 23½ Midvale Rd. St. Helier.
Status Single
Occupation School Teacher.

EX I

Fig. 6.21 Mabel's Identity Card 1941

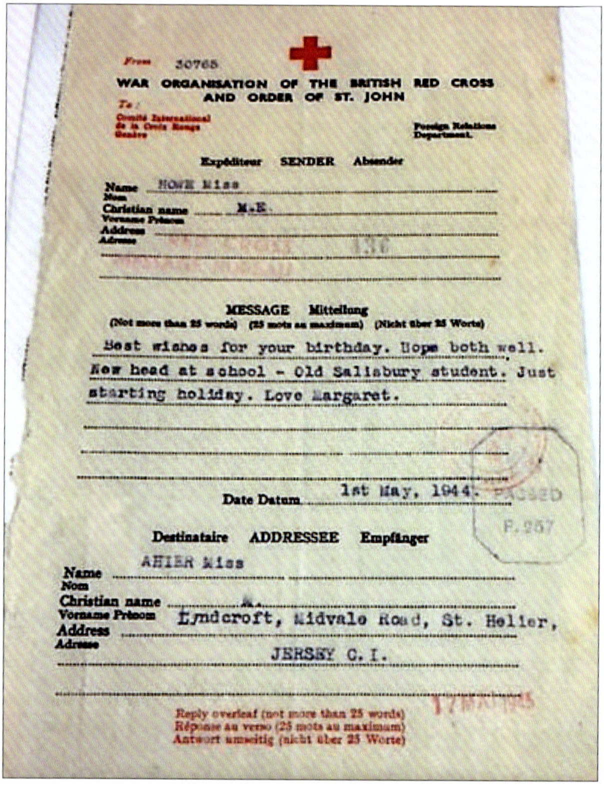

From 30765

WAR ORGANISATION OF THE BRITISH RED CROSS AND ORDER OF ST. JOHN

To:
Comité International de la Croix Rouge Genève

Foreign Relations Department.

Expéditeur SENDER Absender

Name / Nom: HOWE Miss
Christian name / Vorname Prénom: M.E.
Address / Adresse: RED CROSS 136

MESSAGE Mitteilung
(Not more than 25 words) (25 mots au maximum) (Nicht über 25 Worte)

Best wishes for your birthday. Hope both well. New head at school - Old Salisbury student. Just starting holiday. Love Margaret.

Date Datum: 1st May, 1944. PASSED P.257

Destinataire ADDRESSEE Empfänger

Name / Nom: AHIER Miss
Christian name / Vorname Prénom: M.
Address / Adresse: Lyndcroft, Midvale Road, St. Helier, JERSEY C.I.

Reply overleaf (not more than 25 words)
Réponse au verso (25 mots au maximum)
Antwort umseitig (nicht über 25 Worte)

Fig. 6.22 Red Cross Message, 1944

In 1952 Mabel moved to Trinity School, where she stayed until she retired in 1963. The occasion of her retirement was written up in the local paper and mention was made of her 'loyalty and devotion to teaching and her wonderful work in teaching Needlework and French'. Like her father, Philippe, Mabel had a real love of the French language and she had had considerable influence on the teaching of French at Trinity School. A spokesman from the Education Department expressed gratitude for Mabel's long service to the island and commended her 'and other teachers like her' for their 'enthusiasm and loyalty in the face of many difficulties'. This had often gone unpublicised. During the days of the occupation, even reaching school had required great personal efforts. In reply, Mabel spoke of her happy years at Trinity, the kindness of parents, the friendship of teaching colleagues, the support of the Education Department and, especially, the children who had given her so many years of happiness.

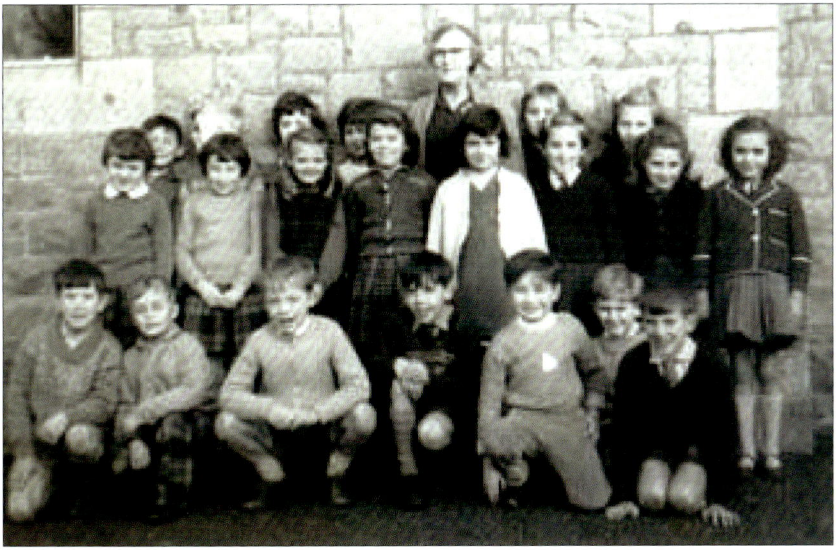

Fig. 6.23 Mabel Ahier with her class at Trinity School 1963

Guernsey Grit!
A Glimpse of Guernsey during World War One

Approximately 3,000 Guernsey men served in World War One. Around one third of these served in the Royal Guernsey Light Infantry (RGLI) which was formed in 1916.

Many Guernsey men had already volunteered for regiments in the British Army before the foundation of the RGLI, but it was created in order that there was a Guernsey named regiment which reflected the island's loyalty and devotion to the Crown.

The regiment saw much action on the Western Front as part of the British 29th Division. They fought in a major battle at Cambrai and suffered huge casualties, with almost 40 per cent of the regiment killed, injured or missing. They fought in part of the Third Battle of Ypres and experienced the terrible horrors of Passchendaele. The conditions were unimaginably dire; mud and disease were rife. Three hundred and twenty seven soldiers of the RGLI died and six hundred and sixty seven were wounded.

In Guernsey, as in the other Channel Islands, the huge loss of life in World War One was a terrible shock. A generation of young men had gone.

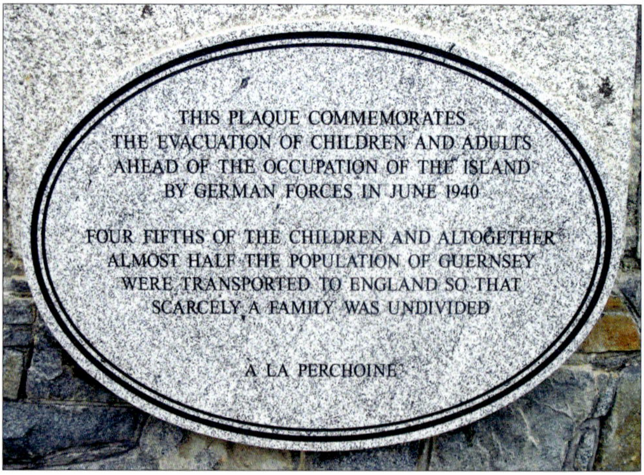

Fig. 6.24 Plaque erected in June 2017 in the Town Church Guernsey

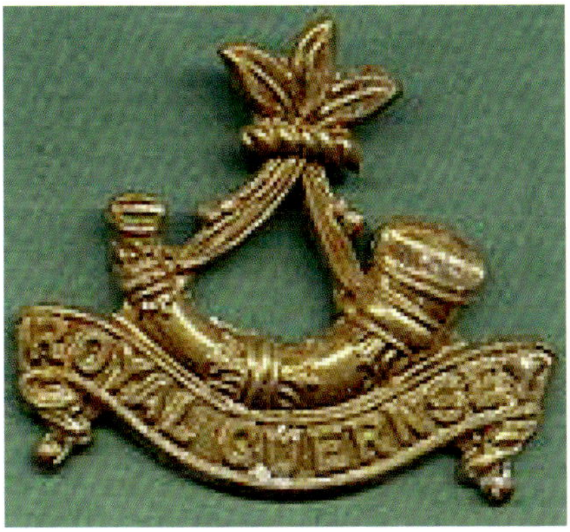

Fig. 6.25 Badge of the Royal Guernsey Light Infantry

Life was hard, especially for those who were widowed and fatherless. Living costs had risen during the war and post-war there was a shortage of jobs and housing. Urgent action was required and committees were set up in 1918 to tackle the housing crisis and to try and provide jobs. A limited low interest loan scheme for people wishing to build their own homes was introduced. In 1920 a compulsory repair scheme for sub-standard housing was also introduced. In 1921 a scheme for building some social housing was started, which helped to improve the situation, although there was still much poverty.

Edna Amy Bisson: 1913–1915

Edna Amy Bisson was born in the parish of St Andrew's Guernsey in 1894. The 1901 Census shows that at that time she lived with her parents and sister at Les Blicqs. Her parents, Frederick and Amy, were fruit and vegetable growers and had three children in total. By the age of sixteen, Edna was working as a pupil-teacher at St Peter's in the Wood Boys' School. She worked there for four hard years – showing true Guernsey grit by sticking at it! The 1911 Census shows that her father's occupation was that of a farmer and they now lived at Le Chene Forest.

In 1913 Edna left for Salisbury, determined to be a teacher. She worked hard and completed the course, at a time when conditions were very difficult. Food was scarce and College was an uncomfortable and cold place to be. Like most Channel Island students, Edna lived at Barnard's Cross and found solace and comfort in the friendship of other students.

Edna returned to Guernsey after her training and taught at Torteval Mixed School. In 1922 she met and married Oscar Ozanne. Oscar had enlisted as a private for the Light Infantry Regiment in 1918, when he was aged eighteen. He was fortunate to recover from a severe attack of influenza during his years as a soldier. After his recovery he rejoined the troops in France, survived the bombardment and served bravely until discharge in 1919, when the SS *Lydia* brought most of the remaining troops back home to Guernsey.

Edna and Oscar led a more peaceful and contented life after the traumas of World War One. Edna's family were involved in farming and possibly this may have been an occupation which Oscar followed. They were married for 36 years and had six children. Oscar died in Guernsey in 1959, but Edna lived until 1984, when she died in St Peter Port.

What were the conditions in Guernsey schools during this difficult time? Edna Bisson and her colleagues had a challenging task, but demonstrated their stamina and determination to succeed.

The inspection reports published during the difficult years of World War One show that there was a strong desire to ensure children in Guernsey received a thorough education in suitable buildings. The children were often praised in the inspection reports. In the report for 1915, the inspector praised the teachers for their hard work and effort but also stated:

> 'The Guernsey boy seems to be above average as regards brains and power of independent work. He resembles curiously enough, in many respects boys one meets in Lancashire in his practical outlook on life and common sense grasp of things in general...Guernsey children have a genius of their own and it is by discovering and developing this in suitable directions that the schools will reach their highest development'.
>
> Mr A F Page, HMI

Mr Page was particularly impressed with:

> ... ' the taste and commonsense shown by Guernsey parents in the dress of their children, the charming manners of the children, and the friendliness displayed to visiting inspectors by the teachers and managers of the school'.

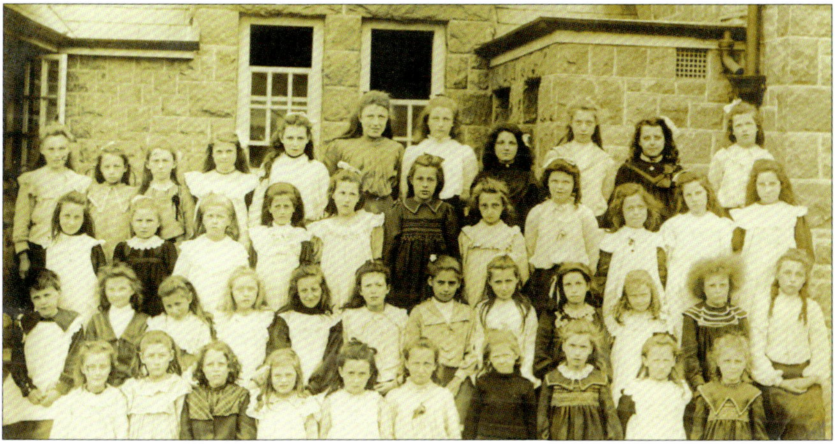

Fig. 6.26 Guernsey school girls in the early Twentieth Century

In 1916 Mr Page once again praised the children:

> 'The natural capacity of the Guernsey children and their quickness of comprehension will raise the work above the level found in the average English school'.

There are several comments in the reports on the health of the children, particularly with regard to school attendance. During the war special permission for school absence was given for children of 'parents in poor circumstances to help tide them over these times of stress'. When Edna Bisson was teaching there were serious influenza epidemics. A widespread measles epidemic caused 'the resulting delicacy of many of the children during the succeeding months'. Schools were encouraged to promote health and the well-being of the children. Practices such as folding their arms when seated and sitting at desks of unsuitable size were frowned upon.

Teachers were in short supply during the years of World War One. The Educational Council worked hard to ensure that the situation improved and that Guernsey had a regular supply of trained teachers. In 1919 several student teachers had been recruited from the Ladies' College and Girls' Intermediate School to train in England. This would have included several students who trained in Salisbury.

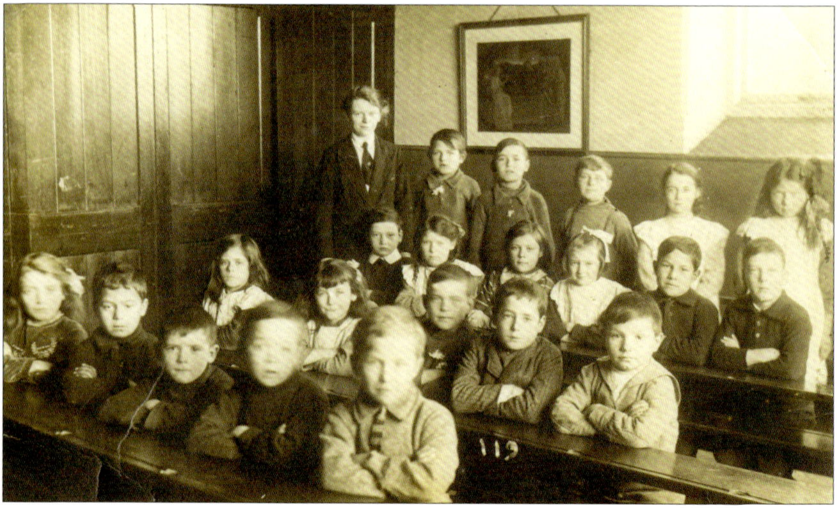

Fig. 6.27 Children at St Andrew's School

'Six teachers emerged from Training Colleges, out of which five returned to the island'. There was a significant increase in the number of Guernsey students who trained in Salisbury between 1919 and 1939 – at least 28 students!

The inspection reports generally praise the teachers for their hard work and also their kindness:

> 'As regards the instruction given, the chief point noticed was the kindness of the teachers to the children; this is a very considerable part of good teaching in the case of the younger children'. 1917 report

It was at the Vauvert School, which opened in 1909 that several Salisbury students worked as pupil-teachers, including Marjorie Falla (College student 1912–14) who worked with the infants:

> 'In some cases the teaching struck me as too wordy, and in almost all cases as too noisy. To raise one's voice above the necessary pitch is a waste of energy and a bad example. The general impression produced

on me was distinctly favourable. The teaching is zealous and efficient, and the children's response is encouraging'.

John Penfold, Religious Education Inspector: 1914 Inspection Report

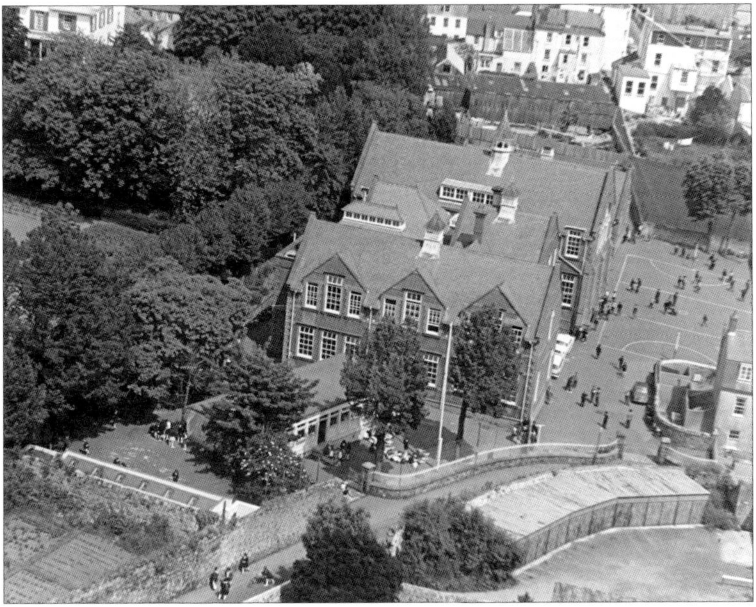

Fig. 6.28 Vauvert School

In 1913 Ethel Hamel (College student 1911–13) was appointed to Amherst Girls' School where Marion Cumber (at College 1913–1915) had worked as a pupil-teacher. In 1914 the school was praised for its teaching of Religious Instruction and the general 'tone and discipline'. Several school buildings were occupied by the Military during the war but they were not occupied for long and the standard of school buildings gradually improved.

'The general standard of school buildings in Guernsey appears to be on the whole superior to that in the English County. The schools in the island are as rule well-built and well planned'.

1916 Inspection Report

The playgrounds of Guernsey schools, including that of Amherst School, were praised in the 1916 report as being much above average:

> 'A comparison is made between the often 'Barrack square' playground of schools in England and the Guernsey playgrounds which often had a field adjoining the school and 'an abundance of flowers throughout the season'.

Unsatisfactory premises were surprisingly few, although some schools were criticised for being ill-lit and having inadequate toilet facilities and uncomfortable backless desks.

When Edna Bisson and other qualified teachers returned from Salisbury Training College to Guernsey, which subjects were they expected to teach? The reports show that the key subjects were Reading, French and Religious Knowledge. The 1915 report found that the 'weakest subject on the island' was Reading. The children did not read enough books and those that they actually did read were uninspiring. The 1916 report stated that there had been a 'vigorous' response to the earlier comments.

Salisbury students had some lessons in the teaching of French – about two hours a week. Some island children spoke Guernsey island Patois at home and others, especially Town children, spoke English, which made for a challenging situation. The 1919 report included a special report on the teaching of French. One finding was that the training of teachers in teaching French was inadequate. Many books were outdated and fit only for 'the lumber room or fire'. Mr Edwards HMI was not without hope, as he had met several headteachers and teachers 'who would welcome the chance of doing what they could to make the Channel Island Schools a model for the British Empire in the teaching of French'.

The importance of Religious Education is evident, as it had its own inspection for many years. Most comments on the teaching of the subject were positive. Salisbury students certainly had a very thorough grounding in the subject during their College years. Considerable time was devoted to teaching arithmetic. Problems occurred due to the complicated system of coinage and weights and measures. The inspector recommended more simple mental exercises and relating arithmetic to real life wherever possible. There were insufficient drill periods but much Physical Education was good. Teachers taught Nature Study – a subject much loved by

Salisbury students, Geography and History. Music and singing were part of the curriculum as were Drawing, Gardening for boys and Domestic Subjects for girls.

The teachers did enjoy some free time and relaxation. The Salisbury Training College Magazine for Whitsun 1915 contains a report of a happy day in July 1914 when seven former students met with Dr and Mrs Baker for a reunion picnic. The report written by former student Dorothy Falla, describes what a memorable day it was for them all. They met at L'Ancresse Common – a favourite picnic spot.

> 'It was a sunny Saturday afternoon. We all met at a pre-arranged meeting place and took a tram to the Common, which, being at the extreme north of the island, has a good stretch of beach. We settled ourselves amongst the rocks and fell at once to talking over old times. Mrs Baker and Mrs Cochrane (Ethel Anley) told us tales of olden days when students got up at an unearthly hour in the morning'.

The inspection reports provide a fascinating overview of life in Guernsey schools around the time of the First World War. Children who were often a delight to teach in spite of the difficulties of the time; teachers who worked hard in challenging conditions; pupil-teachers who worked long hours with determination, spirit and 'Guernsey Grit' in order to progress to Teacher Training College; and an optimism and desire by the States to take on board the criticisms and recommendations of the successive inspectors and improve education for the children of Guernsey.

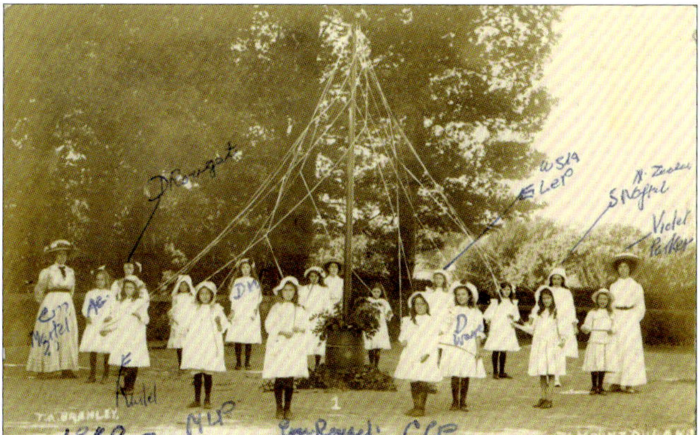

Fig. 6.29
Maypole Dancing
at St Andrew's
Girls' School ,1910

7 Worthy of Remembrance

Settling into Salisbury between the Wars

What did the many Channel Island students find when they arrived in Salisbury between the wars? It was a time of hardship: the impact of the First World War had left its mark on Wiltshire and on the city. Salisbury Plain was full of the remains of army camps, which had housed thousands of men on training.

Many soldiers who returned from the war were homeless. Salisbury Council began to build Council houses in the city, which was an enormous help. War memorials were erected, including that in Salisbury Market Place, unveiled by Lt Tom Adlam VC, born and educated in Salisbury. It was a time of unrest and strikes, and in the 1930s, of recession and financial gloom. Unemployment rose sharply and many people had cuts to their pay. By 1930, 2.5 million people in the country were unemployed. In 1932, at the height of the Depression, there were 2,286 people unemployed in Salisbury.

The students would have been surprised by the noisy streets crowded with both motorised transport and horse drawn vehicles. There would have been so much more noise and confusion than at home in the Channel Islands. By 1928, 21 year-olds would have been able to vote for the first time. One can imagine them having lively debates about life and the many changes which they were witnessing.

How did they spend their limited and precious free time? In 1932, Salisbury's new open-air swimming baths were opened. The water was icy, but many took the plunge! Students complained that there was no 'ladies only day', but were pleased to have any change in College routine. Visits to the cinema were rare, due to the expense, and many films were frowned upon by the staff, as they were thought to be unsuitable, but, by 1930, there were three cinemas open in Salisbury.

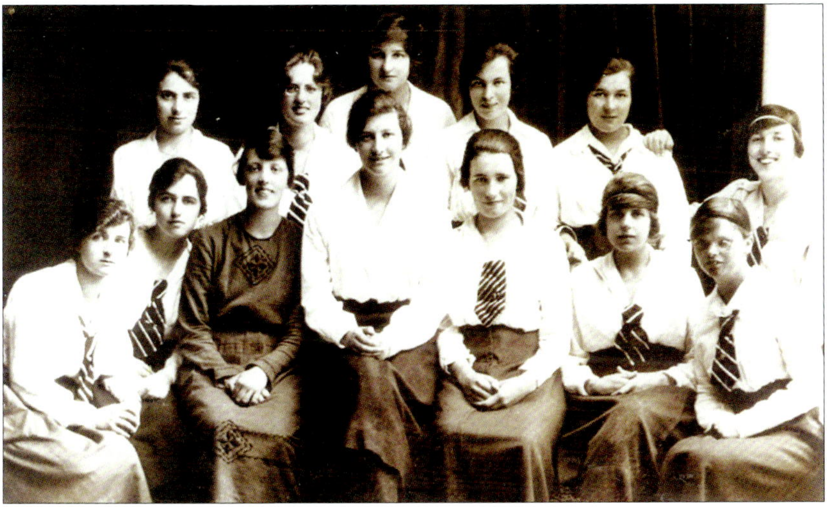

Fig. 7.1 Students from the era

Students enjoyed simple pleasures in and around the city. In 1928, a Barnard's Cross student recalled:

> 'We seldom went into the city as students had little or no money to spend. It was a pleasure, early in the year to pick bunches of snowdrops, for a few pence from a cottage garden. In Spring we picked catkins, primroses, bluebells and periwinkles to decorate our cubicles. Later on we found orchids. Sometimes we picked flowers specially for children in London. These were packed and sent to Old Students teaching in deprived areas for use in Nature lessons. We could readily walk up Fowler's Hill; at the top was open country'.
>
> Lucy Sanderson Taylor: *College in the Close*

There was keen rivalry in sports matches between Barnard's Cross and King's House.

A busy College timetable left little free time for students to be involved in city life.

However, the College students always took a lively interest in what was happening in the Cathedral and the city. In 1920 students joined in

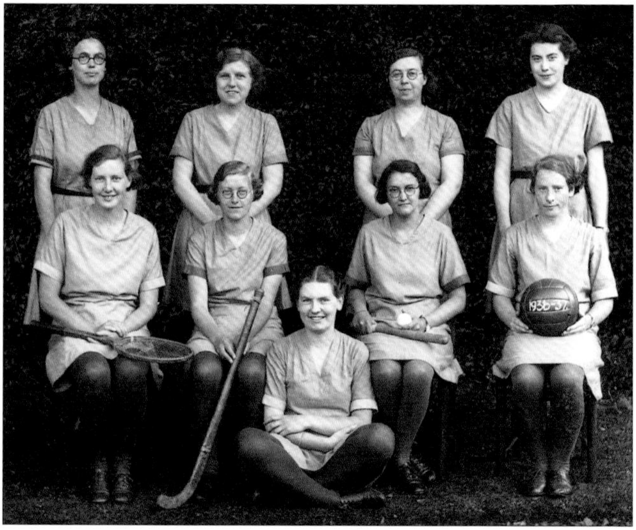

Fig. 7.2 The winning team

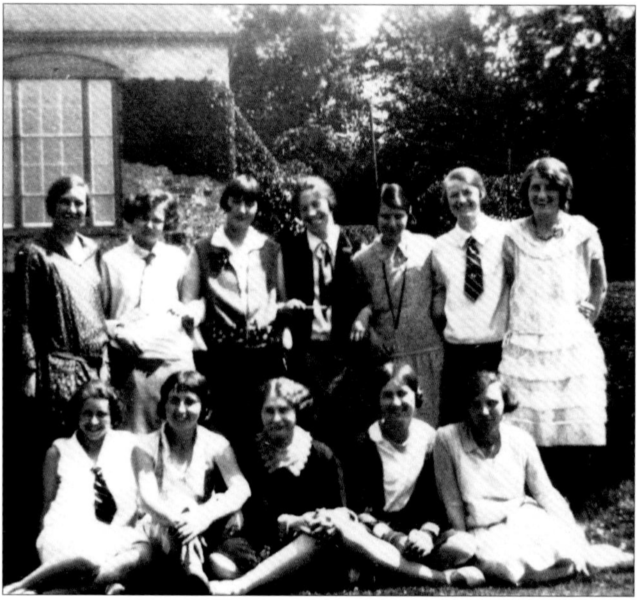

Fig. 7.3 A happy group of students

the 700th anniversary of the laying of the foundation stone of Salisbury Cathedral.

They attended a special celebration service for the opening of the new City Council House and watched a great historic procession move through the city, which commemorated the history of Salisbury's schools. National events were celebrated, with bunting decorating the city streets and tea parties on the College lawn.

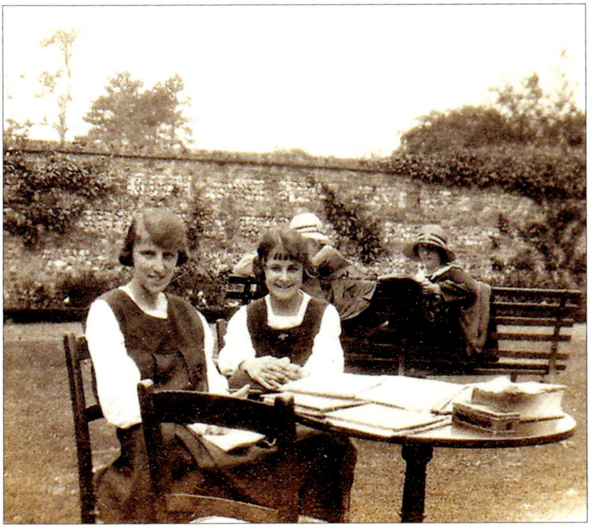

Fig. 7.4 Enjoying the College Garden

A student from Barnard's Cross hostel, described Sunday tea at College in 1925:

> 'In our Junior year we took it in turns, two at a time, to prepare our Sunday tea. We each paid 3d to the two on duty, who bought salmon for sandwiches, and cakes, usually doughnuts. During our Senior Year arrangements were quite different. We had each brought a teaset from home. On Sunday morning we 'bagged' a small table from a classroom, library etc. by chalking initials on it. In the afternoon we set up our tea parties. We were allowed to invite visitors from outside, members of staff etc'.

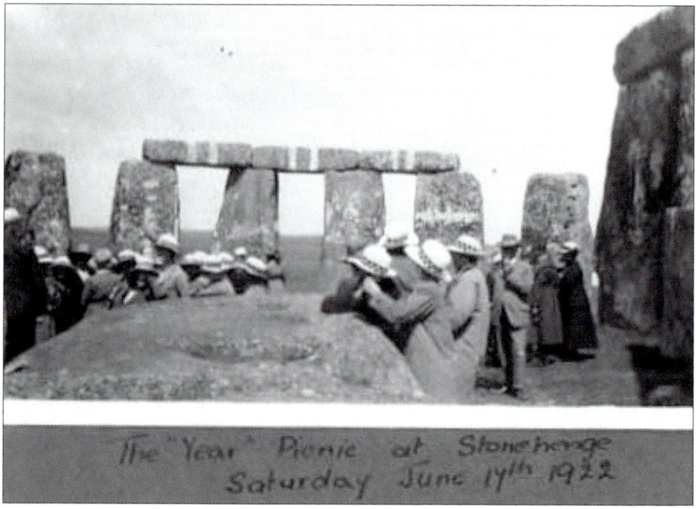

Fig. 7.5 A trip to Stonehenge

Annual picnics to local places of interest were highlights of the year. Events such as this must have helped the Channel Island students, who were so far from home, to settle as smoothly as possible into College life.

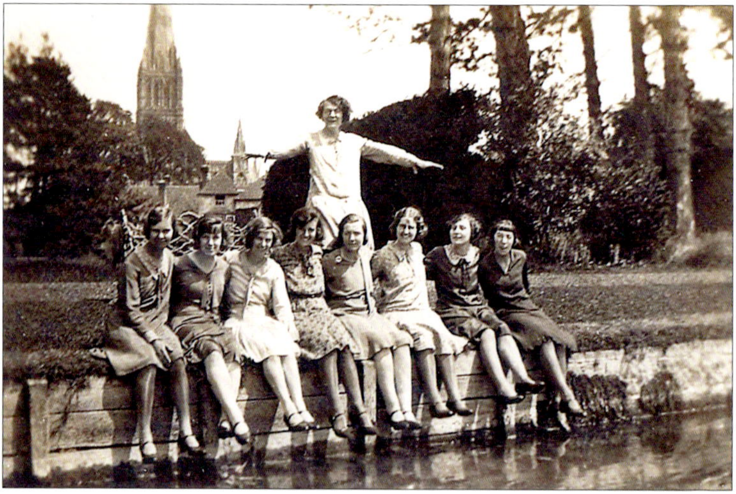

Fig. 7.6 Fun by the river. College reunion 1930

A time of uncertainty lay ahead, but the proximity of the Cathedral and the peace and beauty of their surroundings provided the students with strength, dedication and determination to succeed.

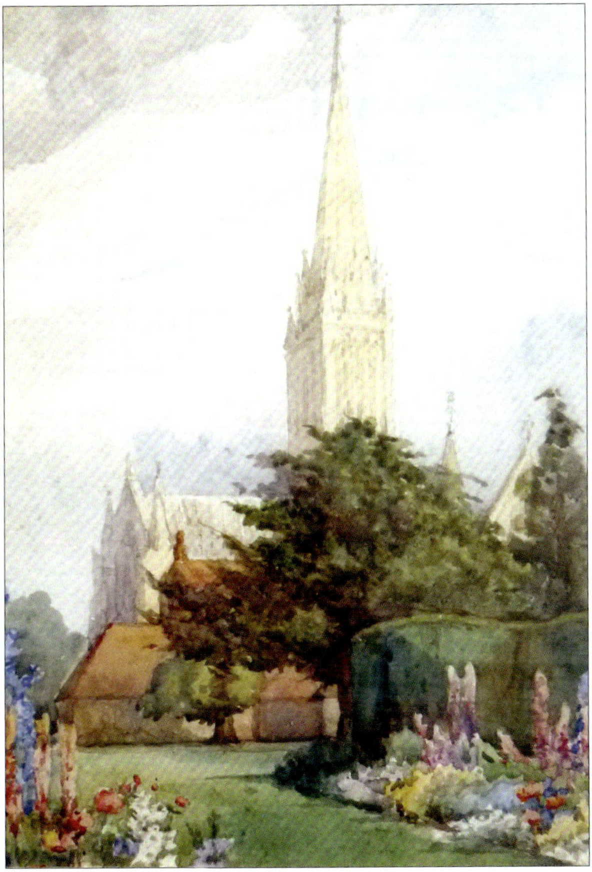

Fig. 7.7 The Cathedral from the College grounds, in 1935

Edith Albiges 1921–23
'One of the best practical teachers of the year!'

Salisbury Teacher Training College report:

> ' I have lived and served in a young world, always thinking and planning for tomorrow, hoping for the future and helping to shape lives yet to be'.
>
> Edith Albiges, on her retirement from teaching in July 1963

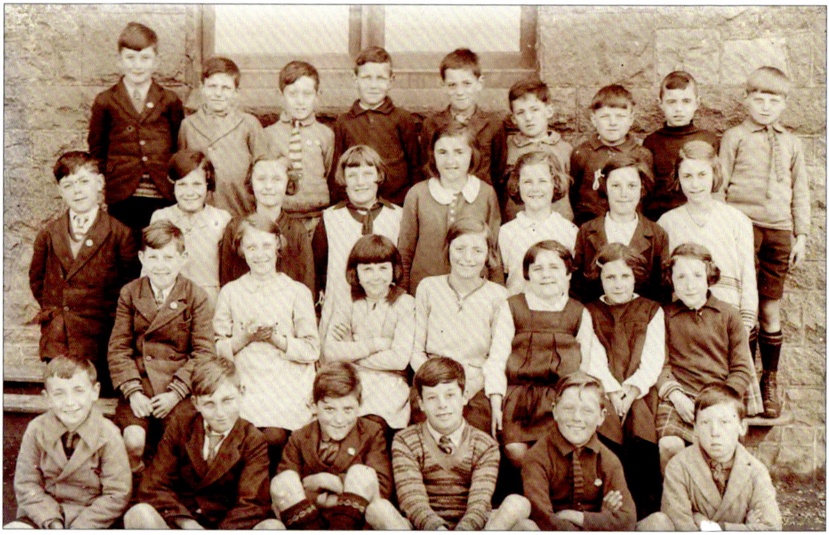

Fig. 7.8 Happy Guernsey primary schoolchildren, 9th May 1932

Edith Albiges was born in St Peter Port, Guernsey on May 7th 1902. Her long life was dedicated to education and to serving the Guernsey community as a member of the States. How proud her parents, Hector Thomas and Edith Annie, would have been.

Edith was educated at Melrose Girls' School, which was a States elementary school in Rosaire Avenue. She decided that teaching was to be her chosen career and later enrolled as a student at the Guernsey Pupil Teacher Centre. Between 1915 and 1920 Edith worked as a pupil – teacher at St Andrew's Girls' School.

Her College entry form states that her address was 'Brookwood', St Mary's and that her father was a bootmaker. In 1921 she set sail for Salisbury, where she appears to have been an excellent student. Like many other Channel Island students, she was housed at Barnard's Cross. Her teaching practice reports show that she was enthusiastic and energetic:

> 'She shows great powers of adaptability, having done teaching of merit with boys and girls, top standards and with infants. She has shown skill in applying her knowledge of the theory of teaching in the planning of lessons, and she shows enthusiasm and energy in the handling of a matter with a class. She has dramatic power and is occasionally inclined to use it to excess'.

After finishing her training, Edith returned to Guernsey where she taught at Saward Infant School for two years. She then moved to Melrose Girls' School and after three years joined the staff at Vauvert School.

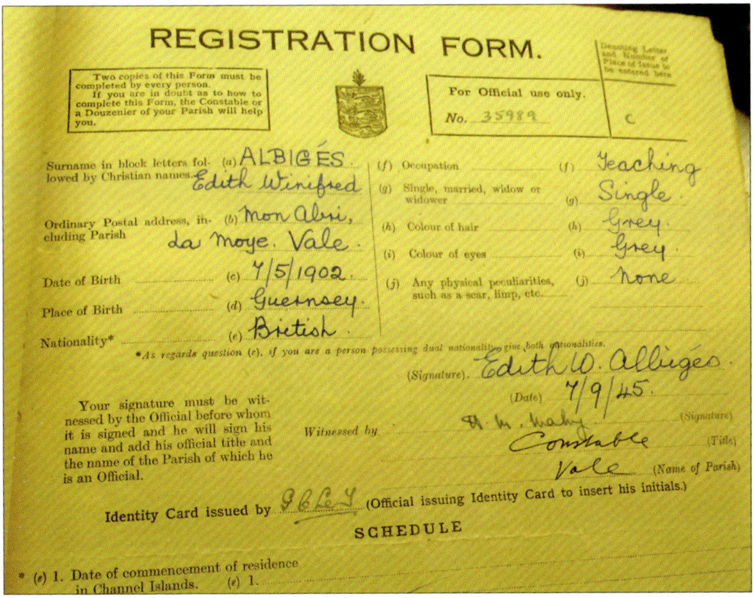
REGISTRATION FORM.

Two copies of this Form must be completed by every person. If you are in doubt as to how to complete this Form, the Constable or a Douzenier of your Parish will help you.

For Official use only.
No. 35989 C

Surname in block letters followed by Christian names. (a) ALBIGÉS Edith Winifred

Ordinary Postal address, including Parish (b) Mon Abri, la Moye. Vale.

Date of Birth (c) 7/5/1902.

Place of Birth (d) Guernsey.

Nationality* (e) British.

(f) Occupation (f) Teaching

(g) Single, married, widow or widower (g) Single.

(h) Colour of hair (h) Grey.

(i) Colour of eyes (i) Grey.

(j) Any physical peculiarities, such as a scar, limp, etc. (j) None

*As regards question (e), if you are a person possessing dual nationality give both nationalities.

(Signature) Edith W. Albigés.

(Date) 7/9/45.

Your signature must be witnessed by the Official before whom it is signed and he will sign his name and add his official title and the name of the Parish of which he is an Official.

Witnessed by (Signature)
Constable (Title)
Vale (Name of Parish)

Identity Card issued by (Official issuing Identity Card to insert his initials.)

SCHEDULE

* (e) 1. Date of commencement of residence in Channel Islands. (e) 1.

Fig. 7.9 Edith's Registration Form

In 1940, just prior to the Occupation, Edith was evacuated with the school to Polockshields Senior Secondary School in Glasgow. She was her usual active self and she worked with the Womens' Voluntary Service (WVS) and was honorary secretary of the Scottish Channel Islands Society.

The school returned to Guernsey in 1945 after the German Occupation had ended. It became a mixed secondary modern school and Edith was eventually promoted to Acting Headteacher of the school. In 1954, she became the Headmistress of St Pierre du Bois School, where she had previously worked as a pupil-teacher. By then, the school was an all age school with 250 pupils. In 1963, having completed 42 years as a teacher, Edith retired – but certainly not to a quiet life.

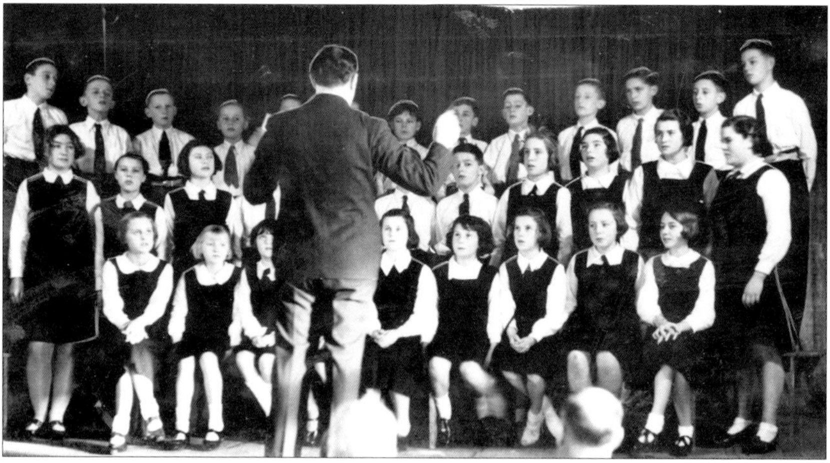

Fig. 7.10 St Peter's School Choir, 1938

Edith was involved in numerous organisations including the Guernsey Teachers' Association. Several charitable organisations benefitted from her knowledge and skill. There was never a dull moment. She was even an honorary manager of the Guernsey Savings Bank. Her diverse interests included serving on the St Peter Port Hospital Board and she was also a member of the Board of Directors of the Ladies College.

In 1964, Edith gained a seat as People's Deputy for The Vale in the States of Guernsey. She remained as a member until 1976. Her links with education continued, as she served on the Education Council and many sub-committees. The welfare of children was always close to her heart.

Edith was always willing to take on extra responsibilities. One of these was as the vice-president of the Bathing Places Committee. The Bathing Places are beautiful seawater swimming pools built in the Victorian era. Thousands of Guernsey children learnt to swim in them. In earlier times the students from the Pupil Teacher Centre held races there with prizes for different races – including one for 'the prettiest swimmer'.

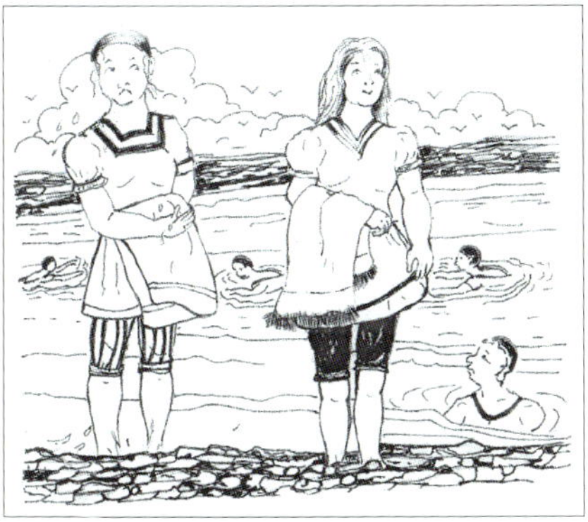

Fig. 7.11 The prettiest swimmer?

There are several pools all refreshed by the sea every day. They are still very much in use today, having been restored and renovated by local volunteers.

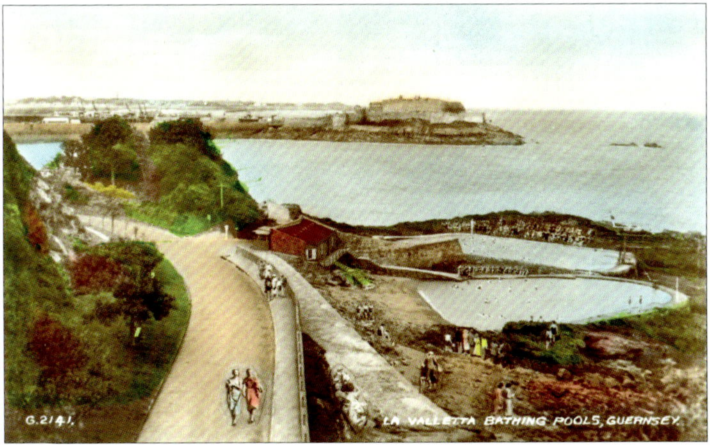

Fig. 7.12 The popular bathing pools

The energy and enthusiasm which Edith Albiges showed at College remained with her all her life. After a fulfilling life dedicated to serving children and the community, Edith died in Guernsey in February 1999, aged 96.

1922–24 Beatrice Le Huquet – a life of dedication to others

Beatrice Le Huquet was born in the Parish of St Martin's on March 20th 1903. She died in 2006 aged 103 years. The 1911 Census shows Beatrice, an eight year old schoolgirl, living at Elmore, St Martin's with her parents and her younger sister Phyllis. Her father, Philip, was a builder and all the family had been born in the parish.

St Martin's is in the north east of the island and even today remains a rural parish with a large farming community. It includes the famous Mont Orgueil Castle that overlooks Gorey harbour on the east coast, St Catherine's Bay with its long breakwater, and the attractive fishing harbour at Rozel. The parish has many incomparable views and a visitor to Jersey in 1926 might well have been thinking of St Martin's when he

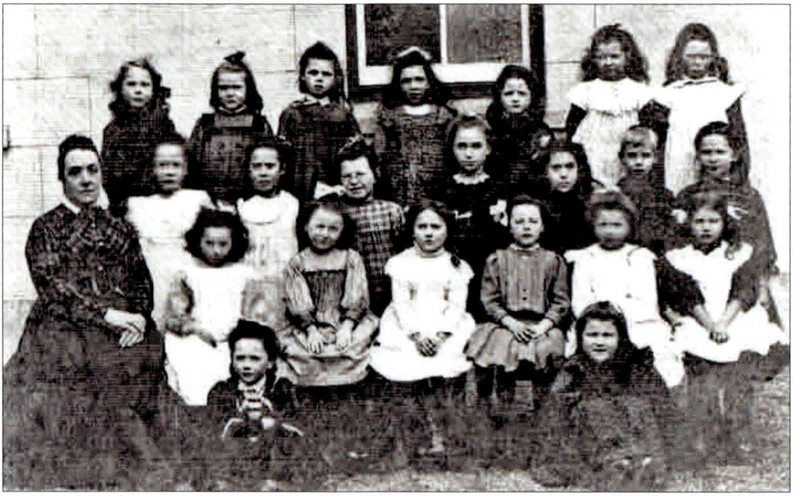

Fig. 7.13 St Martin's Parish School in about 1910

wrote on a postcard: 'Jersey is a wonderful place – everything is of such a vivid colour: rocks, seas, sky and vegetation is like none I have ever seen'.

St Martin's Parish School had opened in 1900 with 59 pupils. The introduction of free compulsory education in 1899 was controversial in the island. In a rural parish such as St Martin's, parents preferred to keep their children at home to help on the family farm. They objected to compulsory attendance at school, as it deprived them of the help on which they were so reliant.

> 'Country parents wished for a basic education and nothing more. The demands of the family took priority over those of school and at harvest time this meant an empty classroom'.
>
> John Kelleher: *The Triumph of the Country*

The summer holidays were also times of work, for they were geared to the potato season. Children were roused before daybreak to pick the Jersey Royals, which were then put in barrels and taken by horse and van to the Weighbridge. Doris Carter, who grew up in Jersey commented:

> 'We were so tired at the end of the holidays that it was almost a relief to go back to school – to be able to sit down and use our brains instead of our brawn'!
>
> Doris Carter: *A Jersey Childhood*

The school was one of the fourteen Parish Schools to be taken over by the States in 1913. It then became known as St Martin's Central School.

We can imagine young Beatrice, who lived in the village, walking to and from school. On arrival, the children were expected to wait in the playground until the bell rang. The school day started with prayers and a hymn. School was still a daunting place in the Edwardian era. Children were sent to learn, rather than to enjoy themselves. Non-attendance was seen as a crime and attendance medals were awarded at the end of the year. The Headteacher was frequently the only qualified member of staff and the only person to have been paid a 'proper' salary. On starting school, the infants faced considerable difficulties as they were used to speaking Jerriais at home, but now had to learn to speak, read and write in English. The Three R's (reading, 'riting & 'rithmetic) formed the basis of education and great emphasis was placed on neatness and accuracy. In Jersey, the most important subject in the school curriculum was French and each year the Public Instruction Committee set examinations in French, with rewards. Physical exercise consisted of drill in the playground, with exercises such as arm swinging, skipping, hopping and balancing.

Looking back today at the challenges that faced both pupils and teachers one hundred years ago, we respect their fortitude, drive and ambition.

Important events were happening in Jersey whilst Beatrice was growing up. The Battle of Flowers, which had started in 1902 to mark the Coronation of King Edward V11, quickly became an annual event. In 1912, when she was nine years old, Beatrice would have heard about the landing of the first hydro-planes on the sands of St Aubin's Bay. Perhaps she was there amongst the crowd of excited onlookers as they caught a glimpse of the future.

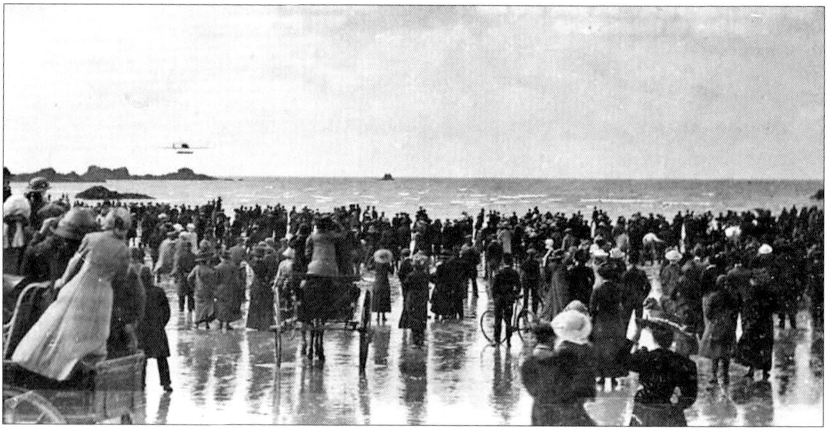

Fig. 7.14 The first airplane lands in St Aubin's Bay, 1912

Beatrice and her friends probably attended Sunday School and would have revelled in the excitement and adventure of the annual Sunday School picnic. Children and adults climbed into two-horse vans and visited remote parts of the island, singing hymns on the way and enjoying the feast that was provided. On special occasions Beatrice would have tasted *merveilles* (Jersey Wonders), which are traditional biscuits made with butter, flour and eggs, and boiled in lard. Her family may have taken their crocks of beans to the bakehouse on Saturday evenings, when no bread was in the oven. The baker, who was paid a penny, baked the beans for Sunday breakfast. In the autumn, neighbours gathered together to make Black Butter, which is an apple preserve, so named on account of its colour when cooked. The stirring went on for hours and was a community event.

Beatrice went on to become a pupil-teacher at St Martin's, as is recorded in the school log book: 'September 13 1920: Beatrice Le Huquet commenced duties today as Pupil Teacher in this school'.

School log books reveal so much about life and a month later, the fact that there were 77 cases of measles in the school was also recorded. It is probable that Beatrice worked part-time at St Martin's, whilst also studying at the Jersey Pupil Teacher Centre in Rouge Bouillon. The Principal, Miss Montgomery, encouraged her to train in Salisbury and on July 21st 1922 the log book records: 'Miss B Le Huquet is leaving the school this afternoon having gained admission to Salisbury Training College'

Beatrice's time in Salisbury was important to her and she became a keen member of the Salisbury Club in later years. Whilst at College, she lived at Barnard's Cross with others from Jersey. One of them wrote the following short article for the July 1923 issue of the Barnard's Cross Magazine:

A Defence of My Island by Une Jersiaise

'According to the many of the uninitiated, Jersey consists of a small patch of land on which are found a few inhabitants of doubtful intelligence who speak a queer language, tethered cows and many potatoes. Strange to say, there are a few other things here. We possess waterworks, buses, trains, telephones, a museum and even wireless. With wondering eyes we have gazed upon aeroplanes and patent knife cleaners. We are able to dance a little and sometimes we produce operas.

Jersey is beauty. Surrounded by seas of changing blue, she is far lovelier than eastern gardens. She has a peculiar charm belonging to jagged cliffs tumbling into rough seas, fields of trembling grasses and meadows of golden buttercups. Skies are often blue, the sun shines for many long hours and the air is fresh and keen. Yes, Jersey certainly is one of the chosen places of this earth.

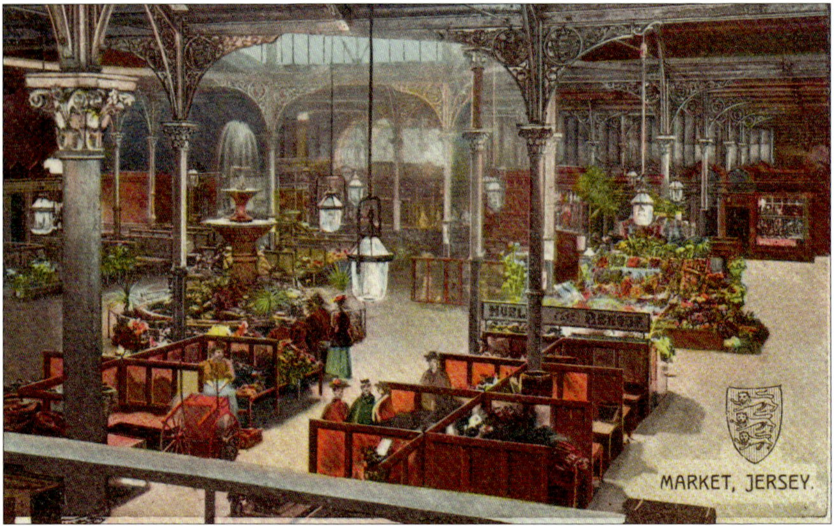

Fig. 7.15 Central Market St Helier before the First World War

On leaving College in 1924, Beatrice taught at First Tower School which had been founded by the Parish of St Helier in 1865 and was also taken over by the States in 1913. On November 5th 1926 she is again mentioned in St Martin's Central School Log Book: 'Miss B Le Huquet having been appointed to the staff commenced duties today. She will be in charge of Standard I'.

Beatrice, born and bred in St Martin's, was surely delighted to return to her old school. The Log Book ends in 1948, but Beatrice was in for the long haul. A former pupil, writing his memories, spoke warmly of the 'good discipline and the stimulating teachers.'

Jersey in the 1930s was a pleasant place in which to live. The island had a population of about 50,000 and an economy that was based on agriculture, mainly early potatoes. Tourism was growing in importance and the holiday atmosphere of the island was beginning to be felt. As the decade drew to a close, however, islanders began to realise that their way of life was going to change.

Ann Cardew (Beatrice's great niece) remembers two stories that were passed down the family:

> 'Beatrice's family owned guns ('they were country people and they just did') and when the German invasion was imminent, Bea, as she was known, and her father took their guns to St Catherine's Breakwater. They threw them off the end into the deep water to avoid them being taken by the incoming troops.
>
> During the Occupation, Bea used to listen secretly to the news on a wire radio. She took down notes in minute handwriting and would fold them very carefully and hide them in her shoes. She would then walk to school saying hallo to any soldiers she passed. Once at school, she would read the news to her fellow teachers'.

Beatrice's 1940 registration card shows her as a certificated teacher who was living in St Martin. She trained as an ARP (Air Raid Precaution) warden and continued to teach at St Martin's Central School during the Occupation and until her retirement in 1966. One of her colleagues was Agnes Machon, a former student who retired from St Martin's in 1965. They were just two of the many stalwart teachers who did their best in very challenging circumstances.

When the island celebrated the 50th anniversary of the Liberation, Beatrice made a scrapbook to present to St Martin's Parish. 'I wanted to give something to the parish as a permanent souvenir of that wonderful time of freedom'.

St John's Ambulance continued to work during the Occupation, offering First Aid courses and distributing the Red Cross parcels that were sent to the island towards the end of the war. Beatrice became increasingly involved and joined the organisation in 1947. It became a very important part of her life and she quickly formed a division of nursing cadets at St Martin's School. Faith Herbert remembers visiting Auntie Bea with her mother (Marjorie Starck, the lighthouse keeper's daughter) and seeing her proudly marching in her uniform. When Beatrice celebrated her 100th birthday in 2003, she asked relatives and friends to give donations to Family and Nursing Care instead of presents. In 2006 she became a Life Patron of the Jersey branch for 'services to the island and to St John in First Aid, going back as far as the Occupation years'.

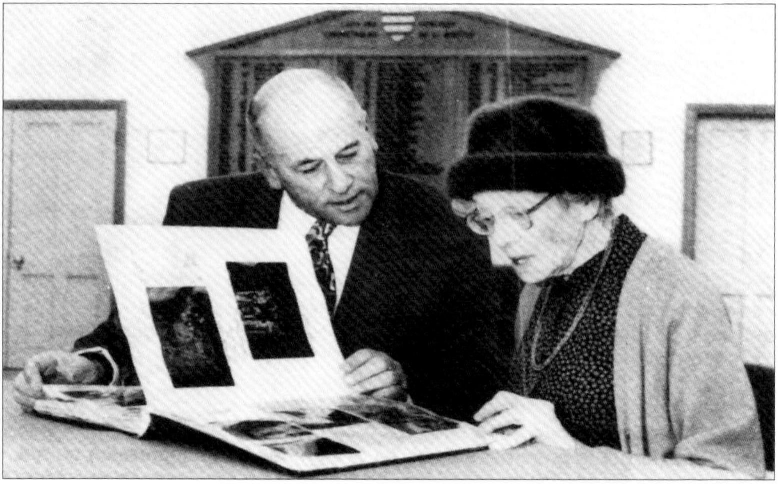

Fig. 7.16 This photograph of Beatrice Le Huquet with her scrapbook and John Germain. Constable of the Parish and former pupil, appeared in The College Newsletter in 1999.

Beatrice also loved painting and the walls of her house were covered with her canvases. She kept painting until the last few years of her life, despite her failing eyesight. She would have liked to have known that her great-niece is one of the artists who produced the cover of this book. Beatrice died on 3rd October 2006. She was 103 years-old and one of the island's oldest residents. In an article in the *Jersey Evening Post*, John Germain, former Constable of St Martin and former pupil of Miss Le Huquet, said that she had been dedicated to St Martin's School and scholars during her many years as a teacher.

1927–29 : Florence Mary Renouf – zest for life and care for others

Mary Renouf (she was always known as Mary) was born on July 8th 1909. She was born into a Jersey family whose fascinating history was recorded by her in articles for the Channel Islands Family History Society.

Our thanks to David Guy, who compiled the stories into a booklet and allowed us to use some of the material. The history of Mary's family provides a vivid background to her own life.

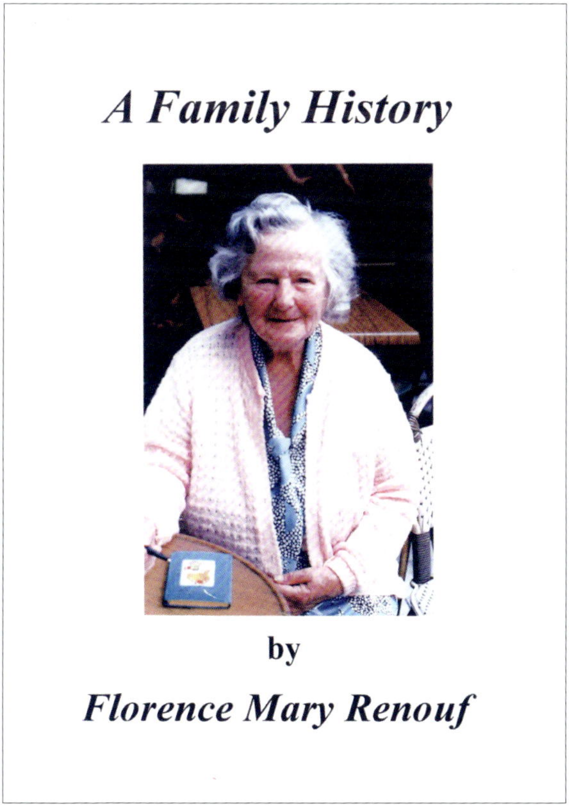

Fig. 7.17

The family history goes back to the Huguenots who had sought refuge in Jersey so as to avoid religious persecution. As the years passed, they intermarried with the Jersey people. Mary's great-grandmother, Nancy Fauvel, who was born in 1798, was of Huguenot descent. She was sent to Mile End finishing school in London, but crossing the Channel had become fraught with danger. Great Britain was locked in conflict with France in the early 19th century and two young ladies, returning from a finishing school in England, were captured and taken as hostages to France. They were eventually released and returned home, but it is not surprising that Nancy's parents decided that she would not return to the finishing school for a second year. In 1818 Nancy married the Revd Philip Dupre, who was subsequently appointed the Rector of St John's. Nancy, a resourceful, active and determined woman was, to quote Mary, 'a Rector's wife, worthy of remembrance'. After her husband's death, Nancy moved into La Franchise in St Martin with her daughter and family. Mary Renouf, Nancy's great-granddaughter, was born at La Franchise in 1909.

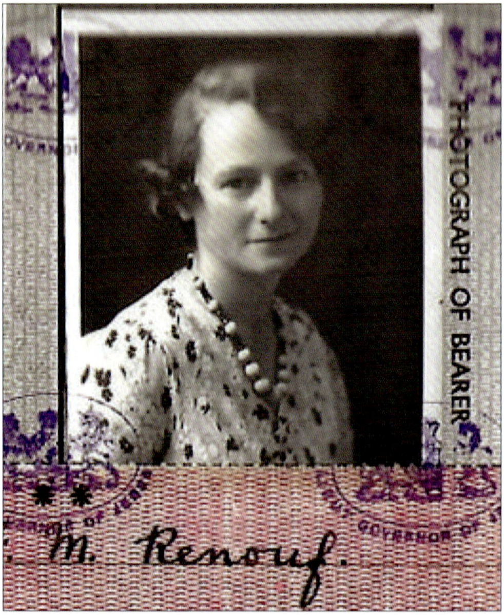

Fig. 7.18 Florence Mary Renouf

Mary's father, Elie George Dupre Renouf, a farmer, owned his own property and employed farm labourers. Mary had fond memories of her early years. Living in this rural part of the island, it was exciting to drive from St Martin into the busy town with her father on Saturdays in Touzel's two-horse bus. She remembered watching horse-drawn vans queuing up at the Weighbridge to have their potatoes weighed before being exported. Sometimes there was a cargo boat or a collier being unloaded in the harbour. It was a vibrant scene. The coal from the collier was hoisted out of the hold and tipped into horse-drawn carts that took it to the Gas Works. It was a special pleasure to catch a glimpse of the train puffing its way out to Corbiere. 'It was busy, but we knew everybody' commented Mary.

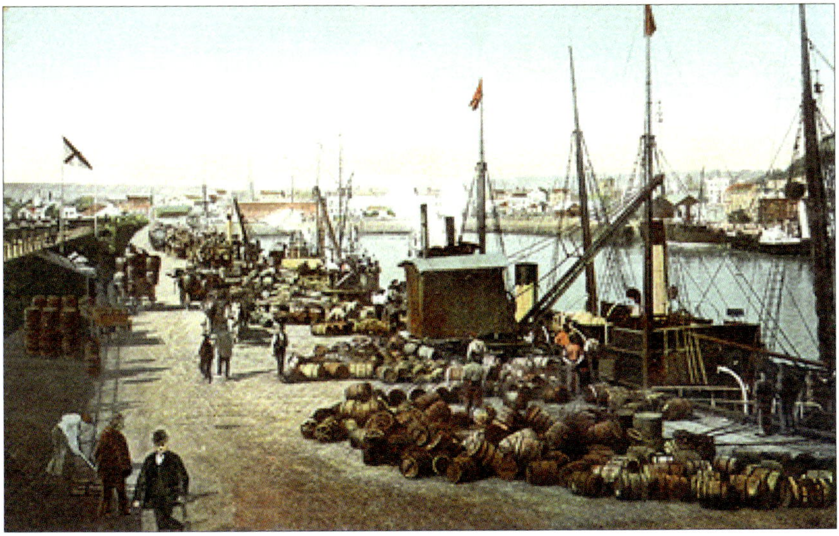

Fig. 7.19 A busy time on the Albert Pier during the potato season

The parish of St Martin included a number of private schools and Mary's education started at Miss Laura du Feu's school near St Martin's Church. When she was older she attended the Jersey Ladies' College for five years and two terms. She then spent one term at the Jersey Pupil -Teacher Centre and this was followed by six months as an 'observation teacher' at Trinity Central School, formerly the Parish School. This was in preparation for her two year course at Salisbury Training College. Miss Montgomery, writing about Mary in 1926, commented: 'She is a quiet girl and a hard worker, ready to do her best'.

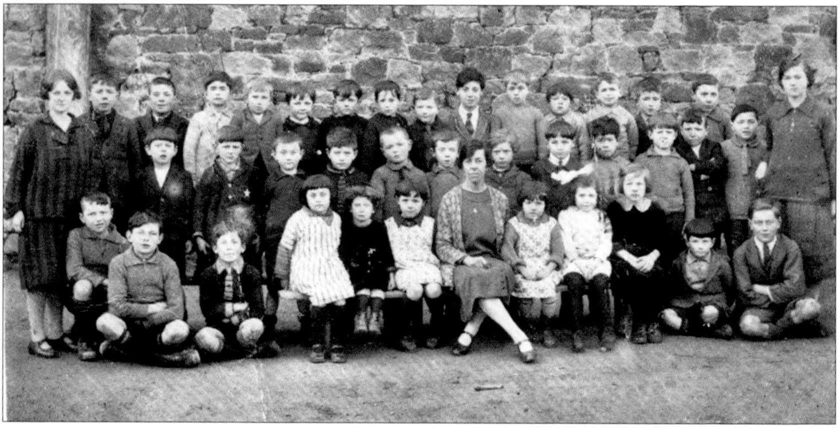

Fig. 7.20 Trinity School in 1927

Mary started at College in 1927, the same year as Ivy Le Blancq, Eline Burman and Kathleen Brookes. No interviews were held, but the girls required good medical reports and credits in London General or Cambridge exams. On reaching Salisbury, they lived in Barnard's Cross and Mary had a horse-box (cubicle) that was close to the fire escape. During her second year she shared a room with two friends at Number 8 in The Close. It was exceptionally cold and snowy and the water in their jugs froze overnight, cracking the jugs. One night the water tank in the attic burst and water froze on the stairs, forming icicles as it cascaded over the bannisters. They were so cold that they did not sleep a wink. In the morning, they passed the White Hart Hotel, which had opened up its disused forge and were invited to 'take a handful of warmth' as they made their way to Barnard's Cross for breakfast.

Mary remembered the arrival in the 1920s of the *Isle of Guernsey*, one of several new mailboats in which the students travelled to the mainland.

When they reached Salisbury, the students stayed at Barnard's Cross for half term as it was too far to go home. Rules were relaxed and they could even go into Salisbury on market day and to the cinema to see a film. Mary remembered how Dr Baker (the Chaplain) and his wife hired a charabanc and took them for a drive in the New Forest before entertaining them in their home. 'Tea was served in tiny china cups – such a change'.

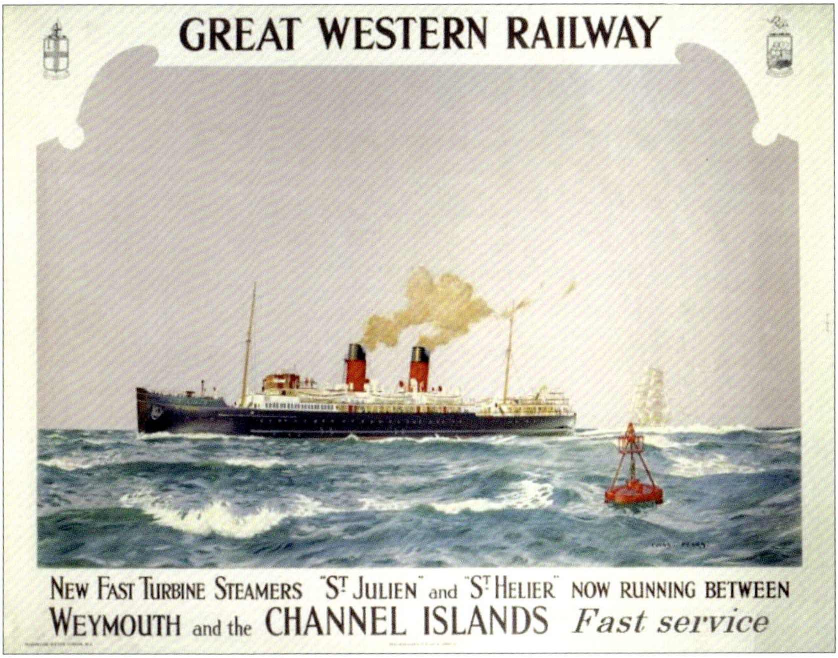

Fig. 7.21

The College curriculum was expanding and by the 1920s students were doing courses in Theory of Teaching and Psychology. Mary and Ivy both chose to do Advanced French and Ivy's college report mentioned her good accent. Her individuality, zest for life and dramatic ability were also commended. Mary's report focused on her good language, pleasant manners and irreproachable standards of conduct.

School Practice was a time of hectic activity, but Mary, having spent six months as an 'observation teacher', was only required to do a total of six weeks in schools. 'However for many, the ordeal lasted twice as long', was her wry comment.

Mary looked back at her college years with nostalgia and affection, but she missed her native island. Returning by boat in 1929, emotions must have been running high when she spotted the cliffs of Jersey, the wide sweep of St Ouen's bay and the lighthouse at Corbiere. There's no place like home and this is where Mary wanted to be. She taught for 41 years in Jersey, working with children aged from infants to fourteen and over. She particularly enjoyed teaching reading, mathematics and nature study, but she did not appreciate changes in education.

After doing some private tuition for a few months, Mary was appointed to Faldouet School, which was the Dr Barnardo's and Jersey Home for Boys. Following this, she taught for 25 years at St Saviour's School. Her younger sister, Madeline, followed her to College and, on returning to the island, the sisters shared La Franchise, the family home in St Martin. Madeline sadly died in 1958, probably as a result of the deprivation she had suffered during the Occupation. By 1945, she had weighed only four stone and eleven pounds.

Mary was quite a character and perhaps she was rather like her great-grandmother, Nancy Fauvel. Mary was, like Nancy, good at looking after people and during the Occupation she cycled into town to visit friends. She always had a little basket that contained a few eggs in a box, or perhaps vegetables, wrapped in a napkin. Living on a farm meant that she could provide a few 'treats' for those in St Helier. The five years of Occupation ended on May 9th 1945 and Mary went to the pier in St Helier, where she and others stood silently and watched proceedings. 'We all cried when we listened to Churchill's speech'. A tremendous sense of relief swept over her when she climbed on the 7 o'clock bus to go home.

Mary was a keen gardener, but she didn't enjoy housework. According to a member of her family, being driven by her was a hair-raising experience and passengers were recommended to shut their eyes!

She was a faithful member of her church but was not slow to complain if someone had the temerity to sit in her pew. She also reprimanded the vicar if she didn't like his sermon, or if it was five minutes too long. Her funeral outfit must have seen plenty of use as she attended every funeral in her church, regardless of whether or not she knew the person who had died.

During her retirement Mary enjoyed talking to schools and telling children about life during the Occupation. Bob Le Sueur, who remembers her well, commented: 'She became a legendary, surrogate-mother to half the parish. Almost everyone in the parish had experienced her jolly, smiling, stand-no-nonsense attitude and her concern with individuals'.

In her interview with Kevin Le Scelleur in 1993, Mary explained how the Jersey that she had known as a child had changed. It was now a much more anglicised place. Whilst this was a matter of regret, she went on to talk about the indomitable spirit of the islanders, which was something that would never change. Mary, or Auntie Flo, as she was known to some, died on April 19th 1999. Many former pupils attended her funeral. Like Nancy Fauvel, her great grandmother, Mary is indeed 'worthy of remembrance'.

1918 – 1939: Jersey between the Wars

The Armistice in 1918 was a time for rejoicing, but also for sorrow. Hard times lay ahead as families mourned those that they had lost, and gradually came to terms with a changed world. Senator John Le Marquand, a former President of the States of Jersey Education Committee, wrote:

> 'These were years of decay in the history of Jersey Education. This blight on the pages of our educational history is all too dramatically portrayed by the fact that Grouville Elementary School was the only States School built between the two world wars. This was at a time of drastic overcrowding, persistently reported by HM Inspectors, in the classes of many elementary schools, particularly in St Helier. The example of the distressing overcrowding at St James's Elementary School was symptomatic of the deplorable stagnation. The Committee of Public Instruction recorded in its 1925 Report to the States that the available space for the number of pupils at St James was 102 girls in five classes in one room. There was no political outcry. Nothing whatsoever was done to alleviate the unacceptable overcrowding in urban elementary schools, mainly caused by the building of many small houses at St Luke, First Tower and St Clement'.

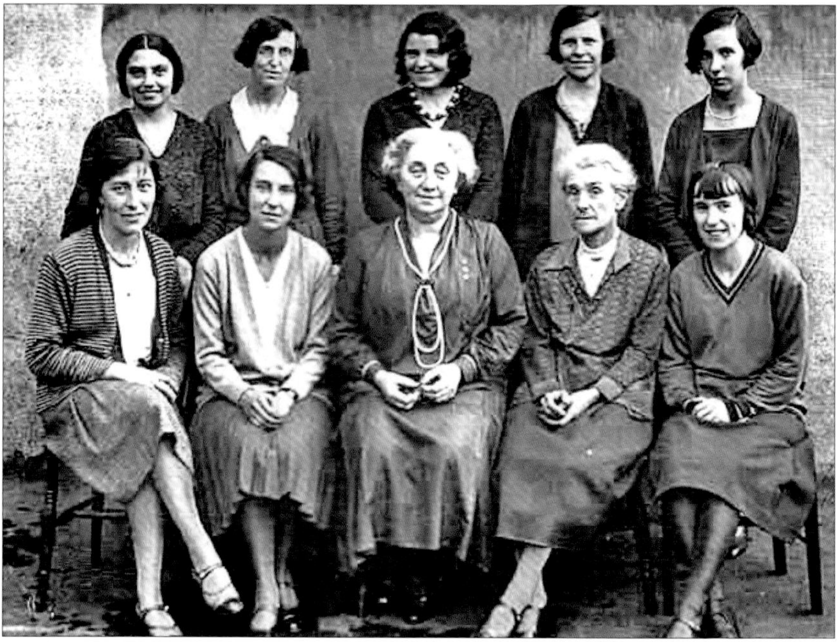

Fig. 7.22 Teachers at Halkett Place School in the 1930s

Quite apart from overcrowding, some of the rural schools also had problems. An HMI who visited Trinity Central School in 1933 reported 'serious defects regarding the supply of water in the cloakrooms and lavatories, which should receive early attention'. He then turned his attention to the staff:

> 'Some of the teachers have reached what may be described as the veteran stage, adopting methods of instruction to which they have been accustomed for many years, while others are still recruits, and are influenced by modern tactics, the effectiveness of which has still to be proved. Up to the present, the two have still not succeeded in achieving a blend which constitutes complete harmony of treatment'.

The Hadow Reports, which were issued between 1923 and 1933, came from the Consultative Committee of the Board of Education in

England. Two principal recommendations were the raising of the school leaving age to fifteen and the introduction of secondary education for every child, following six years in primary education. Her Majesty's Inspectors, nominated by the Board of Education, promoted these recommendations in both England and Jersey. In England it became the policy to build new, modern secondary schools. In Jersey the recommendations were ignored. Inspectors persistently stressed the need for a new school building to accommodate the Intermediate School, thereby releasing modern classrooms for the children from Clearview Street and Saint Mark's Elementary Schools, but nothing happened. The school leaving age was raised to 15 in both England and Jersey during the Second World War.

The 1931 Report of the Committee of Public Instruction stated that no school building had been undertaken on a large scale in Jersey for many years. The reaction from the States, written in French, as was still the custom, was one of complacency:

> "Le Report est tres interessant au point de vue d'un Inspecteur de Sa Majesté que fait sa critique basée sur des idées anglaises. Il est bon de noter que notre administration en général et le personnel de nos écoles meritent un éloge".
> (The Report is very interesting from the point of view of Her Majesty's Inspector, whose criticism is based on English ideas. It is good to note that our general management and the people in our schools deserve praise)

Senator Le Marquand wrote that this 'was indeed a shameful time of neglect, deprivation and hypocrisy'. The States of Jersey failed 'dismally and disgracefully' to address the situation regarding education.

This neglect of public education led to the growth of many small private schools. In 1925 there were thirty-eight States Public Elementary Schools and fifty-five fee-paying private schools that offered a form of elementary education. Fee paying secondary education was available at Jersey Ladies College, and Victoria College, but only a small number of pupils stayed on for the Higher School Certificate, which was the precursor of A Levels. Neither Beaulieu nor De la Salle, both Roman Catholic schools, had a

Sixth Form. The co-educational Jersey Intermediate School was selective, but there was no Sixth Form and pupils left after taking the School Certificate. Cyd Le Bail, a former pupil, commented: 'The brighter ones sailed through School Certificate without much effort'. Very few pupils then had the opportunity to go on to Further Education.

More than 60 percent of pupils in Jersey stayed on in their elementary schools from the age of 11 to 15. This continued until the early 1950s.

It is remarkable, given the inadequacy of secondary education in the island, that so many young women were accepted for teacher training in Salisbury between 1918 and 1939. The amount of time that they spent at the Pupil Teacher Centre in St Helier was probably variable. Pupil-teachers were useful, especially in elementary schools that had few teachers. Eline Burman worked at St Clement's before going to College and was also a Sunday School teacher for three years. Kathleen Brookes taught at La Moye, where she 'satisfactorily replaced an adult teacher'. Comments in college reports suggest that a few students arrived with inadequate preparation, but then made good progress. Their experience as pupil-teachers must also have helped with the acquisition of some classroom skills.

Gladys Gruchy was a pupil-teacher at New Street Girls' School and she also attended the Pupil Teacher Centre before entering College in 1921. Her particular strengths were Needlework and Music. Gladys returned to Jersey after her training and taught there for 44 years.

Constance Renouf lived in Stopford Road, St Helier and she attended St James's Girls' School before moving to the Pupil Teacher Centre for her secondary education. She passed the Cambridge School Certificate examination in 1924, gaining Distinction in French. Constance went to College in 1925.

Vera May Le Seelleur, whose father, Thomas, was secretary to the Constable of St Helier, also arrived at College in 1925. She had been educated privately at La Chasse School before going on to St Luke's Mixed School where she was a pupil-teacher. St Luke's, in the expanding suburbs of St Helier, was one of the overcrowded schools. Thomas Stent, the Headmaster, warmly supported Vera's college application:

'Vera Le Seelleur was attached to this school for practical work during her apprenticeship. She shows great aptitude for teaching. Her mother was a teacher and her aunt is the Headteacher of the most successful Infant School in the island. I am sure she has chosen the right vocation'.

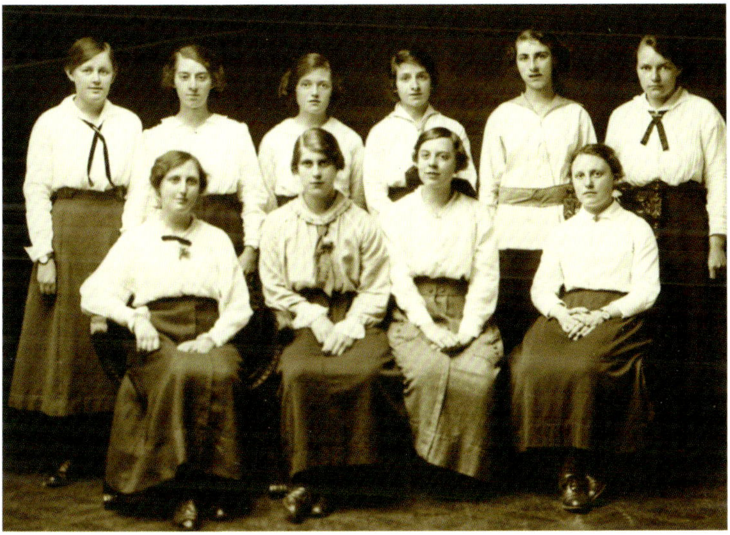

Fig. 7.23 Jersey pupil-teachers

Vera also attended the Pupil Teacher Centre. Miss Montgomery's report stated that Vera had given complete satisfaction. 'She works hard, has grit and does not suffer from mental fatigue'. Vera returned to Jersey after her training and had a long and successful career in the island.

The Pupil Teacher Centre developed into the Intermediate School in 1929. By this time it had built up an enviable reputation and was highly regarded in the island. Iris Le Feuvre, former President of the Education Committee, remembers that it was such a privilege to be awarded a coveted place:

'It was a great honour to have been selected to go to the Intermediate School in 1939. This was a big deal for a tenant farmer's daughter from St Peter's School. It was not every year that someone went to the school and all the others remained where they were until they were fourteen or fifteen'.

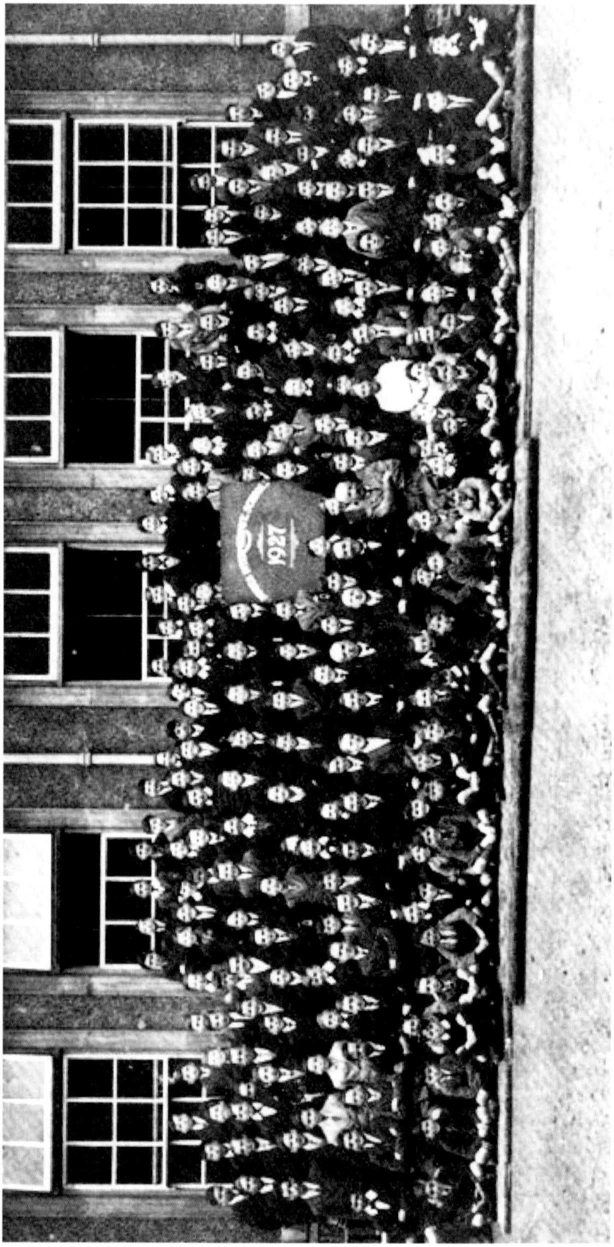

Fig. 7.24 Jersey Intermediate School

A steady flow of Jersey students continued to enter Salisbury Training College through the 1930s. Cecile Blacklin arrived at College in 1931, together with Dorothy Duffett and Marguerite Luce. Cecile had been educated at FCJ Convent, as had Madeleine Norman and Janet Tarr. Madeleine's school report commented that she 'always upholds authority and has not been known to break any school rules'. In Salisbury, Barnard's Cross continued to be the house where most of the Channel Islanders lived. Beryl Woodsford arrived there in 1932.

Beryl's ambition developed early! Miss Montgomery, Headmistress of the Intermediate School, commented that she 'had entered this school in 1927, aged eleven, with the intention of becoming a teacher'. Beryl's college reports show that she spoke French well and was considered to be an enthusiastic, intelligent student who showed promise. It was felt that she was a genuine influence for good and that her 'kindliness and vivacity endear her to the children'. Beryl returned to Jersey in 1934 where her first job was at New Street Boys' in St Helier. She later taught at Victoria College Preparatory School.

These young women were fortunate. They had reaped the benefits of the limited secondary education that was available in Jersey and they had been prepared well for College. Many of them returned home after their training and gave long years of service to island schools.

By the 1930s, communications were developing and Jersey was becoming more prosperous and outward looking. On December 9th 1933, Jersey Airways Ltd was formed and nine days later the first aircraft took off from the beach at West Park, bound for Portsmouth. By the end of the year the airline had carried 20,000 passengers. The States of Jersey Airport opened in St Peter four years later, in 1937. Air travel was augmenting shipping services, but there was no decline in travel by sea. New ships were built for the GWR route and also for the Jersey to St Malo route. Tourism was becoming 'big business' and hotels were springing up. The principal exports from Jersey in 1939 were potatoes, tomatoes, grapes, granite and cattle. The island was prospering, but the storm clouds were gathering.

Guernsey between the Wars – 'The Child of Today is the Adult of Tomorrow'
(JNO. Roussel: President Education Council)

During this period numerous Guernsey women trained to teach in Salisbury, with several returning to teach on the island. The States was eager to recruit more qualified teachers and wholeheartedly supported their applications. Students known to have returned to the island included: Edith Albiges, Nora Birch, Phyllis Burgess, Kathleen Clarke, Freda Flambard, Ivy Gillam, Daphne Lacey, Renée Le Messurier, Minnie Nevitt, and Lorraine Le Page. Other students arrived in Salisbury in 1938, just prior to World War Two.

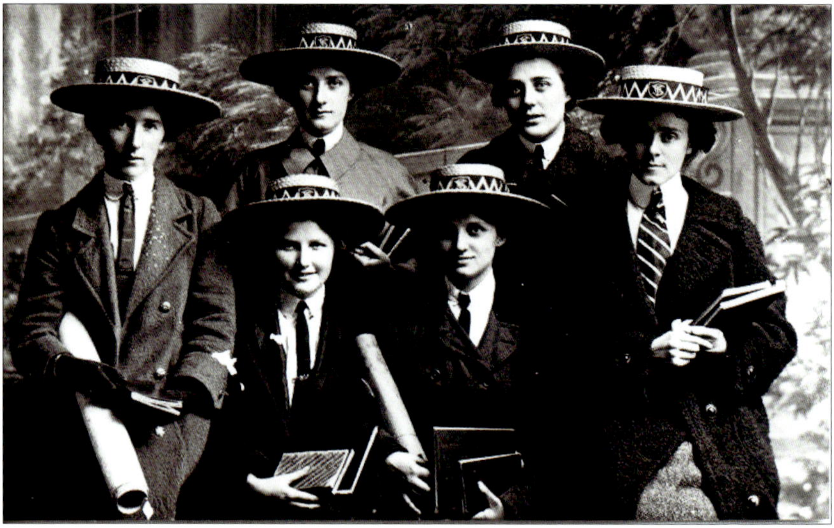

Fig. 7.25 College Students in the 1930s

In 1925, The Education Council had approached the States with a request for teachers' salaries to be paid in line with the Burnham Scale, which had been adopted on the mainland. This was agreed in 1925, and replaced the local scale.

It was in 1925 that Phyllis Burgess attended College in Salisbury as a student at Barnard's Cross. She died in 1996 aged 90. Her obituary in the 1996 College Magazine described her as a dedicated teacher:

> 'Her entire teaching career was one of devotion to her scholars: she was most respected by colleagues, ex-pupils and parents of the children in her care. She taught in Guernsey, first as an assistant at St Sampson's Infant School and, post-war, as headmistress of St Martin's Infant School… Phyllis was a faithful and devout member of her church. She was quiet, purposeful, had a lovely sense of humour and a merry chuckle. She was a well-loved lady'.

In 1940, Phyllis was evacuated to Glasgow with St Sampson's School until the German Occupation ended.

Times were hard for the general population in the 1920s. In 1926, the first Guernsey Old Age Pensions Law was passed, although this was only for people aged over seventy on a low income. Conditions began to improve as other social legislation gradually followed.

In 1935, teachers agreed to a temporary reduction in their salary to help overcome the financial crisis. Life remained very tough as the economic depression impacted. Many employers ran small scale businesses and employed only a few people. Some employees were only able to find work for a few months of the year and often combined different jobs. Unemployed men were given work building roads or maintaining sea defences.

Life gradually improved; modernisation was in the air. A new jetty was built at the harbour, and a reservoir was constructed to increase water supplies for the expanding horticulture industry. Cinemas opened, providing new entertainment for residents. The airport opened which made the links with the mainland much speedier.

What were Guernsey schools like during this time? A 1934 School Inspection Report mentions the uncertain situation regarding the organisation of elementary education. Some schools were overcrowded, especially the town schools, where two teachers sometimes shared a room. 'The sharing of a room involves loss of teaching efficiency and imposes undue strain on teachers and children'.

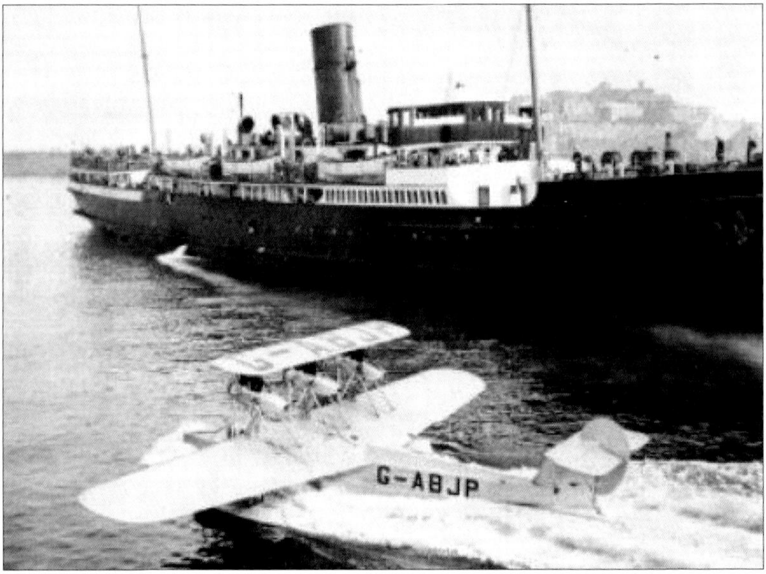

Fig. 7.26 The mail steamer St Helier, and a seaplane of Guernsey Airways in St Peter Port 1938

The number of pupils was still increasing with 4,982 pupils on roll. In addition to the lack of practical instruction for boys, there was an inadequate supply of home reading material. There was above average progress in the teaching of French, although it was uneven. Teachers showed 'praiseworthy zeal and keenness'. On average, four hours a week were allotted to the study of French.

The health of the pupils was a concern, as was the impact of poor health on their education. The school nurse was fully occupied dealing with many children. It was hoped that Guernsey could appoint a School Medical Officer at the earliest opportunity: in 1935 the first school Medical Officer, Dr. William McGlashan, was appointed. The importance of physical exercise was emphasised and lectures and demonstrations related to the subject were given to school teachers.

The teaching of Religious Knowledge was praised in the 1934 report. This subject was a key strength for many Salisbury trained students such as Marjorie Sarchet, who was born in St Peter Port in 1903. She lived in a small four-roomed cottage with her parents and brother. Before training in Salisbury, Marjorie taught at Amhurst Girls' School and then, after qualifying, at St Sampson's Infants. The 1938 Salisbury Training College Magazine gives an account of the events of the Guernsey Branch of the Salisbury Club. Dr Baker had been in the island for two weeks in September and assisted at Marjorie's wedding, before the summer branch meeting on the next day. How special it must have been for Marjorie to be married by Dr Baker, Chaplain of the College Chapel and a favourite College lecturer. A student from Barnard's Cross in 1926 described Dr. Baker and his work:

> 'His was dedicated work; performed with care and devotion...He was a kindly bearded and spectacled person who always appeared in cassock and clerical collar. When he saw students crossing The Close he would doff his mortar-board and sweep it low in a bow of acknowledgement. He kept a store of little jokes and anecdotes with which he was always ready to lighten conversation'.

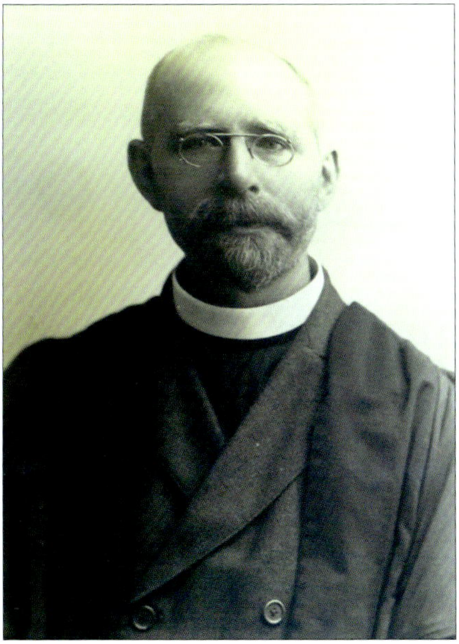

Fig. 7.27 Revd Dr Baker

An Interlude in Alderney

The island of Alderney is part of the Bailiwick of Guernsey and is the closest island to France and the United Kingdom. It is about three miles long and one and a half miles wide. A letter written in 1925 by Margaret Montgomery, who was a former College student and lecturer, indicates that a former College student was working on Alderney at this time. Doris Noel, from Jersey, trained in Salisbury around 1913. Miss Montgomery wrote to the head of Salisbury College, commiserating about the influenza epidemic, but also mentioning Doris:

> 'I suppose you know that Doris Noel is in Alderney, where apparently education was previously optional. She seems to have the organisation in her hands under an untrained (perhaps unqualified) master. So far she appears to like the work.'

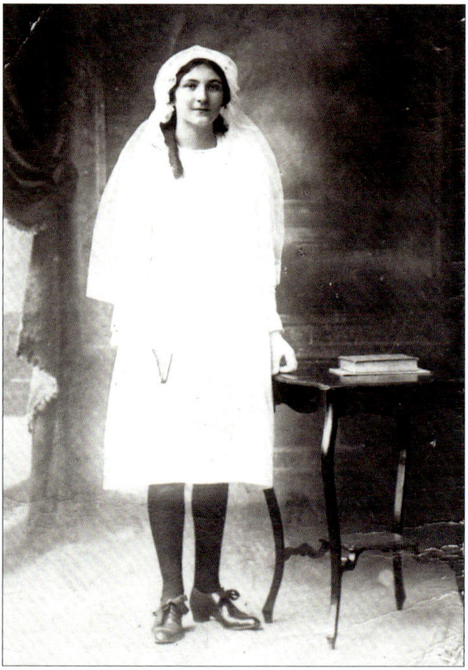

Fig. 7.28 Doris Noel in 1918

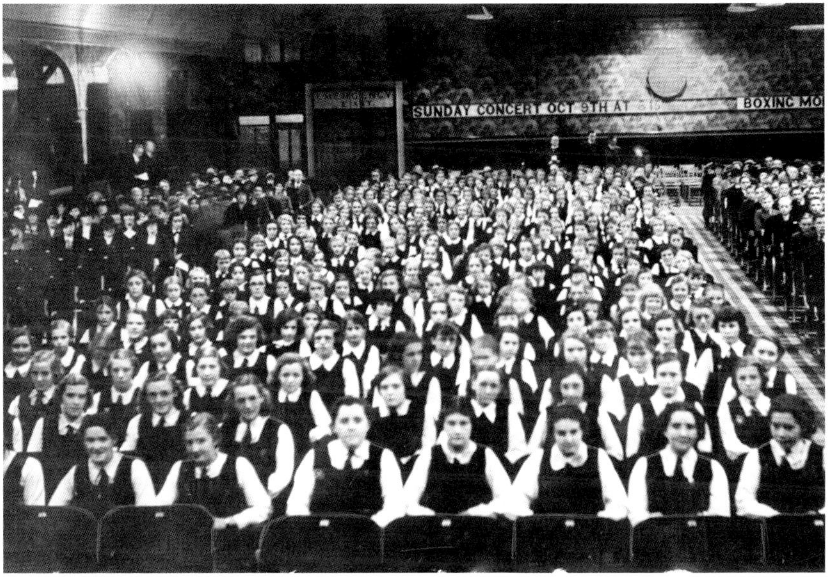

Fig. 7.29 Prize-giving at The Girls' Intermediate School in 1938

Life went on in Guernsey, and conditions gradually improved, but as World War Two loomed, life, education and the lives of children on the island were about to undergo a dramatic change!

8

The Years of Occupation 1940–1945

'It was the Vega that saved us'

'The *Vega* was an International Red Cross ship that was sent to the relief of the Channel Islands in 1944. In September 1939, when Britain and France declared war on Germany, no one could have imagined that just five years later, the islanders would be near starvation. 'It was the *Vega* that saved us' wrote Philip Le Sauteur in *The Occupation Diaries*.

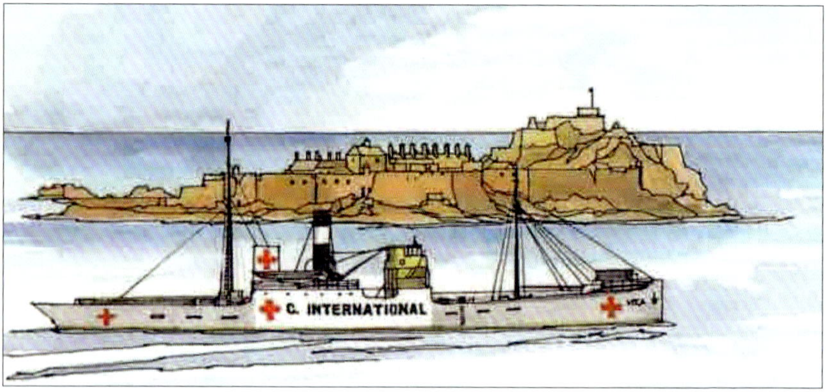

Fig. 8.1 The *Vega* depicted on a phonecard

On September 3rd 1939 Britain declared war on Germany. The initial reaction in Jersey was similar to that in England. People felt shocked and alarmed as emergency measures were put into action. Blackout was enforced, gas masks were issued and the air raid sirens started to wail. At sea the buoys and lighthouse lights were extinguished at night. British and French reservists could be seen at the harbour in St Helier, preparing to rally to their country's call.

It was, however, all rather unbelievable. If there was a war, it surely wouldn't last long and after all, Jersey was part of Great Britain and would be defended to the hilt. Life settled down again. Outwardly all was peaceful. 1940 began calmly and life went on as usual. The economy was booming and Jersey was advertised in the English newspapers in March as 'the ideal resort for wartime holidays this summer' (Michael Halliwell: *Operating Under Occupation*).

The front cover of a pamphlet produced by Tourism proclaimed '*Facts and General Information on Wartime Holidays in Jersey, Channel Islands*'. The wildly optimistic message to tourists was that:

> 'the island with its eternal sands, sea and sunshine is far removed from the theatre of war. Jersey offers you a haven for repose and recreation and it is in such calm surroundings that you will, at least temporarily, be able to banish the spectre of war from your mind'.

The enemy, however, swept across France and islanders became increasingly aware of the seriousness of the situation and of their own vulnerability. British residents did their utmost to return to the mainland. At the end of May, by which time there was much confusion and anxiety, some country schools closed to 'allow pupils and staff to assist in potato digging and export'. Jersey Intermediate School in St Helier, decided to keep going as they had few staff or pupils to whom this was applicable. Pupils and staff were dismissed on June19th and told to return later for the second half term. That same day, there was a message from King George VI to the Bailiffs of Jersey and Guernsey:

> 'For strategic reasons, it has been found necessary to withdraw the armed forces from the Channel Islands. I deeply regret this necessity, and I wish to assure my people in the Islands that in taking this decision, my government has not been unmindful of their position. It is in their interests that this step should be taken in present circumstances'.

The Channel Islands were declared a de-militarised zone. The islands would be declared 'open towns' and no attempt would be made to defend them. Troops and stores that had started to arrive for the defence of

Jersey were withdrawn. Fighting the enemy was now out of the question. The British government announced that ships would be sent to evacuate all those civilians who wanted to leave, but all civil servants were expected to stay. Never before had people had to make such an agonising decision – shall we stay or shall we leave?

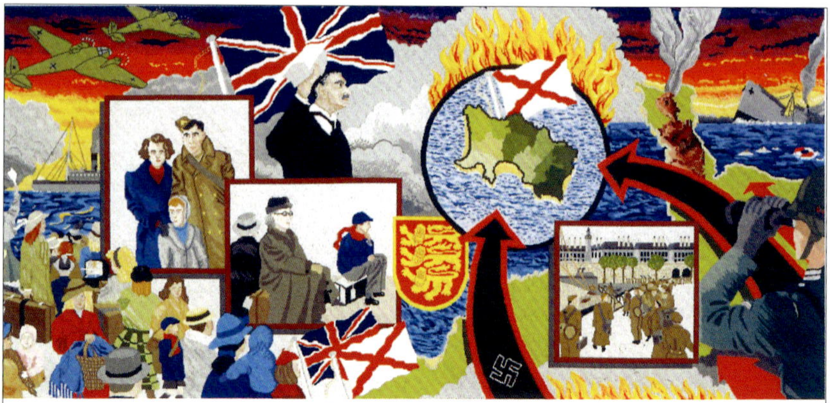

Fig. 8.2

OUTBREAK OF WAR

Embroidered by the Parish of Trinity

Despite the sacrifices of the Great War and German assurances of "... peace in our time..." hostilities become inevitable when German armies attack Poland on 1 September 1939.

The 19th of June was described by the diarist, Leslie Sinel, as a 'day of wild rumour' and, he added, 'the suddenness of the decision flung the island into a panic'. Telephone lines were choked and long queues of islanders waiting to register for evacuation formed at the Town Hall. The piers were crowded with people, luggage and abandoned cars. The evacuation boats, many of which were small cargo vessels, were crammed to capacity. Ethel Meldrum, whose teacher training in Salisbury had finished in 1924, was on one of these boats with her husband. She worked in munitions during the war. Sybil and Kathleen Ahier also travelled in a cargo boat with their family.The last boat left at about midday on June 21st.

In Jersey, about one fifth of the population chose to leave, contrasting with Guernsey, where many more were evacuated. Perhaps the newspaper headlines were an influence. On June 19th the *Guernsey*

Press announced 'Evacuation of Children', whereas in Jersey, the Evening Post stated 'Grave decision. Island to be demilitarised'. It is likely too that the words of Alexander Coutanche, the Bailiff and now Jersey's Civil Lieutenant Governor, had an effect. He felt sure that those who had their roots in the soil would not want to leave. Many islanders would have related to this announcement. Living quietly in their parishes, they led secure and stable lives, many coming from families who had lived in Jersey for generations. The decision as to whether to stay or go had only one answer. It was unthinkable to uproot themselves and their children and leave their homes, farms and communities for unknown destinations over the sea.

Jersey settled down and waited, but not for long. 'Hold Fast' were the words of advice in the *Evening Post* and they did, for just over a week. Devastating air raids took place over Jersey and Guernsey on June 26th, with a considerable number of casualties. The BBC reported later that day that the enemy had not been informed that the islands were undefended. On June 30th a message was sent to the Germans via the United States Embassy in Berlin, telling them that people had been evacuated and that the islands were demilitarised and could not be considered a legitimate target for bombardment.

On July 1st the occupying forces arrived. Shortly afterwards, a notice on the Post Office in St Helier announced: **ALL COMMUNICATION WITH THE MAINLAND HAS NOW CEASED**.

Islanders felt abandoned. They were marooned, cut off from the outside world and now facing life under an occupying force. A. Downer, writing in *The Channel Island Schools 1940–45* recorded:

> 'The schools in Jersey re-opened on July 2nd. A roll call of staff and pupils found that roughly half of the children and one third of the teachers had been evacuated. A re-shuffle had to be made; teachers were sent to other schools and some schools were amalgamated. The children were in fair spirits but the teachers wondered what the final outcome would be. The Germans were openly boasting that they would be in London by the middle of August'.

As the troops settled in, they requisitioned houses and supplies and confiscated cameras and wirelesses. The islanders planted vegetables in anticipation of food shortages. Life was going to be very different.

A sizeable contingent of former Salisbury students was amongst the stalwart teachers who kept the schools going during the next five dark years. Glimpses of life during the Occupation, along with some of the teachers' experiences, help us to paint a picture of what school was like at this time.

Jersey Intermediate School was under the headship of Miss Coad, who had succeeded Miss Montgomery a few years earlier. Evelyn Hoyles, a former Salisbury student joined the staff in July 1940 (see Chapter 9 for her story). Her family lived on the island and Evelyn managed to get on the last boat home before Jersey was occupied. Another student stayed on the mainland, having been told by her parents earlier: 'Go to your new job, the Germans are coming'.

In September 1940, Harold Carter became the Headmaster of St Lawrence Central Mixed School. He took on a school of approximately 100 boys and girls aged 6–14, three teachers and a deplorable lack of books and equipment. This was typical of many rural elementary schools in the island. Cecile Blacklin, a former Salisbury student who had left College in 1933, was one of the teachers. She was remembered as a 'devoted teacher who cycled to school every day from her home in St Saviour's Road'. Marguerite Luce, who also trained at Salisbury, taught the infants. Miss Laurens, another 'devoted teacher' who may have trained at Salisbury, was 'handy with the ruler and accurate with the blackboard cleaner'.

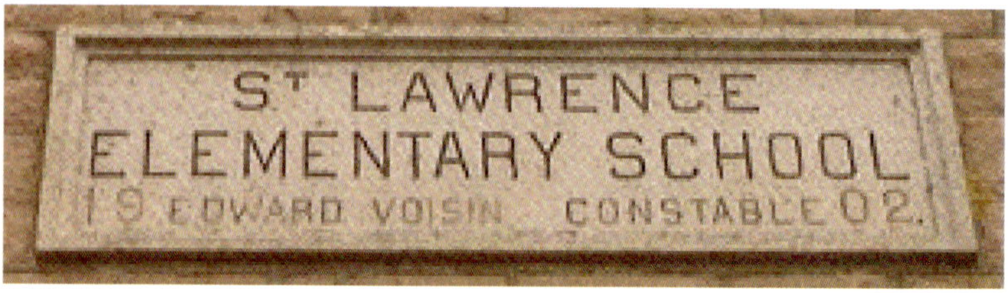

Fig. 8.3

Providing children with a sound, basic education was a challenge. Schools had mostly foreseen the shortage of materials in the event of war and had a supply of exercise books, pencils, chalk and ink. Pencils were treasured possessions and exercise books were used at both ends for different subjects and were only replaced when each full page had been seen by a teacher. Cecile Blacklin sometimes had to ask children to rub out a whole page of writing and then re-use the page. When the exercise books completely ran out, the island was given surplus stock by Guernsey, as their schools didn't need the books due to their depleted school age population. Girls learnt practical skills such as sewing, patching and darning, but teachers felt that giving their pupils some knowledge of English literature and poetry was very important, in case the war was lost. Children were also taught patriotic songs.

> 'It was wonderful to hear the lusty singing of 'Rule Britannia' and the 'British Grenadiers' whilst the German Feldwebel drilled his squad in the adjacent field'.
>
> Barbara Journeaux: *Our Wartime Parish*

Beatrice Le Huquet, who had left College in 1924, was living in St Martin's and teaching at the parish school, where she had herself been educated. A horse and trap delivered dustbins to the school every day throughout the Occupation. The dustbins contained vegetable soup and by the time Monday's ration, which had been cooked on Friday, arrived, the children were complaining 'Miss, it's sour'. In fact the soup, which was provided for all the schoolchildren, helped to nourish them and to maintain their health, as did the ration of one third of a pint of Jersey full cream milk. At Halkett Place School in St Helier, the soup was brought from a communal kitchen at the Chelsea Hotel. It was the Headteacher's responsibility to heat it on a gas stove. In 1940, the school Log Book reveals that she also 'packed the oven with potatoes and vegetable dishes brought by country children for their midday meal'. Despite the fact that islanders were without toothpaste and toothbrushes for most of the war, there was an improvement in children's teeth. This was thought to be partly due to the lack of sweets and the chewing of vegetables and wholemeal bread.

Food was the most prized essential and those who lived in country parishes such as St Martin's, fared better than those in the town, who had nowhere to grow vegetables. Potatoes were not rationed, and neither were carrots, swedes and parsnips. Ground carrots and parsnips were used as substitutes for tea and coffee and other substitutes included sugar beet syrup and potato flour. Seaweed jelly was made and families kept chickens and rabbits. Fish was not an option as the beaches were eventually sealed off. Meagre rations kept body and soul together, but people were inventive and nothing was wasted. An egg, an ounce of butter or a tin of peas was manna from heaven.

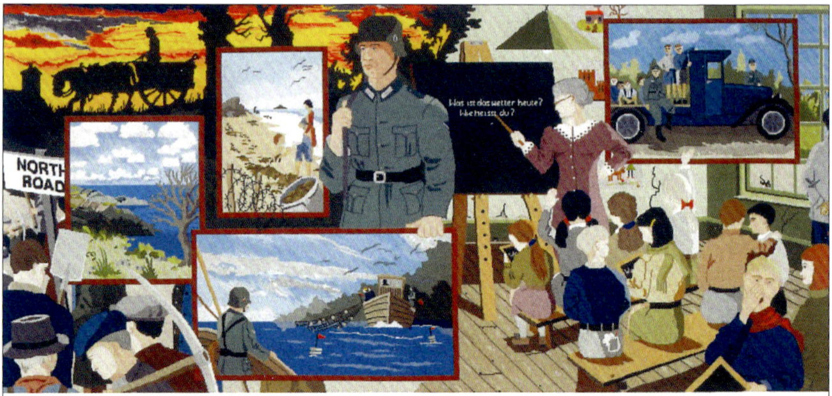

Fig. 8.4

SCHOOL AND WORK

Embroidered by the Parish of St Lawrence

As a result of the restrictions imposed, working practices and schooling have to change.

Teachers were concerned with education in its fullest sense, including their pupils' emotional and physical wellbeing. This was particularly important during the Occupation when parents struggled to clothe and feed their children. Getting to know families and watching out for those children who were especially deprived or anxious was all part of the teacher's job. It was difficult for them to talk about the current situation when so many of their pupils had German soldiers living in their homes. Mabel Ahier , Janet Tarr, Beryl Woodsford, Mary Renouf, Dora Hacquoil, Phyllis Perchard, Madeleine Norman, Margaret Cadiou, Constance Renouf, Florence Hacqoil, Muriel Le Breton and others were all teaching in Jersey during the Occupation.

At Christmas 1940 the pupils at St Lawrence School enjoyed a special Christmas Tea with meat paste, jam, cakes and sweets, but as time passed, the weekly rations steadily decreased. The Medical Officer of Health recommended that all competitive athletics should stop in schools, owing to the shortage of foodstuffs and insufficient diets. The children looked well, but they were lethargic and lacked concentration. Muriel Le Breton, who left College in 1917, also noticed the lethargy:

> 'This was due to lack of food. No fats and no sugar. Bread made from pig-meal, tea from scraped potatoes or beetroots and five pounds of potatoes per week (mostly bad) were the staple diet. Little faces became more and more pinched and little bodies became thinner and thinner'.

Phyllis Perchard and Madeleine Norman were infant teachers at First Tower. They would have seen how hard it was for parents to provide shoes for their children's ever growing feet. At first, people exchanged outgrown footwear, but by 1943 the problem was getting worse At first shoes were mended with parts of motor tyres, but when the uppers had gone, wooden clogs with straps were given to them. The clogs, which were made from beech trees, were made at Summerland Factory and were clumsy and uncomfortable. A. H. Downer, writing in *The Channel Island Schools 1940–45*, described how 'children sometimes walked home from school barefooted, with their boots hanging round their necks. The clatter of the clogs in the classroom was one of the minor annoyances of the Occupation'.

Alice Hambly and Dorothy Mauger, former Salisbury students, were amongst the staff at Halkett Place School during the Occupation. The school log book reports that when the school reopened on July 2nd, there were 86 pupils present, but 94 were absent, having left the island. 'Dorothy Mauger was not at school on July 2nd as she was attending the funeral of her father, who had been killed in one of the recent air raids on Jersey'.

In September 1942 the Halkett Place school log book records that 'a number of families with pupils in this school or children about to start here have received notices that they are to be evacuated by the German authorities'. This deportation of hundreds of British-born residents to

Germany took place over the next few days, arousing considerable public indignation and sympathy. Those who were deported remained at camps in Germany until the end of the war.

In 1941 the schools were ordered to teach German. The States Department of Education made desperate attempts to avoid the German language becoming a compulsory subject. Delaying tactics such as the introduction of voluntary classes after school were started. Mr Carter at St Lawrence refused to find a teacher as he thought it would be unpatriotic. The teaching of German from the age of 12 became compulsory in 1943. Some pupils decided that it was patriotic not to be very good at it. Herr Bleuhl, the German Education Officer, was sent to interview headteachers regarding the length and number of their German lessons. He had many rude shocks and was not well received.

Concerts, plays and community singing helped entertain people and keep spirits up. Cecile Blacklin took part in some of the shows that were put on by Donald Journeaux to raise the morale of the war-torn islanders. Young children did not feel the deprivations as much as their parents, as they had never known anything else. The island was still a good playground, even though the beaches were out of bounds. They made their own fun and found ways to explore, climb trees and throw snowballs. They knew interesting rude German words and sometimes even played games with the German soldiers. John Hibbs, former Headmaster of Victoria College Preparatory School, remembered his own childhood during the Occupation:

> 'For us there were aspects of those years which made it a less frightening time to grow up – there was little traffic and none of the dangers of our overcrowded island to fence us in, no television or long hours of schoolwork to inhibit our play'.

By 1944, the island transport situation had become impossible and children from rural areas such as St Ouen and Grouville could not reach the Intermediate School in St Helier. Many dropped out of education, whilst others returned to their elementary schools. Iris Le Feuvre, former President of the Education Committee, has always regretted her own truncated secondary education. Her experiences shaped her career, leading her to become passionate about education and the opportunities that it could bring. For teenagers, the Occupation had more serious consequences. Being cut off from England meant being cut off from examining bodies and from further education on the mainland. Cecily Hoyles was one such person. She was ready to follow her sister Evelyn to Salisbury Training College, but instead she spent the war years working as an 'observation teacher' in Jersey.

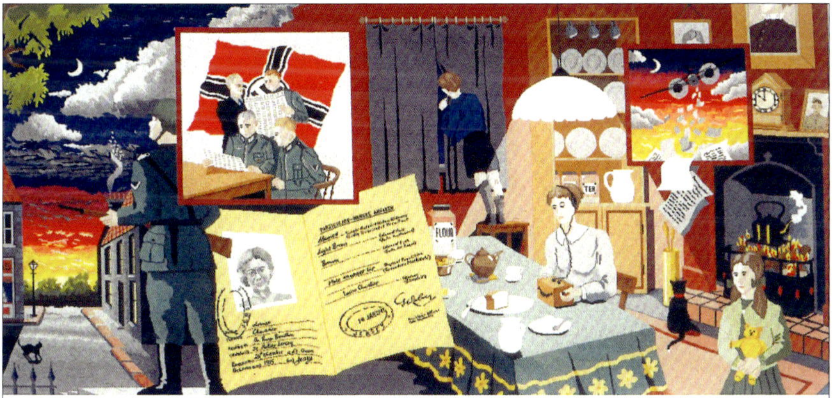

Fig. 8.5

RESTRICTIONS

Embroidered by the Parish of St Helier

To enforce the Occupation, the Germans restrict civilian movement; identify certain groups and curtail the exchange of information.

Following D-Day on June 6th June 1944, liberation became a real possibility in islanders'minds, but the hardest times were still to come. Rations were reduced from autumn 1944 and by Christmas there was no sugar or butter, and soap and fuel was non-existent. Pupils and staff at the Intermediate School hurriedly prepared a pantomime, 'aimed at a cheerful ending to term, to offset shortage of food – and Christmas cheer being limited'. Gas supplies had ended in the autumn and there was no electricity from January 26th 1945. The last bread ration was February 19th. Islanders were literally starving and so too were the occupying forces. At night, children helped their parents to carry items of food upstairs to prevent soldiers from breaking in and getting them. The bitter winter of 1944–45 was the worst one. Many people had no outer clothing and children who arrived at school shivering and wet were sent home as there was no means of drying them. Teachers lacked energy and were strained to the limit.

It is hard to imagine the gnawing hunger, the chilling cold and the deprivation that people endured, but it is interesting to notice that the Intermediate School log book contains less information between December 1943 and April 1944. Any note of buoyancy has gone and the scant information reflects the worsening conditions. Coughs, chills, chilblains and skin infections compelled the Education Department to close the schools just before the Christmas that was described as the 'Black Christmas'. The cheerless and unheated classrooms could be borne no longer. The schools stayed shut until February, then only opening for half time. When children attended school, they took their blankets with them.

The population was only saved from starvation by the arrival of Red Cross Parcels. The arrival of the International Red Cross ship *Vega* in January 1944 was the result of an appeal for aid by the Bailiffs of Jersey and Guernsey. There was another visit from the *Vega* in February and the third, in March, brought flour. At last there was bread in the shops.

The name *Vega* remains cemented in memories today

By spring 1944, news from the battle fronts was improving daily and a feeling of euphoria was creeping across the island. The islanders knew that the end was near and the Halkett Place school log book speaks for itself:

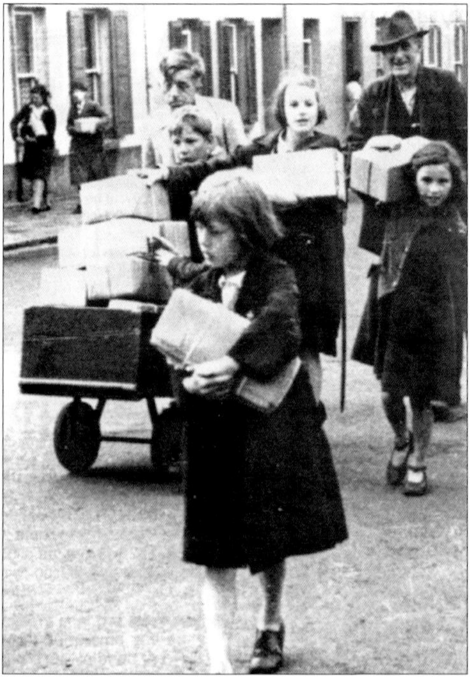

8.6 Vega Parcels

"May 8th: In anticipation of peace being proclaimed this afternoon, the school closed this morning, to resume next Monday.

LIBERATION OF JERSEY

After nearly 5 years of German occupation, Jersey was liberated on Wednesday May 9th and the rest of the week saw scenes of unparalleled joy and enthusiasm. British troops now occupy the Channel Islands. Germany has unconditionally surrendered and the war in Europe is over'.

May 14th: School re-assembled this morning. The Headmaster addressed the boys on the happy situation. Attendance 148 out of 190. German language lessons discontinued forthwith. Senior boys are writing a composition on their experiences in Liberation Week."

After the war, the island fairly quickly returned to a kind of normality. People wanted to shut the door on the Occupation years and get on with their lives. This is reflected in a comment made by John Hibbs, former Headmaster of Victoria College Preparatory School:

'For those of my parents' generation, the fear and deprivation of those five years were something to be swept away and forgotten like an unhappy nightmare'.

Lieutenant-General Sir Edward Grasett, who was the Governor of Jersey from 1945 until 1953, appreciated the contribution made by teachers in the island during the Occupation:

'I have been greatly impressed by what I have heard of the way teachers carried on during the Occupation. They did a great job and did it well. The thanks of the community are certainly due to the teachers of the Island who kept the schools together in such a fine way and so ably taught the children in their charge under difficult conditions'

Evacuees began to return to Jersey. Marguerite Le Chasseur wrote a poignant account of her return home:

'The breeze freshens, the dock lights grow dim. Adieu, England, great country of great people. To have lived with you in the shadow has been an inspiration and a privilege. May we never forget your kindness, courage and fortitude, your happy, friendly children. May that faith which sustained you in your darkest hour help us to meet the future. Dawn. The mist clears. It is a radiant summer morning, clear blue sky and shimmering blue sea. Impatiently, intently, we stare and stare. Yes, there it is at last! Jersey, the most beautiful island in the whole world! Grosnez, St Ouen's Bay, Corbiere, St Brleade's, Portelet, Noirmont ..... we disemabark. Our friends welcome us. How good that is! They still have a strained look about the eyes, their cheeks are hollow, their figures slimmer, but they are free and they are happy'.

It is recorded that as former evacuees returned home by sea and rounded Noirmont Point, they burst into joyful song and sang the anthem, *Beautiful Jersey, a* traditional Jersey anthem still sung on May 9th (Liberation Day)

Beautiful Jersey, gem of the sea,
Ever my heart turns in longing for thee;
Bright are the memories you waken for me,
Beautiful Jersey, gem of the sea.

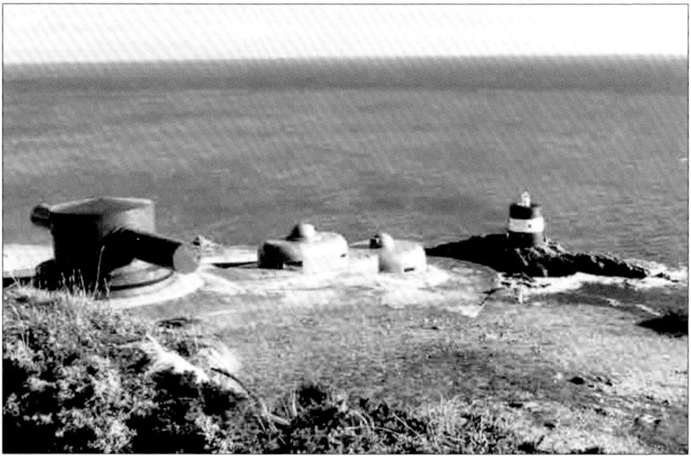

Fig. 8.7 German defences visible on Noirmont Point

Once the Occupation had ended, Cecily Hoyles wasted no time in applying to College for places for herself and Jeanne Dorey. They both arrived in Salisbury in September 1945, together with Fay Arthur and Ruth Le Boutillier. Pat Prosser, who was in their year, remembered the thin, pale islanders who ate everything on their plates and made sure that nothing was wasted. They began to understand that although life had been very hard in England, people in the Channel Islands had suffered far more. Despite this, the spirit of the islanders had prevailed and the Salisbury trained teachers had played their part in steering the children of Jersey through to a brighter future.

A Gruelling Time: Life in Guernsey during the Occupation

'Even the darkest night will end and the sun will rise'

Victor Hugo: *Les Misérables*

Those who did not experience the German occupation of Guernsey can never fully understand the suffering and hardship which the children went through. Some were evacuated at short notice to England with their schools, unable to return to their homes and families for five years. Others remained on the island with their families and endured dreadful hardship which, after D-Day, became near starvation. During 1942–43 over 2,000 Channel Islanders were deported to Germany and housed in internment camps. Five children from the Intermediate School were amongst those deported.

In the log book of the Intermediate School, the much respected Head-teacher Peter Girard wrote:

> 'A notice appeared in the newspapers saying that certain British subjects were to be evacuated to Germany. These included persons who have permanent residence elsewhere than the Channel Islands and also men

> not from the Channel Islands between the ages of 16 and 70. In the latter case families were ordered to be evacuated with the men. This notice concerned many members of the staff and many members of the School Committee were also involved.'

It was a terrifying time. In Peter Girard's booklet *My Occupation Memories (1940–1945)* he explains that his wife was due to give birth to their first child in June 1940. There was no Red Cross (Hospital) ship to provide medical support on the sea crossing and so they were both 'fated to remain on the Island'.

Channel Islanders pride themselves on their qualities of independence and loyalty. Guernsey people are proud to be known as tough, resilient and determined and it is these qualities which enabled the children and adults to survive the gruelling years.

Germany invaded France in May 1940, and at that time Channel Islanders were unsure as to whether their islands would be attacked. Guernsey was only thirty miles from the French coast and residents became increasingly concerned that a German invasion was imminent. In London there was a debate about the fate of the Channel Islands. Although Winston Churchill had no desire to abandon the Channel Islands, he was advised by the Vice Chief of the Naval Staff that there was insufficient arms and equipment to ensure the safe defence of the Channel Islands at that time. The Cabinet Office announced:

> 'The Channel Islands are not of major strategic importance either to ourselves or the enemy…we recommend immediate consideration be given by the Ministry of Home Security… for the evacuation of women and children on a voluntary and free basis'.

In early June any British troops on the island returned to England. Guernsey headteachers were invited to an emergency meeting and the States agreed that it would support the evacuation of Guernsey children if recommended. It was agreed that the evacuation of the children would take place on a voluntary basis. It was an agonising time for all.

Two Guernsey sisters vividly recalled their childhood days on Guernsey from 1940–45. An early memory was the sight and sound of the German soldiers marching in St Peter Port. It was to become a familiar sight.

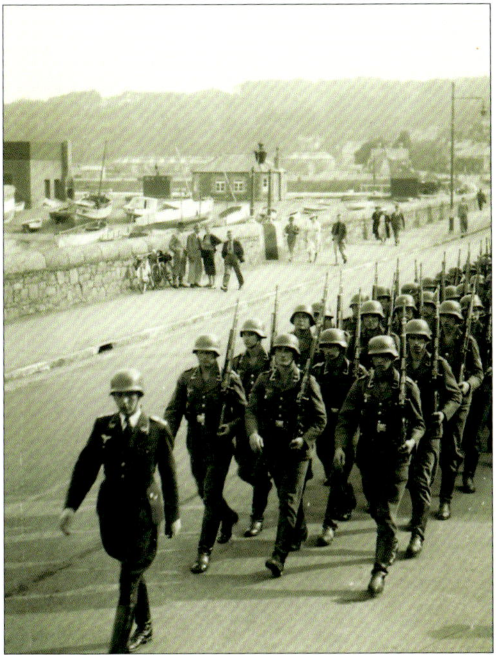

Fig. 8.8 German troops marching along the Esplanade 1940

During the Occupation food became very scarce. People grew what they could – potatoes being a staple food. As folk became hungrier, careful watch had to be kept over food which was often hidden as everyone became more desperate for basic essentials. Children were allowed one third of a pint of milk a day and families were given two ounces of butter a week.

During the early years of the Occupation there was no schooling, but the States was determined that children would receive as good an education as possible. Many school buildings were commandeered by the Germans for use as their billets and quarters.

Peter Girard was appointed Headteacher of Castel School and the Intermediate School. Pupils were admitted to the school as a result of passing a test. Although the main focus was often on mathematics and English, other subjects were taught in the schools, which often depended on the teacher's main interest and knowledge. Some schools which had been single sex, became co-educational. Peter Girard was much in favour of this. It became compulsory for older pupils to learn German, which was not popular with them.

On May 13th 1942 German forces commandeered the Intermediate School. All school equipment such as pens and paper was thrown upon tarpaulin sheets and dumped in a heap. Peter Girard stated:

> 'All the cupboards and desks were emptied and all material not required by the German forces was put outside or piled in doorways…we managed to keep the material and books of the reopened Intermediate School separate from the rest'.

Schools had to be housed in a variety of different buildings such as Sunday Schools, large private houses and even a teashop! Children often had to walk a long way to school. Some fortunate children had bicycles and when the tyres wore out hose pipe or rope was used as a substitute – until that also ran out. Peter Girard was a common sight at auctions where he bought rope and rubber hoses to use on the bicycles.

The Intermediate School was housed in the school in Burnt Lane. After the Allied bombing in the Town after D-Day, it was considered a dangerous position and the school closed from May to August.

Peter Girard ensured that the children had some soup which was made from whatever vegetables could be found – turnips were often a main ingredient. In the log book of the Intermediate School on May 7th 1942 he recorded:

> 'First soup day. Soup provided by nuns on full school days…not on half days. Children brought some vegetables especially potatoes. Other vegetables bought. Children paid 1 penny for soup and vegetables are to be bought from them. Bones obtained through Essential Commodities Committee – also salt'.

The Island Potato Controller took great risk in hiding tons of potatoes for the schoolchildren. Peter Girard stated 'Due to this I was able to feed 280 children during the breadless period'. How thrilled the children would have been when Peter Girard distributed one and three quarter pounds of biscuits received as a gift from the French Société National. A favourite Guernsey dish was the Bean Jar: meat and vegetables would be cooked slowly in an earthenware jar with dumplings. As the Occupation set in this became more and more watery. Potato peelings would be mixed with water and baked in the oven for tea – until the electricity and gas ran out. Children were weighed at school and given extra milk if very underweight.

At Christmas Peter Girard was determined to ensure it was a special occasion: school Christmas dinner consisted of rabbit stew and vegetables followed by Christmas pudding. Music was provided on piano and drums. 'Paper hats presented by Royal Hotel which also gave whistles, teasers and noise makers which added to hilarity'. Father Christmas always arrived at the party, although it was difficult to fill his sack.

After Christmas the weather was dreadful and influenza spread with staff and pupils absent. Teachers were in very short supply as so many had been evacuated. A letter from the secretary of the Guernsey Education Council detailed the number of children who remained and were being educated in Guernsey on 13th March 1942:

> 'On Friday last there were 1,117 children in Guernsey State Schools. The approximate number of children of 10 years of age and over in State-aided schools is 460. Twelve States-aided schools are open and are accommodated in 22 separate buildings. After the general evacuation of school children in 1940, only 12 of the council's permanent teaching staff remained in Guernsey'.

The letter continues to say that the teaching staff was supplemented by 50 other people including several young girls. In addition there were 155 children being educated in private schools.

People who had qualifications other than for teaching were able to do some retraining to help out. Retired teachers were asked to return to the profession, as were female married teachers. They were known as 'dugout teachers'.

Renée Le Messurier 1931–1933

One of these teachers was Renée Le Messurier, born in Guernsey in 1913.

Renée attended College between the years of 1931–33. She was educated at The Intermediate School and worked as a pupil-teacher at St Saviour's School. Her College record states that she spoke 'very good French …and she has a 'very good brain and is bilingual'. Renée was very much in demand as a teacher and had no problem teaching French. She later became Head of Infants at Torteval Primary School in Guernsey. Renée left teaching when she married, but returned to the profession during the Occupation, when teachers on the island were in very short supply.

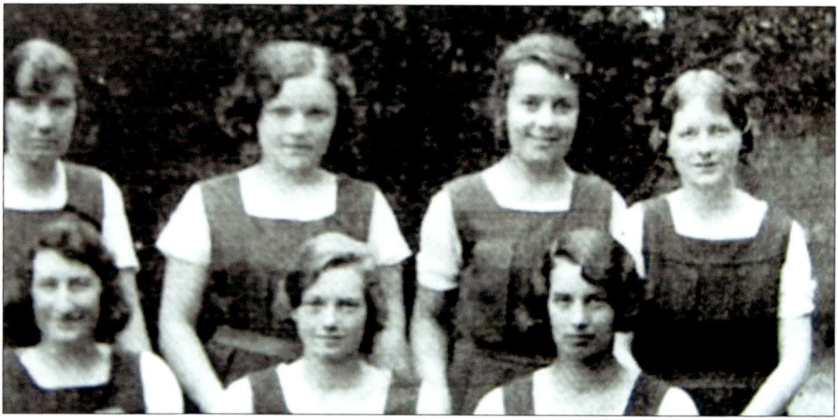

Fig. 8.9 Renée Le Messurier at College; Back Row, 2nd from right

In 1939 Renée married Frederick Jehan and they lived with his parents on their farm. They were undecided about whether to evacuate or not: in the end they decided to stay. This was partly because when their animals were let loose they were unable to fend for themselves. Guernsey cattle were especially valuable. In addition, it was becoming much too dangerous for boats to cross the English Channel.

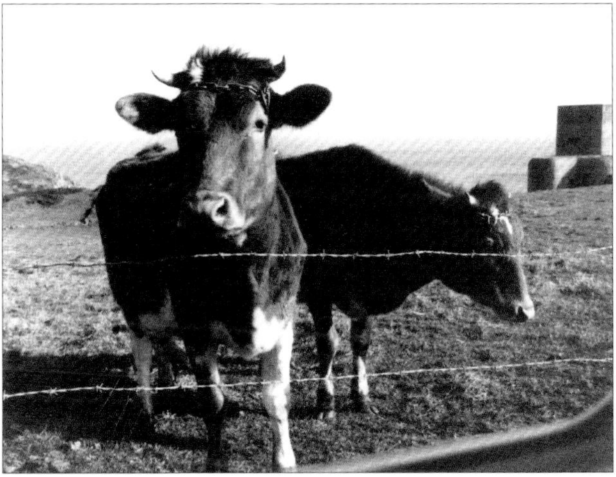

Fig. 8.10

Renée continued to teach at a school which was set up in a large private house located in the Le Vallon area in St Martin's. Fortunately for the pupils, there was a sizeable garden and Renée took the children out there for lessons in suitable weather. At College she had studied Botany and probably encouraged the children in this subject. Renée composed a book of poems in Guernsey French. They were mostly about nature – a subject always dear to her heart. Renée's poems are still recited by adults and children in the Guernsey French section of the island Eisteddfod and printed in the annual magazine of the Guernsey French Group:

'he Soleil'
Hes berbiyaettes ouvrent leux visages
Et mourtent leur belle radiöànce
Daöutes fllieurs etou forche leur images
En couleur déà brilliance.

The daisies open their faces
And reveal their beautiful radiance
Other Flowers also open their images
Of shining colours

Renée showed great courage by writing to the German Commandant when food on the island became even scarcer. She requested that the petrol allowance could be increased so that they and other farmers could grow more produce, which would benefit everyone. The Commandant agreed!

Renée retired from teaching in 1944, when her son was born. She continued the College connection by regularly meeting up with the Salisbury Club.

During the Occupation there were strict laws and people were imprisoned for the slightest thing. Having a gun was strictly prohibited and could result in deportation of the owner.

Wirelesses were forbidden, as were cameras. Radios had to be handed in, but many people made crystal radios and became very clever at sharing the BBC nine o'clock news with their friends and neighbours. There were frequent searches and the radios had to be hidden very quickly. The headmaster of Vauvert School was found to be in possession of a wireless set and was waiting for trial by the German authorities. Peter Girard recorded: 'This was an unfortunate incident from many points of view, especially owing to the very depleted state of the staffs of the Island Schools.'

There was a strict curfew; if any candle light shone through a window a search and warning would follow. People went to bed as soon as darkness fell. Gas and electricity were rationed to a few hours a day. Towards the end of the Occupation there was very little fuel – all the twigs had been collected and many trees felled and burnt.

The lack of food meant many people became malnourished. Rations for the week commencing 27th March 1944 for an average person aged ten or over were:

1 oz coffee substitute
3 oz of butter or cooking fat
4 oz meat
1 oz macaroni
8 oz split peas
Half a pint of milk per day
1lbs 8 oz bread

There were no stocks of tea, coffee, cocoa, sugar or potatoes.

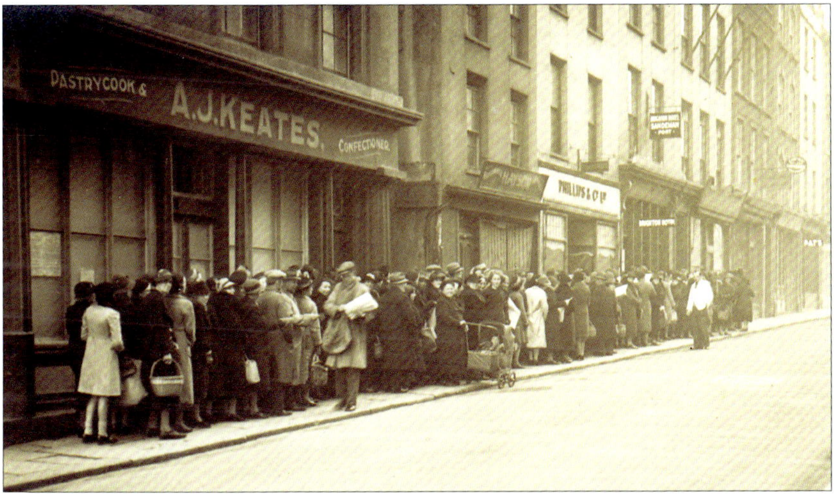

Fig. 8.11 Queuing for rations in Fountain Street, St Peter Port

Islanders were skilful at growing what they could and used seaweed in cooking, produced salt and drank bramble and nettle tea. Medical supplies soon ran out. The skilled pharmacists copied the ingredients printed on the containers of the remaining medicaments in order to make substitute remedies, which helped many children survive. Magnesium was used from sawmills, but eventually there was no pain relief available.

When the Germans arrived they bought many of the items left in the shops. Clothing was scarce and people made garments from curtains or whatever they could find. They often swapped clothes if they had been outgrown.

Fuel to keep warm was often a problem but enough fuel was found for the schools and people became skilled at making briquettes out of tar, coal dust and cement.

The children's lives went on, but they experienced many unforgettable sights and sounds: starving prisoner slaves from the camps shuffling along in formation to do forced labour; a mother rushing out to give one man a hot potato; heavy banging on the door for a night-time search of the house and the dreadful fear of the radio being found.

A wonderful sight was that of the Red Cross ship the *Vega*, which brought food parcels, saving the islanders from starvation. In all it made six trips to the island. When it arrived shortly after Christmas in 1944 it caused great excitement! People quickly headed to the distribution centres. Children rejoiced at tasting coffee, tea, biscuits, powdered egg, butter and jam. Parents would have enjoyed the coffee flavoured condensed milk. Strict guards were put in place around the distribution centres – such was the hunger and desperate need for food.

Children from the Intermediate School wrote moving letters to the President of the International Red Cross:

'Dear Sir,
I must begin by thanking you for all you have done for our islands. One has to be in a position such as we are, to be able to appreciate fully the true food value of the Red Cross Parcels.

The Cod Liver Oil is also very good for us, because many of the children are losing weight; and besides it is a treat to eat it.

For three weeks we have been without bread, and so we welcome the Parcels even more than before…Today as I went to the grocer's shop to fetch my fourth parcel, I met many people, wearing smiles on their faces and wheeling small carts carrying their Parcels home.

The children especially were eager to get home because opening a Parcel is as exciting as opening a Christmas stocking. The first thing they look for is chocolate. For nearly five years, except for an occasional ration brought by the Sates from France, we have had no sweetmeats of any kind.

Since Christmas we have been without gas, and it is very difficult to find the necessary fuel with which to cook. For one week we have been without electricity.

I can assure you that every person in Guernsey feels grateful for all the Red Cross Society and the Order of St John have done, and we will never forget it'.

On May 7th 1945 in the school log book Peter Girard recorded:

'Whole island gloomy this evening as everything points out that the Germans will resist to the last. Mines are being laid and soldiers say that they have been told to resist even if the whole of Europe capitulates'.

However on the next day:

'Wonderful news…German officers had visited the Bailiff and had informed him that the War was over in Guernsey as elsewhere and that flags could be put up all over the island after 3 o'clock in the afternoon. School Closed for Peace Celebrations. Teaching suspended– everyone extremely excited. Before going home a Service of Thanksgiving was held'.

The church bells rang out the miraculous message of liberation in May 1945! On Tuesday May 8th Winston Churchill announced:

'Hostilities will end officially at one minute after midnight tonight…and our dear Channel Islands are also to be freed today'.

Parents who had children in England could look forward to seeing them again and families would be reunited. There was real hope at last!

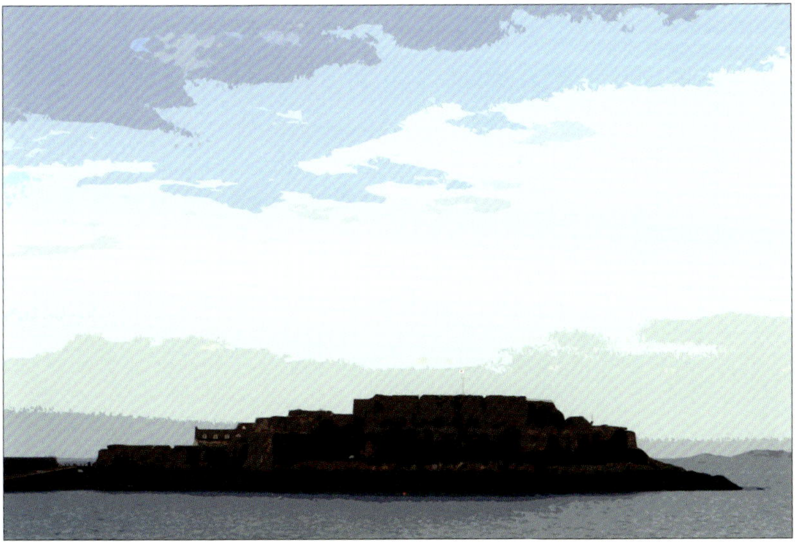

Fig. 8.12 Breakwater at Castle Cornet

1899–1967 Dora Hacquoil ... teacher, friend and political prisoner

Dora Jane Hacquoil was born on April 30th 1899 in St Helier. Her father, Philip, who was born in St Ouen, was described in the 1911 Census as a general labourer and her mother, Marie, was a dressmaker. Dora was an 11 year old schoolgirl and her younger brother, Philip, was also at school. Marie's 82 year old mother shared their home at 18, Vauxhall Street, St Helier.

After attending one of the town schools, Dora moved to the Pupil Teacher Centre in St Helier. In 1916 she passed the Cambridge Senior Examination, with Distinction in French. This was a certificate-based school leaving examination that required candidates to pass in a range of subjects. It was replaced a little later by the Higher School Certificate. Dora probably started her teacher training in Salisbury in 1917 or 1918, but the records for these years are not available. There is also no indication as to where she taught on leaving College, but she is likely to have returned home. It is the log book for Les Landes School in St Ouen that helps to trace her life and career. The log book begins on September 18th 1933 and Dora is named as the Principal Teacher. It is interesting to note that she became Headteacher exactly ten years after Rachel du Heaume retired from the same post (see Chapter 4).

'Hacquoil' is very much a St Ouen's name and the log book includes many pupils and members of staff with that surname. In 1951, for example, Dora J Hacquoil was still the Principal Teacher but Doris M Hacquoil was an uncertificated member of staff and a pupil called Dora F Hacquoil won 1st prize in the Cocoa Competition!

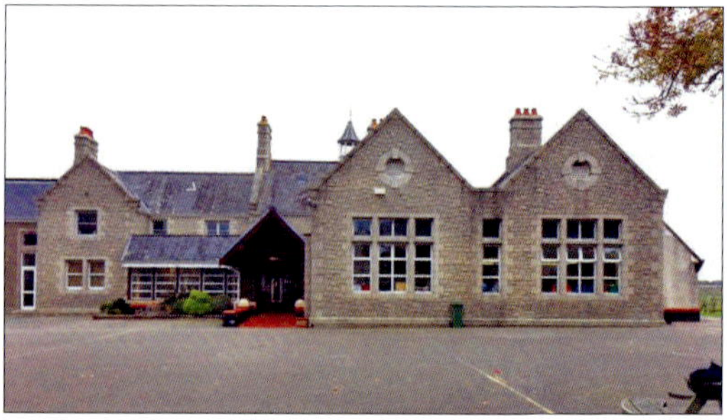

Fig. 8.13 Les Landes School, St Ouen

Dora lived at Les Landes School House, which was where Rachel du Heaume had lived with her family. Rachel had lived there during the First World War and it was there that she had heard about the death of her son, Reginald, in 1916.

Dora was now living through the years of the Occupation in the same house and teaching at the same school.

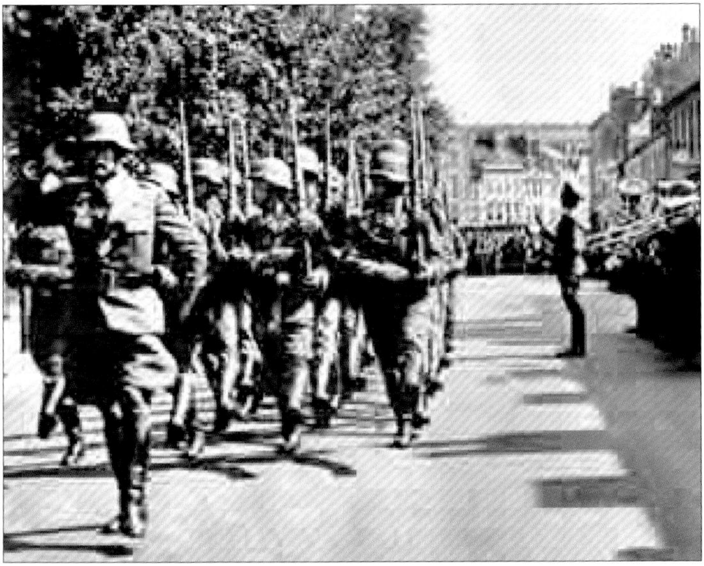

Fig. 8.14 German troops arrive

The main story of Dora's life does not, however, feature school. The first thing to explain is the presence of eastern European slave workers in Jersey during the Occupation. These men had been forcibly transported to Jersey by Nazi Germany's Todt Organisation in order to build fortifications, including an underground hospital. They were cruelly treated, worked long hours and were inadequately fed and clothed. Local people saw them walking past, filthy and close to collapse. They felt compassion for them and sometimes attempted to share their own rations, at great risk to themselves.

Occasionally, slave workers escaped and this is where Dora's life took an unexpected direction.

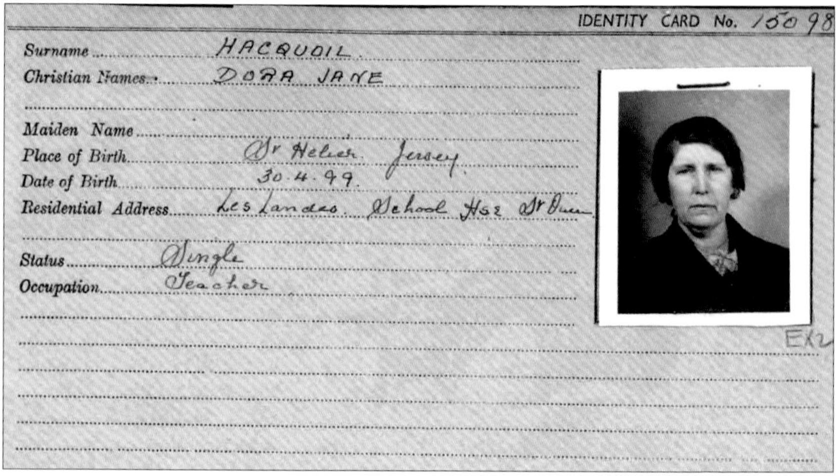

IDENTITY CARD No. 15098

Surname HACQUOIL

Christian Names DORA JANE

Maiden Name

Place of Birth St Helier Jersey

Date of Birth 30.4.99

Residential Address Les Landes School Hse St Ouen

Status Single

Occupation Teacher

EX2

Fig. 8.15 Registration card of Dora Hacquoil

Dora had a friend called Louisa Gould, a hardworking widow who ran a small shop in Millais, St Ouen. Louisa's two sons were both away at war. The following true story was written by Dora and tells how Louisa felt that she had to do something to 'help another mother's son'. It was published in the 1946 edition of the Salisbury Training College Magazine.

1942–1944 Experiences of Political Prisoner No 12184

'In June 1942 our wireless sets were confiscated. This at the time when it seemed that the end of the war would never come, coupled with the removal of this last link with the mainland, had a most depressing effect. Those braver ones, who were in possession of small sets, kept and hid them, sometimes in most unexpected places, and listened in.

A friend of mine kept her set. At this time I was sleeping every night at her place as the school and school house were situated in a rather lonely spot and the field directly opposite had been turned into a camp for Russian prisoners of war. These were very badly treated and ill fed and often at night they managed to go foraging for food and clothes, breaking into houses, and sometimes acting in a very violent manner and generally frightening one and all. It was not wise to live alone.

Later on, one young Russian prisoner managed to escape from his camp. Half-starved and ill clad, he appeared at my friend's door. Full of pity for him, she took him in, Naturally we all befriended him, finding clothes for him and entertaining him at our homes, although we knew we were running great risks in doing so. He quickly learned English sufficiently well to follow the broadcasts. Every night at nine o'clock we would wend our way upstairs, move the duchess table, lift the carpet and then the lino-surround to reveal the floor boards. One loose floor board was then lifted and there, reposing in the cavity underneath the floor, lay the small set. Kneeling down (in the dark in winter) we all listened-in breathlessly, memorising the news to impart it to trusted friends the next day. How eagerly we heard Churchill's speeches and the King's at Christmas. In this way we kept up our spirits.

For nearly two years we pursued the even tenor of our days, till, in May 1944 someone betrayed us to the German authorities'.

Louisa was arrested, but she had sufficient warning to allow Feodor to get away to St Helier, where he was sheltered by other brave people until the end of the Occupation. After much searching, a Russian-English dictionary and Louisa's wireless were found in her house. After three weeks of suspense, Dora and another friend were ordered to the Gestapo Headquarters for questioning.

'In fear and trepidation lest I should incriminate others, I answered the questions with: I'm afraid I cannot tell you, or I do not know, as often as possible. Luckily, we all knew exactly what to confess to having done, as my friend (Louisa) had secretly managed to convey the gist of her first statement to us through someone in the gaol. Needless to say, the Gestapo agent refused to believe me.

My journey through the town to the local prison was one I shall long remember. See me seated in a front seat of a German car, beside the chauffeur, with a fully armed escort in the rear, his rifle with fixed bayonet ready if I should try any funny business. For ten days I was shut up alone in a cell. How hard the prison beds were and how poor and uninteresting the fare – weak, substitute coffee, a hunk of bread, soup and potatoes boiled in their jackets.

After ten days we were court-martialled. This awful experience we had dreaded for days. However we were sentenced to varying terms of imprisonment. My sentence was two months imprisonment. The others had longer terms and three were sent to France, and eventually to concentration camps in Germany. One reached Belsen and was rescued in the nick of time, but his sister, my friend Louisa, died in the camp at Ravensbruck.

So many people were being arrested at this time, more than the gaol could hold, so that there was a long waiting list – one almost had to queue up. Consequently two of us were allowed to go home after the trial until the 6th of July.

This time prison life was a little easier. Three of us shared a large stone-flagged cell with large barred windows, and as political prisoners we were allowed to bring in our own comfortable beds and a sideboard. In this we kept our food and on top the flowers which were sent to us. The German authorities allowed us a parcel a fortnight and friends, often at great sacrifice to themselves, sent us food. Twice a day we exercised in a small courtyard surrounded by high walls topped by broken glass. The time in between was spent in eating, sleeping and playing bridge or other card games with the prisoners in the next cells. Every day we received the 'news' which was passed on to us by men politicals or smuggled in. Several of the men had managed to fix up a lovely crystal set in their cell and so had the latest news. This was right under the nose of the Germans who had actually taken over a third of the gaol.

On August 29th, three days before school began again, I was released from my 'holiday resort'. With mixed feelings of relief at my freedom, regret that others were not yet free and grief that those overseas had no friendly faces to greet them, I met those who had come to greet me and who were laden with flowers. Never did grass seem greener or air fresher and sweeter than when I walked up the country lane to my home. Here I was welcomed by my very loyal friends, teachers and my faithful dog. How lovely it was to be free'!

Dora J Hacquoil
Les Landes School
St Ouen
Jersey

Dora was sentenced to two months imprisonment for 'abetting breach of the working peace and unauthorised removal'. She stated later that she owed her relatively lenient sentence to Louisa Gould's intervention: 'I was charged with listening in, but Lou vowed and declared that I always arrived too late. Louisa's word was accepted. But for her statement, I should have suffered the same fate'.

After intense questioning, Louisa, her friend Berthe and her brother Harold le Druillenec were deported to Germany. Louisa was subsequently taken to Ravensbruck, where she died in a gas chamber in 1945. Feodor (Bill) was sheltered by Bob Le Sueur for a long weekend, before being handed on to someone else. He returned to Russia after the war.

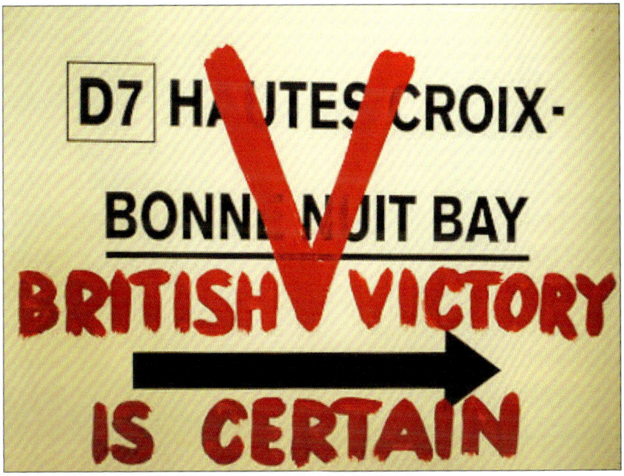

Fig. 8.16 A popular form of dissent

The story of Dora, interwoven with that of Louisa and others, reflects the courage and compassion that was shown by so many islanders during the Occupation. Feelings of despair, horror, shock, grief and anger were kept below the parapet. Resilience, stoicism and unsung determination to 'do their bit' were all part of the spirit of the times. Life had to go on.

As Dora mentioned in her article, term was about to begin when she was released from the gaol. It was time to return to school. She spent a further sixteen years as Headteacher at Les Landes. On July 22nd 1960 the log book records: 'School closes today till Sept 12th for the summer holidays. Mrs Cory leaves for England and was given a handbag. So ends my 30 years of service here, where I have been quite happy'. (Eloquence was not for the school log book!)

Dora Jane Hacquoil of Alanaver, Clairvale Road, St Helier died on the 19th of January 1967. She is buried at Almorah Cemetery.

Footnote: Berthe escaped from prison in France, but Louisa died in the gas chamber at Ravensbrück in February 1945. Louisa's brother, Harold le Druillenec, became the only known British man to survive the horrors of Bergen-Belsen, and he later testified at the Nuremberg Trials. Harold returned to teaching in Jersey and in 1949 he was appointed Headmaster of St John's School, retiring in 1971. The film, *Another Mother's Son*, was released in cinemas in March 2017.

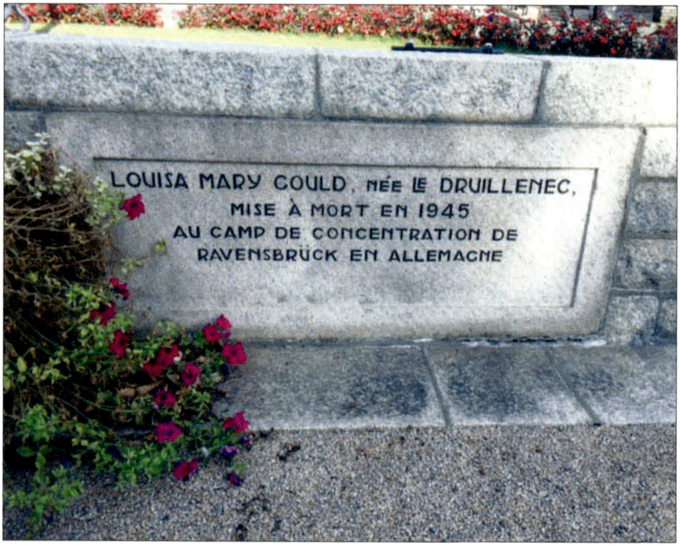

Fig. 8.17 Memorial to Louisa Gould in St Ouen's village

Far and Away – Guernsey Evacuation 1940

What happened to the children, families and whole schools that were evacuated from Guernsey?

Explosions and gunfire could be heard from the French coast! Time was short and evacuation plans were quickly made, as it was understood that several evacuation ships would arrive on June 19th. Teachers were informed and leaflets distributed to parents telling them where to take their children, and what they would be allowed to take with them to England. A free edition of *The Guernsey Star* informed parents that they should register their children at the schools that evening.

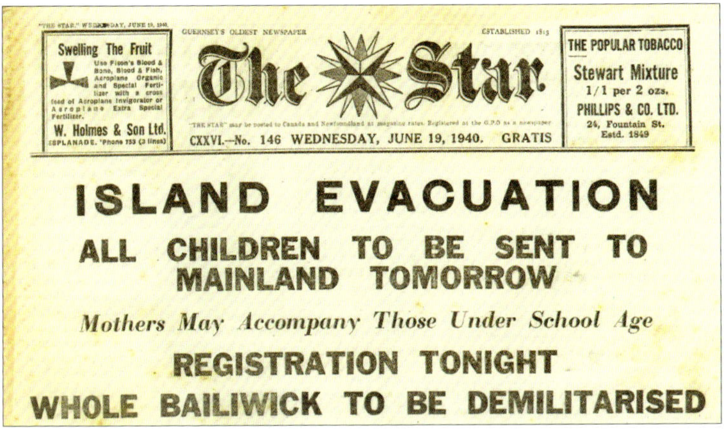

Swelling The Fruit

Use Fison's Blood & Bone, Blood & Fish, Aeroplane Organic and Special Fertilizer with a cross feed of Aeroplane Invigorator or Aeroplane Extra Special Fertilizer.

W. Holmes & Son Ltd.
ESPLANADE. 'Phone 753 (3 lines)

GUERNSEY'S OLDEST NEWSPAPER

The Star

"THE STAR" may be posted to Canada and Newfoundland at magazine rates. Registered at the G.P.O. as a newspaper

CXXVI.—No. 146 WEDNESDAY, JUNE 19, 1940. GRATIS

THE POPULAR TOBACCO
Stewart Mixture
1/1 per 2 ozs.
PHILLIPS & CO. LTD.
24, Fountain St.
Estd. 1849

ISLAND EVACUATION

ALL CHILDREN TO BE SENT TO MAINLAND TOMORROW

Mothers May Accompany Those Under School Age

REGISTRATION TONIGHT

WHOLE BAILIWICK TO BE DEMILITARISED

Fig. 8.18 *The Star* June 19th 1940

Parents had a heart-wrenching decision to make: should their children stay or go? The world was turning upside-down! There was a muddle and panic as people struggled to make sense of the situation.

> 'The question everybody was asking was whether to stop on Guernsey or stop in England. That is, if they could. One minute it was said everybody would have to go; and the next minute that nobody would be able to. Then nobody could make their minds up if they wanted to or not'.
>
> G. B. Edwards: *The Book of Ebenezer Le Page*

Around 5,000 children left the island with their teachers and 500 adult helpers. Overall, approximately 17,000 people left their beloved island at this time. Mothers of infants under five were allowed to accompany their children, but older children travelled with their school groups. The helpers sometimes included mothers. A former College student recalled the anguish of being evacuated as a child with her mother. Her father remained behind, but fortunately he later escaped and joined the family in England.

The harbour was packed and so parents were advised to take their children to the schools and to say goodbye there. Some ships were delayed and children were returned home to have to say farewell once again. For some parents this was too much and they changed their minds, deciding to keep their children with them during the Occupation. Once the final decision had been made, parents then felt anguish about whether or not they had made the right choice. By Friday 21 June the evacuation of children was almost complete. Some children thought it was going to be a big adventure, never having left the island before.

There was often a long wait at the harbour as the ships were sometimes late in arriving. One of the evacuation ships was SS *Viking*. Children, from the age of four to seventeen, boarded the ship in an orderly fashion, carrying their tiny suitcases and their gas masks. The ship was crowded with over 2,000 children, teachers and helpers on board. Many different types of vessels were used for the evacuation. Some had recently been in use to evacuate troops from Dunkirk.

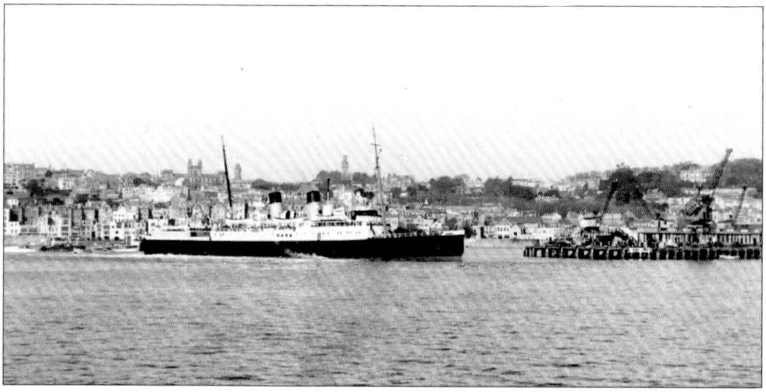

Fig. 8.19 The last passenger boat with Guernsey evacuees leaving St Peter Port Harbour bound for the U.K. June 1940

Many parents planned to follow their children but were unable to do so as on the 28th June Guernsey's harbour was bombed. It would be five long, hard years until they would be re-united.

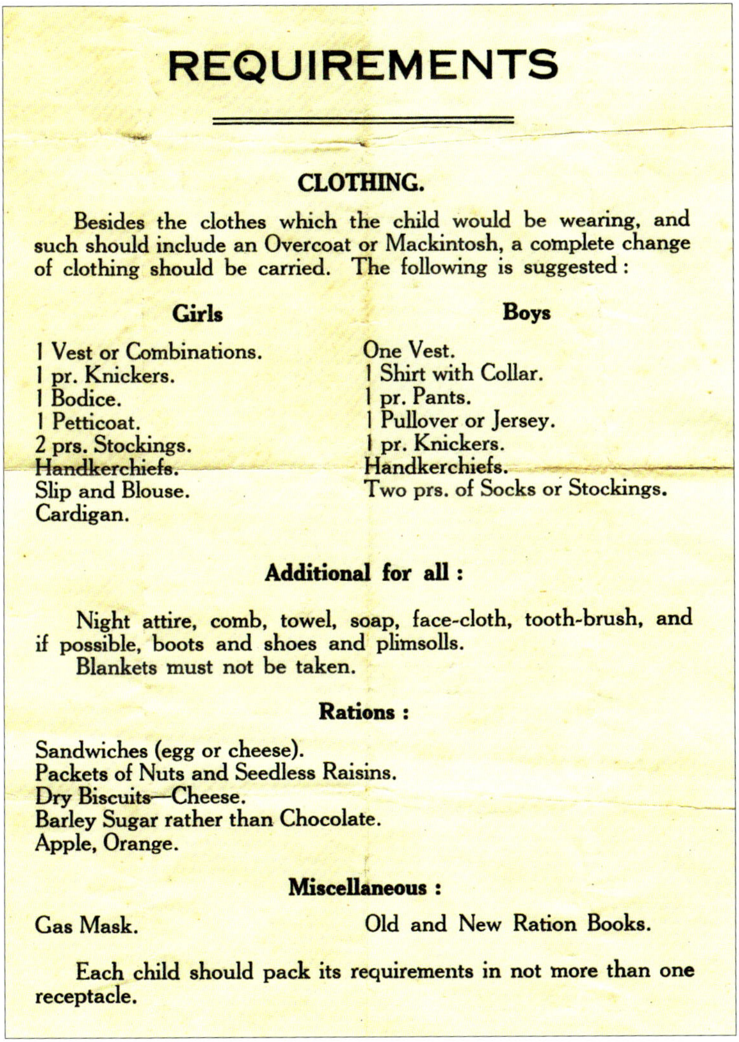

REQUIREMENTS

CLOTHING.

Besides the clothes which the child would be wearing, and such should include an Overcoat or Mackintosh, a complete change of clothing should be carried. The following is suggested :

Girls

1 Vest or Combinations.
1 pr. Knickers.
1 Bodice.
1 Petticoat.
2 prs. Stockings.
Handkerchiefs.
Slip and Blouse.
Cardigan.

Boys

One Vest.
1 Shirt with Collar.
1 pr. Pants.
1 Pullover or Jersey.
1 pr. Knickers.
Handkerchiefs.
Two prs. of Socks or Stockings.

Additional for all :

Night attire, comb, towel, soap, face-cloth, tooth-brush, and if possible, boots and shoes and plimsolls.

Blankets must not be taken.

Rations :

Sandwiches (egg or cheese).
Packets of Nuts and Seedless Raisins.
Dry Biscuits—Cheese.
Barley Sugar rather than Chocolate.
Apple, Orange.

Miscellaneous :

Gas Mask. Old and New Ration Books.

Each child should pack its requirements in not more than one receptacle.

Fig. 8.20 Guernsey evacuation list of items permitted to be worn and taken by children to be evacuated 1940

Jonny Guille was a student in Salisbury during the years 1944–46. She was born in Guernsey and wrote about her experience of evacuation in the College Newsletter of 2010. Her father was the Rector of the parish of St Peter in the Wood. Her Headteacher told the pupils to tell their parents to buy the *Evening Press* which told of the next day's evacuation.

> 'When I arrived home the Rectory was full of people asking my parents what they should do. My mother decided to come with us (my brother, my younger sister and myself) and on the next day we each went to school with one small suitcase'.
>
> As we waited and waited, my mother decided that she could not leave her husband alone (he could not leave his parish) and so she returned home.
>
> Eventually we found an empty troop ship that had unloaded troops from Dunkirk. We all had to go down in the hold, which was very dirty. After zigzagging across the Channel to avoid U boats, we arrived at Weymouth where we were given hot tea and jam sandwiches'.

Girls from the Intermediate School were settled in Rochdale. Perhaps they might have heard of the town because of Gracie Fields, the famous singer who was born there. It was so different from the Guernsey they had left behind.

> 'We were put on a train, together with most of our teachers and a few helpers. When we arrived in Rochdale in Lancashire it was dark and raining and it sounded to us as though the people spoke another language. Soon, however, we found out how kind everyone was– we were all in big houses at first, but by the winter we were billeted with local families. For the rest of the war we only had the occasional Red Cross letter of 25 words from our families'.
>
> Jonny Guille

The children were exhausted from their journey. They were first taken to reception centres, their 'home' for up to four weeks. The local people were welcoming and friendly and generously provided the evacuees with essential items, in addition to treats for the children. Hundreds of families provided homes for the children and many were heartbroken when they eventually returned home.

'Unflagging Zeal' – The Evacuation of Guernsey Schools and Teachers
Dorothy Falla, 1910–1912, and Marjorie Falla, 1912–1914

Dorothy Falla, was born in 1892 in St Peter Port. In the Census of 1901 she was living with her parents, her younger sister Marjorie, three nephews, grandmother and aunt at Higher Hubits in St Peter Port. Her father was working as a drapers' assistant. By 1911 Marjorie, aged seventeen, was working as a pupil-teacher and living at home in Les Hubits with her parents.

Both sisters were educated at The States Intermediate School for Girls, Guernsey and attended the Pupil Teacher Centre at Vauvert. They were hard-working, successful students, winning prizes and certificates.

At College, both students were residents at Barnard's Cross. Marjorie gained a B+ for her work on teaching practice: 'She works continuously with energy and brightness and readily gains the co-operation of the class'. After training they returned to Guernsey. The sisters were dedicated teachers who lived full lives devoted to others.

During the Occupation the sisters were evacuated with their schools. The 1942 College Magazine mentions that the Salisbury Club of former students had made a collection for Dorothy Falla, evacuated to Glasgow with St Sampson's School, and for Edith Albiges who had been evacuated to Glasgow with Vauvert School. Letters of great appreciation were received from both. They hoped to use the donations to provide 'some little outings and reunions' for the girls and take them to the sea for which they are very homesick'.

The teachers found comfort and friendship at meetings of the Scottish Channel Islanders Society, of which Edith Albiges was the secretary. They had enormous responsibility for their young charges. In addition to teaching them they sorted out any problems regarding accommodation, health and general welfare. In the absence of any contact with parents, they made important decisions on behalf of the children.

Some children were homesick, lonely and unhappy but others delighted in the lively exciting life of Glasgow and soon settled in with loving families. When they returned home many talked 'Scotch'. Some found it difficult to settle back into Guernsey life. Many evacuees maintained the many close friendships which they had made in Scotland.

Marjorie Falla did not go to Glasgow, but went with 44 infants from Hautes Capelles School, St Sampson's, to Spurstow Council School, near Tarporley in Cheshire. At that time Tarporley was situated on the main Crewe to Chester line.

One can imagine the kindness, love and care which Marjorie and Dorothy showed to those in their care.

The sisters loved their years at College and after the war made many visits back to Salisbury. They became principal officers of the Guernsey Club and were fully involved in many aspects of island life. In retirement they spent much time in voluntary, educational, social and welfare work. 'They were of a fine character, a noble example and an inspiration to many'. Salisbury College Magazine 1965

They died in Guernsey in 1965, within two months of each other. In the words of their obituary in the College Chronicle of 1965:

> 'Few lives can have been more marked by unassuming modesty, quiet fervent love and deep dedication than those of Dorothy and Marjorie Falla. Their unflagging zeal and enthusiasm for their profession, their high ideals of education and their unfailing concern for the well-being of their pupils were appreciated by all who knew them.
>
> For many years they had been most popular and successful Head Teachers, and many parents will remember, with gratitude, the devoted care they gave to the island children who were evacuated to Britain, in their charge, when Guernsey was occupied by the Germans for those five long years'.

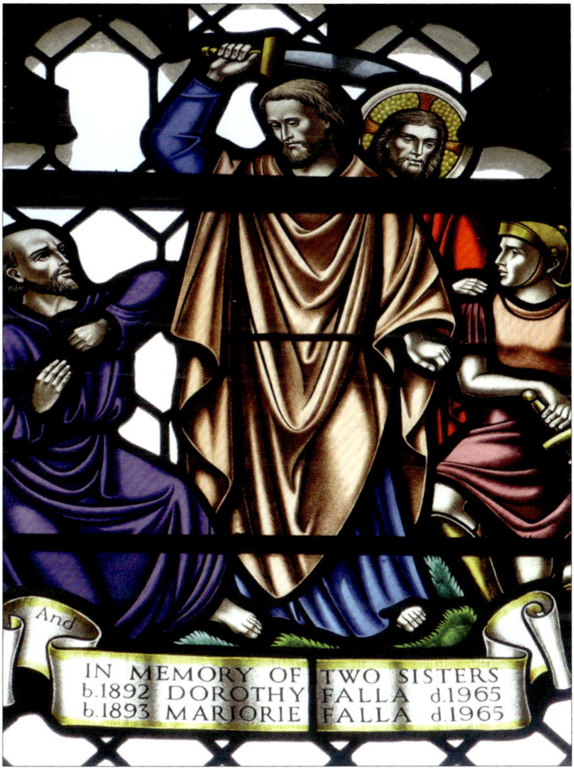

Fig. 8.21 A beautiful stained glass window in the Town Church in St Peter Port provides a fitting memorial to two exceptional sisters.

Minnie Nevitt 1925–1927

Minnie Nevitt was born in Deolali, Maharashra, India around 1907. Deolali was a transit camp for British troops, and at the time of Minnie's birth it was the location of the Army Staff College. The summer heat was intense with much dust, and it must have been a difficult time for the family. By the time Minnie was four, the family was living in the barracks in Portsmouth, where her father, Thomas Nevitt, was a sergeant major. By 1907 Thomas had been posted to the Royal Artillery Garrison on Alderney and Minnie's brother Jack was born there. It is likely that the family finally settled in the Channel Islands.

During her training in Salisbury Minnie was resident at Barnard's Cross.

When she returned to Guernsey, she taught at Vauvert Boys School and then at the Forest Mixed School in 1928. It was with this school that on June 21st 1940 Minnie was evacuated with 132 children. They travelled with many other evacuees on SS *Viking*. The Headmaster, Percy Martel, kept a fascinating diary during their time there. There were four teachers and fourteen other helpers.

After arriving at Weymouth they were sent by train to Stockport, where they arrived at 5 am, 18 hours after leaving Guernsey. The Masonic Guildhall had been prepared for them but there was no privacy and only 4 ft. between each bed. The Stockport community welcomed the evacuees and made generous donations of clothes and other items. The children must have been very distressed, but the teachers including Minnie, focused on comforting them.

A priority was to try and keep the children together. It was a stroke of luck that the local education inspector was a man from Guernsey who had been living in the area for some time. Eventually the Forest School group left Stockport by train and after a short journey arrived at Cheadle Hulme. The school was re-established there in the local parish hall.

The staff did excellent work, visiting each foster home to ensure its suitability and also to form positive relationships. In 1941 a school canteen opened, which ensured the pupils had a hot meal every day. The pupils became a firm part of the local community, putting on plays and concerts as a way of saying thank you.

Links were formed with other evacuated Guernsey schools in the area. When possible, the children enjoyed picnics and staff benefitted from meeting others 'in the same boat'. Red Cross messages were sent to the families in Guernsey who were dearly missing their children.

Percy Martel and his staff felt great responsibility for their charges:

> 'I have acted for the best, no one has been able to guide me…I have done as I would have done for my own'.

News of the German surrender was received on May 8th 1945. We can imagine the teachers and children listening with such joy to Churchill's famous words regarding liberation of the islands. On May 10th the delighted and joyful evacuees took part in a special BBC broadcast to the Channel Islands. Percy Martel read the opening line:

> 'Sincerest Greetings from all Islanders to our Mother Country... We acknowledge your courage and fortitude during the long years of captivity with great pride and thankfulness. We now rejoice at your liberation and the prospect of re-union'.

Minnie would have helped Percy Martel and the other staff to prepare the children for their return home. It was a difficult task! Some of the older children were now approaching adulthood, and younger children who had left as infants were approaching secondary education. Important formative years had been spent away from their parents. Many children had formed happy and strong relationships with their new families and they found it harder to settle in back home. Strong links were made with the communities which had welcomed the evacuees.

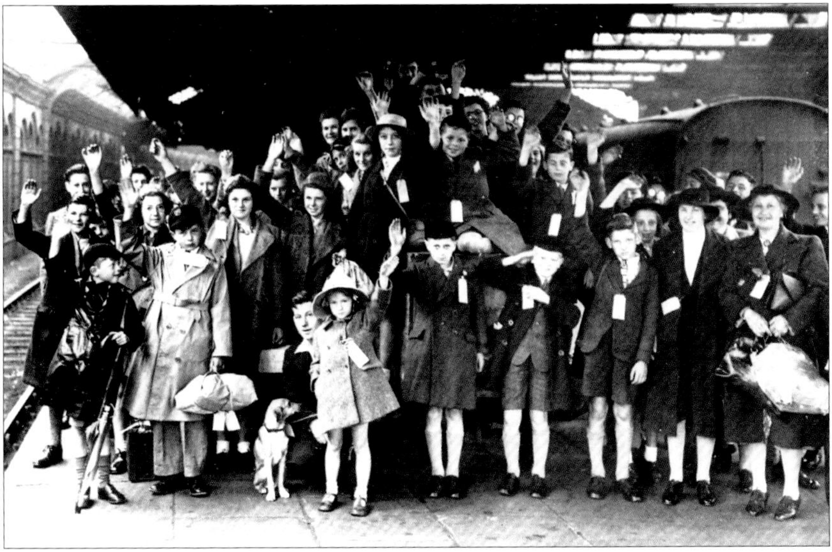

Fig. 8.22 Liberation! Evacuees on their way home at Crewe Station

Although they returned to loving homes, their island home had changed in so many ways. The system of government, society and the general the way of life was much altered. The experiences of the people who had remained on Guernsey were bound to influence their outlook and way of life. Children and adults, who remained on the island, and those who had left, showed typical Guernsey grit, and worked to re-build their lives, which enabled Guernsey to gradually recover and flourish once more.

Once back in Guernsey, Minnie found that Forest School was one of the least damaged buildings on the island, as it had been used as a hospital. The school re-opened in September 1945. The pupils spent the first day of term clearing up. Desks were the only furniture and equipment left. In April of the next year, Percy Martel sent 1,000 bunches of Guernsey primroses to Cheadle Hulme to say thank you. It was a typically thoughtful gesture.

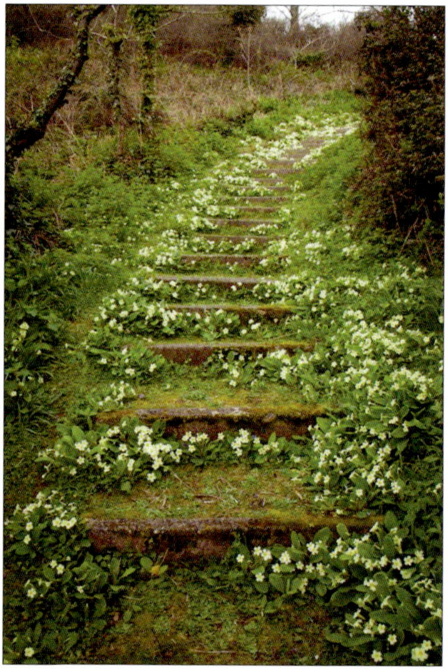

Fig. 8.23 Guernsey primroses

It is likely that Minnie returned to the family home in Guernsey. Her parents died on the island in the 1930s. As for Minnie, eventually she moved to Poole in Dorset, where she died in 1972, aged 65.

1938: Marie Le Lievre and Friends College, Work – and Home at Last!

Several Channel Island students who came to College began their training prior to the start of World War Two. They then found themselves marooned in England until after the war had ended. Marie Le Lievre, born in Guernsey in August 1920, was one such student.

Marie arrived at College in 1938, along with her friends, May and Marion Hamel, who were twins known as Blackie and Whitie. They settled well into College life and their records show that they worked hard. Marie was a keen member of the Senior Girl Guide (Ranger) group at College and was also involved with the Red Cross. During the war the College Rangers made a significant contribution to the war effort, by helping on the domestic side of Salisbury Infirmary. Students worked on a rota each weekend.

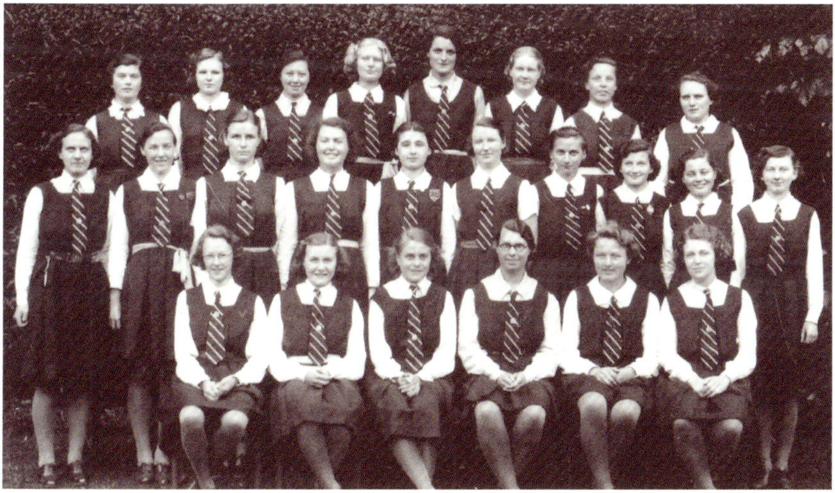

Fig. 8.24 College Student Ranger Group.
Marie Le Lievre front right, Marion Hamel third from the left, back row.

In 1939 Marie and Marion returned to Guernsey during the College summer holiday. They had a hazardous journey back to College for their final year, just after war was declared. Their boat departed from Jersey and called at Guernsey on its way to England. There were six students on board bound for Salisbury. Later, Marion recounted the adventure:

> 'We set sail at about ten fifteen in the morning. It was a lovely sunny day so we stayed on deck most of the time. The journey took double the time it normally did... you had to go through a passage that the Navy had cleared the mines from. By the time we arrived in Southampton it was pitch dark, because there was a black-out. There wasn't a taxi, or a bus... the trains had stopped, we couldn't find anywhere to put up – people had closed up their hotels and vanished.'

The students were stuck, and were just about to go to the police station and volunteer to sleep in a cell, when the two Jersey girls remembered that Miss Montgomery – ex College student and lecturer, and retired Jersey Headmistress, lived in Southampton. They remembered the street where she lived and eventually found a helpful taxi driver who took them there. They divided into pairs and knocked on the doors until they found the right house. What a relief! Miss Montgomery was so pleased to see them. They were fortunate as she was about to depart for Devon the next day, as Southampton was a prime enemy target. In the morning the students telephoned College to say they were safe and on their way.

> 'They were pleased to see us, they thought we had been torpedoed, they were so glad that they didn't make any fuss about the fact that we were nearly twenty four hours late'.

Memoirs of College from students, who were contemporaries of Marie, provide a clear picture of College life at this time:

> 'Despite restrictions and hard work, College was fun, and I don't believe that restrictions or hard work caused us any real suffering. The lecturers were great characters. They were all so enthusiastic and eager for their students to succeed. I feel the influence of the college, its ancient buildings, lovely garden and above all, the dedication of the Staff, has stayed with me'.
>
> Lucy Sanderson Taylor: *College in the Close*

Days were spent in study, and attending College Chapel, known as 'voluntary obligation'. College meals were 'very monotonous and frugal'. Barnard's Cross had closed at this time and Channel Island students were mainly accommodated in King's House, which was often very cold. They slept in small cubicles with curtains to separate them. A pattern of life was established:

> 'Rise at 6.30am and get a bath – anywhere (nobody else was having one) – find a cup of tea, do an organ practice or help in Chapel, breakfast at 8am, short service in Chapel (optional) lectures at 9.30, milk and biscuits in the Milky Way corridor, more lectures, dinner 1pm, games fields or visit schools, tea 4.40, then Rangers, Choir, Drama Group, and other activities before supper, followed by Chapel at 8.30. We were in bed and lights out by 10pm'.
>
> Lucy Sanderson Taylor: *College in the Close*

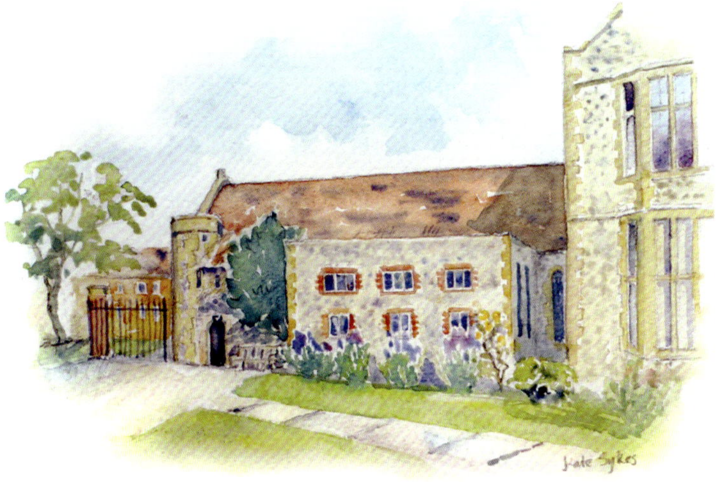

Fig. 8.25 The College Chapel

Although the College was keen on PE, swimming and athletics were limited. Students were not allowed in the river which ran through the College grounds, but they did enjoy long walks in their free time.

Marguerite Le Chasseur from Jersey attended College at this time. Perhaps she was one of the Jersey students on the ferry back to England in summer 1939. She would certainly have known Marie and her friends. Marguerite returned to Jersey and became Headteacher of St Peter's School. She must have loved Wiltshire, as she returned as Headteacher of Mere Infant School in 1963 and Wyndham Park Infant School, Salisbury in 1966.

Eileen Dorothy Connors was a Guernsey student at College in 1941. She had been a brilliant student at the Intermediate School Guernsey and originally came to England to study for a History Honours BA degree at King's College, University of London. However, in June 1941 she wrote a letter to the College Principal:

> 'In June of the following year, however, I was forced to abandon my degree course, as my father who had been paying my fees, was taken Prisoner of War, and at the same time all contact with the rest of my family (resident in Guernsey) was severed owing to the German Occupation of the Channel Islands. I have since been making every endeavour to raise sufficient money to enable me to return to University College, but as this has not proved possible, I am very much hoping that I shall be admitted to a Training College, where the fees are not so high'.

The hardship and reality of these dreadful times is brought home by her words. Did her father return from imprisonment? Eileen was fortunate indeed to have arrived in England in 1939.

Salisbury has a very strong military connection. During this time the city was often full of soldiers based on Salisbury Plain Training Area. The students would have been well aware of the horrors of the war. Although Salisbury was not a main target during the war, from some areas the glow of flames from Southampton could be seen. The Cathedral Spire was used as a guiding landmark by the German Air Force (Luftwaffe) when heading for Bristol and the Midlands.

College staff volunteered as Air Raid Wardens and students took turn at fire-watching on the Cathedral roof. One room in College was permanently blacked out and this was where everyone assembled when the air raid warning started, having collected a tin hat en route. There were no street lights in Salisbury and blackout curtains were everywhere, but living in The Close provided the students with a feeling of relative safety.

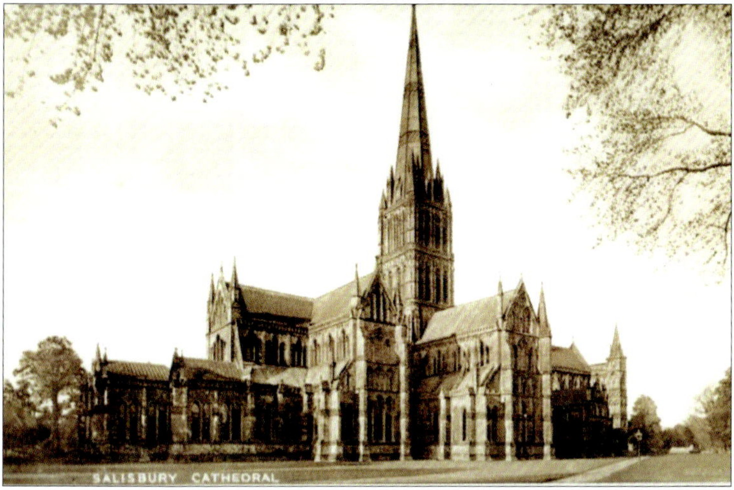

Fig. 8.26

In 1940 Marie Le Lievre was appointed to a secondary school in Eastleigh, which had opened in 1939. The College had strong links with Eastleigh for many years, often placing students there for School Practice, as there was a good rail link with Salisbury.

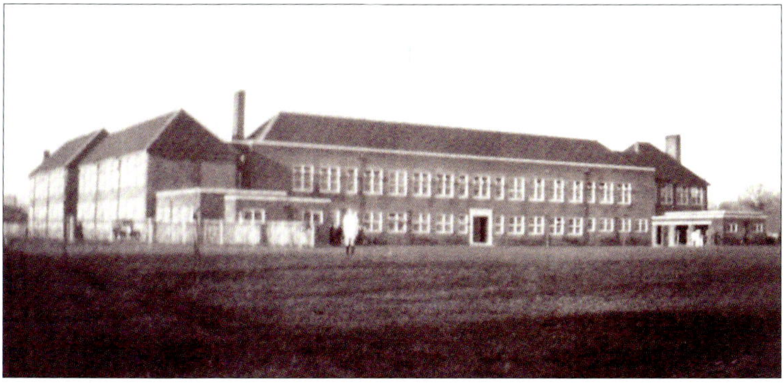

Fig. 8.27 Marie's first school was at North End Senior Council School, Eastleigh 1940

We can imagine Marie settling into her 'digs' which she shared with Marjorie Harkins, another former College student. What a contrast North End School must have been with those at home in Guernsey. Eastleigh was so close to Southampton with its regular air raids and it must have been extremely frightening at times.

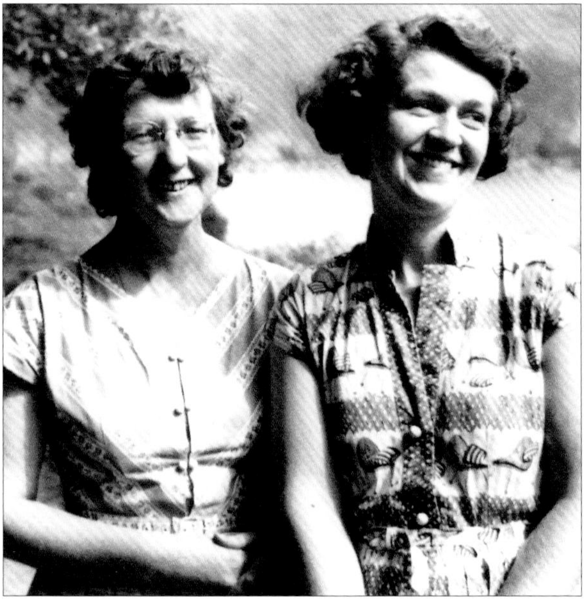

Fig. 8.28 Marie (on the right) and Marjorie enjoying some free time

In 1945, when the war was over, Marie and her friends could finally return home – how overjoyed they must have been!

Marie taught at The Vale School for two years before marrying Herbert Machon, a Guernseyman and an RAF pilot, in 1947. She remained as a teacher at the school until her son was born. May and Marion Hamel also returned to teach in Guernsey after the war. Marie maintained many of the friendships made during her College years. She died in Guernsey in 1981, aged 61.

What strength, determination and endurance it must have taken for Marie and her friends to succeed as they did, during the difficult war years at College and after.

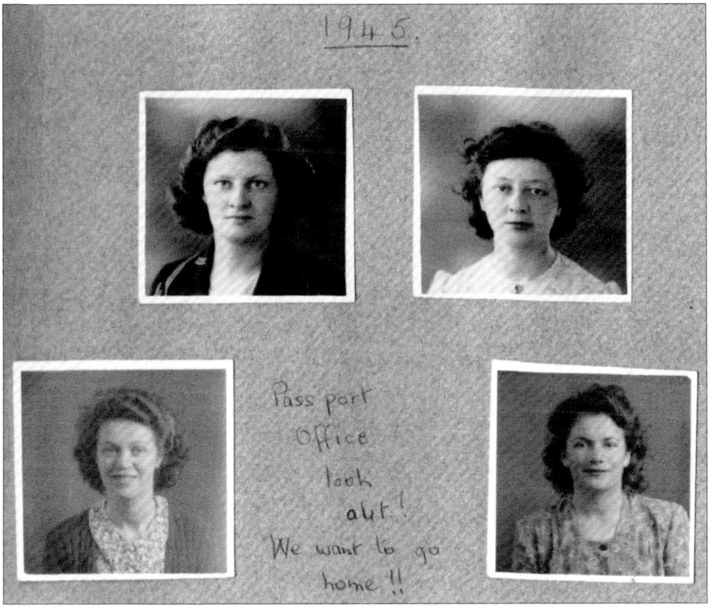

Fig. 8.29 We want to go home! May and Marion Hamel are at the top of the photo. Marie is at the bottom left

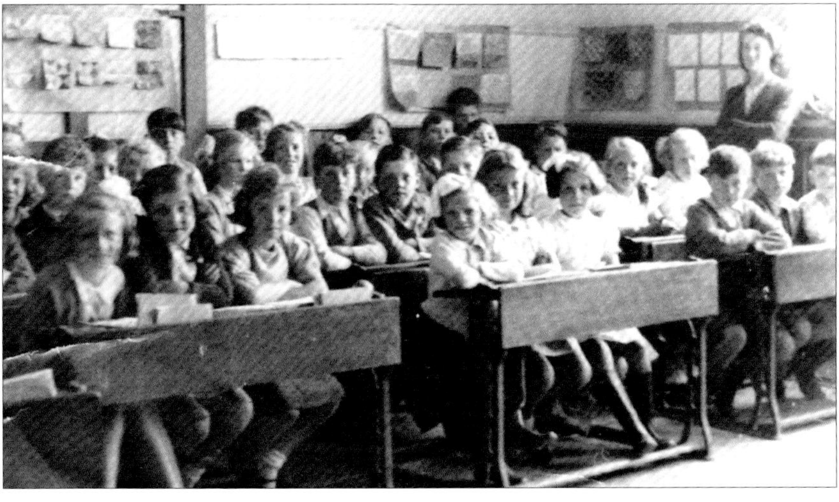

Fig. 8.30 Marie with her class at The Vale School in 1946.

Jonny Guille, 1944–1946

Jonny's Story in her own words

In June 1940 the school I attended was evacuated from Guernsey to Rochdale. After several years I had to decide what to do when I left school after taking the Higher Certificate, (the equivalent of 'A levels').

I would have liked to join the Land Army, but as I was still seventeen my Headmistress was my guardian and wouldn't give me her permission. She suggested I went to College and trained as a teacher.

One year I had been to stay with relatives near Oxford and was inspired by the beauty of the buildings. I had no hope of getting into Oxford University (ironically one of my granddaughters has just graduated from Magdalen College), so I chose Salisbury because of its beautiful setting in the Cathedral Close. One of the pupils from my school, Audrey Hamel, had gone there the previous year and I understand her twin cousins also went to Salisbury. Up to then I had no idea that students from the Channel Islands often went to Salisbury. It was easy to get on the Mail Boat to Southampton and then the train to Salisbury.

I was certainly not disappointed! It was wonderful looking out at the Cathedral from King's House. Being war time there was no floodlighting. The last time I came to a College Re-union I stayed in the old Theological College and got up several times in the night just to gaze at the floodlit spire.

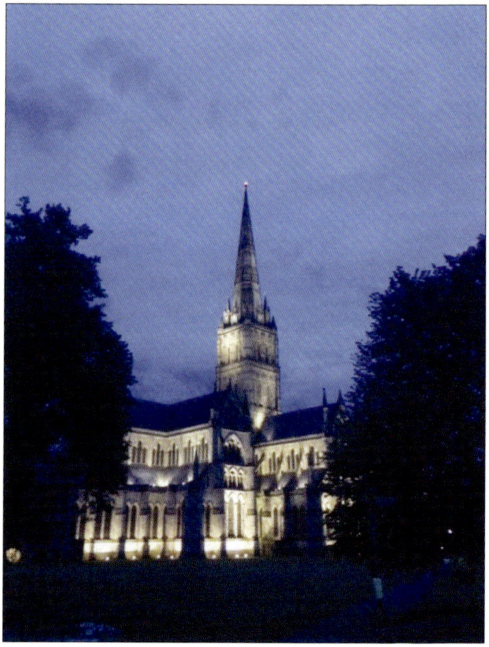

Fig. 8.31
Salisbury Cathedral at night

There were two more Guernsey students in my year, Hazel Maplesden and Enid Falla (1944–46) and Ruth Le Boutillier joined us from Jersey.

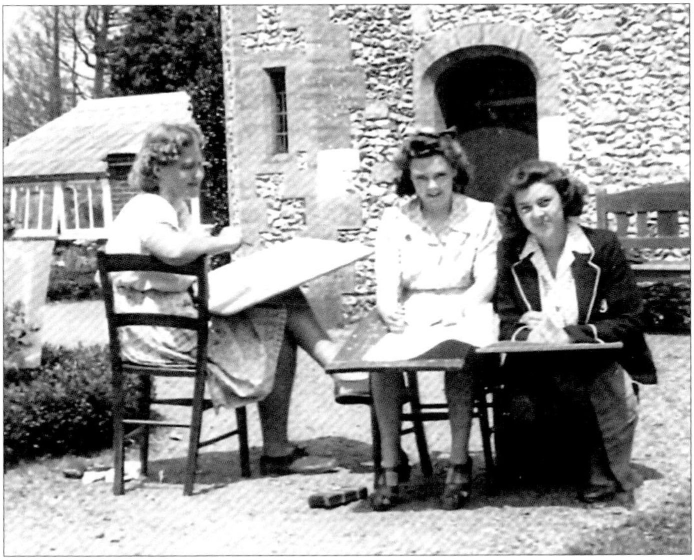

Fig. 8.32 Enid Falla (in her College blazer) and friends outside the College Chapel

My family name was GUILLE – an old Channel Island name. My grandfather was born in Sark – he could trace his family back to 1618 and his was one of the first families to settle on Sark. He married a Guernsey girl and they had eleven children of whom my father, Basil, was the youngest.

My father Basil Guille served in the army in the First World War and went to Palestine as a member of the Church Army. When he came home he stayed in England and trained as a priest eventually marrying a Hampshire girl and moving to Eastleigh as a curate.

When I was eighteen months old my father was appointed to the parish of St Peter in the Wood and we moved to Guernsey.

From 1947–1963 he was Rector of the Town Church in St Peter Port. He also became the Chaplain for the Old Students' Association of our College.

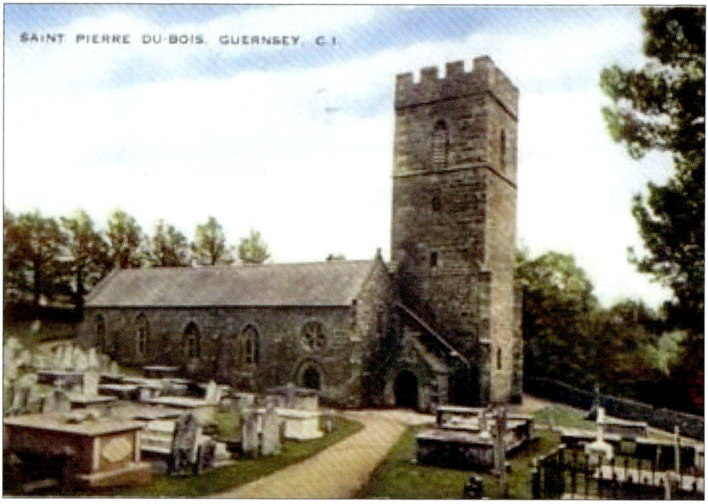

Fig. 8.33

The first teaching practice I did was at St Thomas's School, Salisbury, and on hearing my name one of the masters asked if I knew a Revd Basil Guille – my father had prepared him for confirmation in Eastleigh.

One of my favourite walks was to Harnham Mill. I vividly remember one of my pupils asking why they shouldn't go there. He had misunderstood the words of the prayer: 'Protect us from harm and ill!'

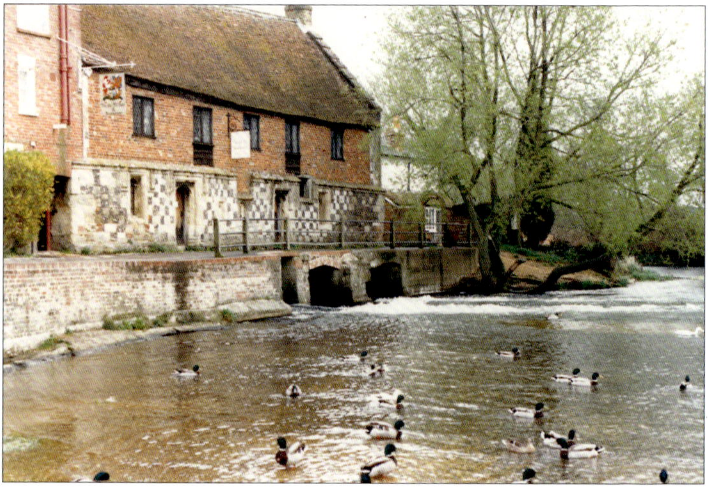

Fig. 8.34 Harnham Mill – one of Jonny's favourite walks

My Christian name is Jeanne – I had always been called Jean but there were so many students named Jean that I decided to use the French pronunciation. On the first time in the lecture room a girl sat next to me and said 'I'm Eve Dunn – who are you?' When I said 'Jeanne' Eve said, 'I can't say that, so I will call you Jon'. Then she turned to another girl called Molly Eaton and said, 'I'm Eve and this is Jonny'. Seventy years later I am still Jonny.

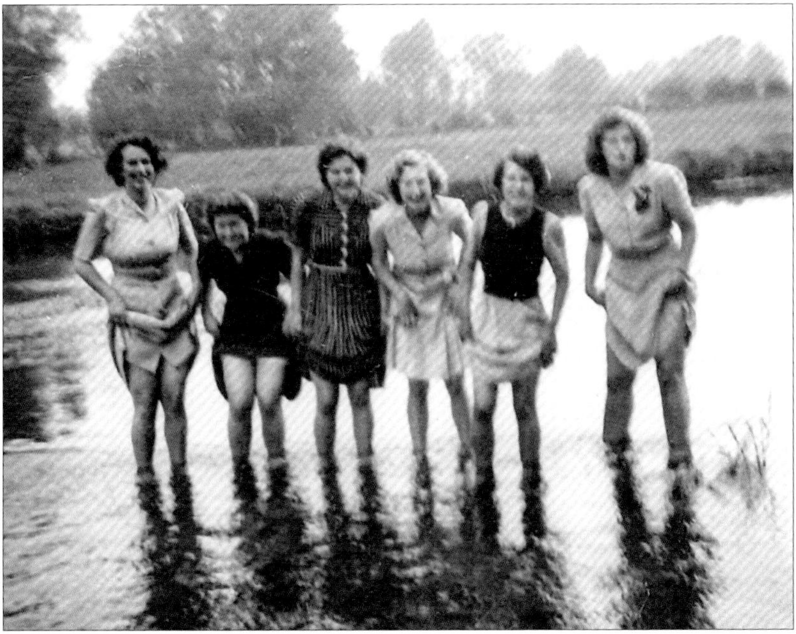

Fig. 8.35 Jonny and friends in the river at College

Eve and Molly were two of my best friends and Molly came and stayed with me in Guernsey. One other person who looked after us well was Matron – Miss Augusta Leest. Later she married an Austrian Count, and so became a Countess. We often visited them in their London flat. So did Nan Brown (1944–46) who to this day, remains a friend.

Altogether, despite the war, my two years at Salisbury were happy ones and becoming a teacher was a good career and fitted in well with having children of my own and shared holidays.

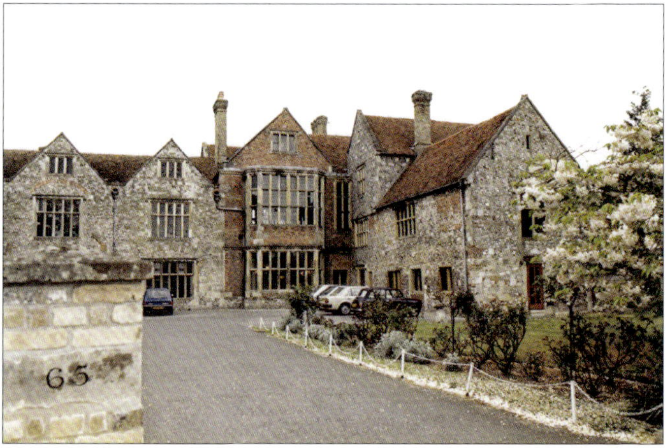

Fig. 8.36 Jonny's room in King's House overlooked Salisbury Cathedral

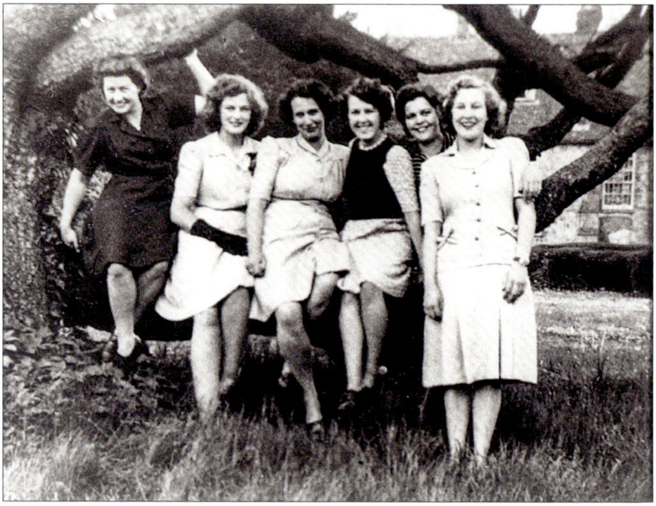

Fig. 8.37 Happy College days in the Old Deanery garden .
Jonny is the 4th from the left

If I were to choose a career today it wouldn't be teaching – it would be gardening!

9

The Post War Years – Looking to the Future

1 Guernsey

After World War Two, fewer students from Guernsey chose to train in Salisbury. More Teacher Training Colleges had opened and there was wider choice available.

Guernsey had to rebuild itself after the Occupation. Evacuees returned home to find that things were vastly different from before: many properties were badly damaged as so much wood had been used as fuel, traditional businesses such as fishing and quarrying had almost vanished and tourism was non-existent. There was a huge debt liability. Freight costs were high and the island had to look to pastures new. The right to supply Mateus Rosé, which became one of the most popular drinks in the world, was controlled by Guernsey. Little did College students who sometimes enjoyed this drink, realise that they were supporting the island!

Rationing continued in Guernsey until the mid 1950s. A former student from this time recalled that a Channel Island student arrived at College without a winter coat, as she could not afford one. On hearing about this, the College Principal ensured that enough funds were found to enable her to buy one.

During the German Occupation the States succeeded in maintaining the education system on the island. In England in 1944 the Butler Act was passed which aimed to provide 'free secondary education for all' by raising the school leaving age to fifteen and developing a tripartite system. Local Education Authorities were to allocate places for children in grammar, secondary modern and technical schools on the basis of an eleven plus examination. As a result of the Second World War, the Butler

Act was not implemented in England until 1947. In Guernsey a start was made on the reorganisation of the education system in 1946, but it was not until 1960 that the reorganisation was completed, with the opening of a third secondary modern school. The 11+ examination was used as a means of selection. Entry to the Intermediate School was by test results and was no longer by payment of fees. The school leaving age remained at 14 until September 1963 when it was raised to 15.

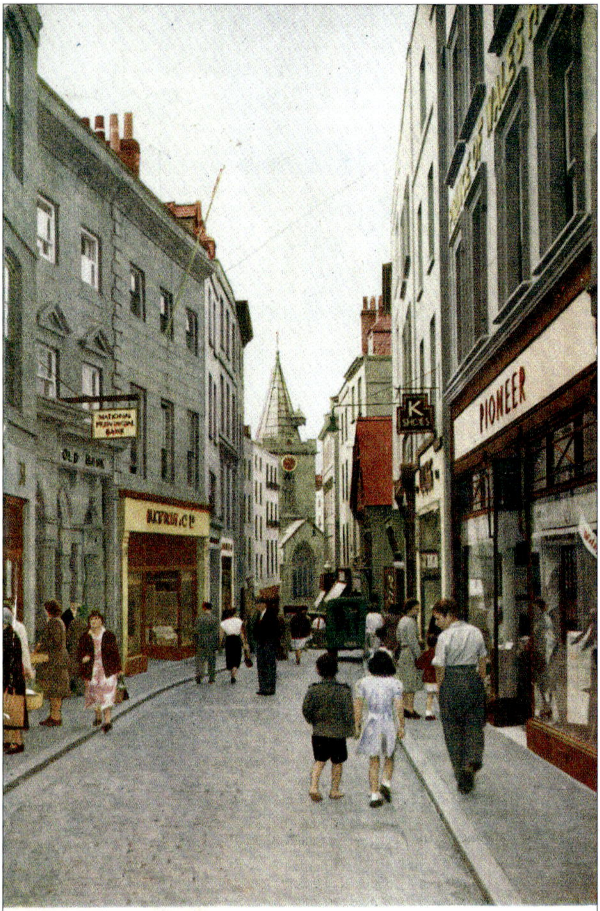

HIGH STREET, ST. PETER PORT, GUERNSEY *Channel Islands*

Fig. 9.1 The High Street in 1952

In 1945 there were 157 boys and girls on the register of the Intermediate School in St Peter Port, under the headship of Mr Peter Girard.

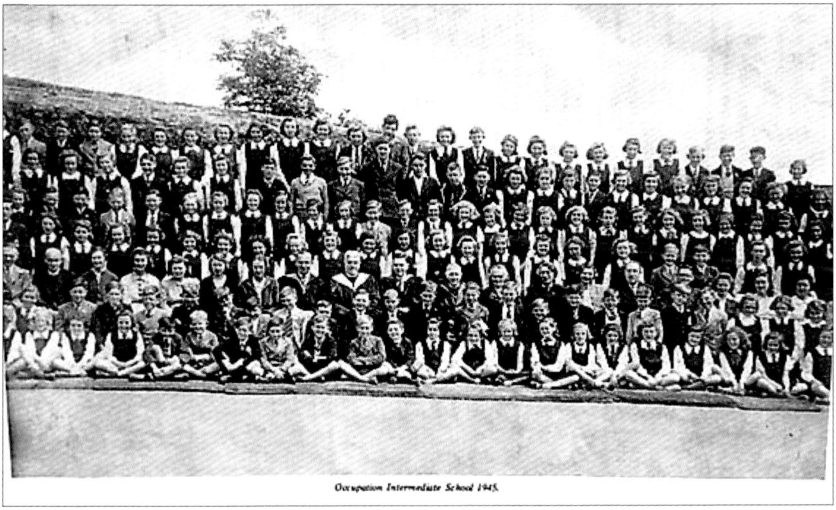

Fig. 9.2 The Occupation Intermediate School 1945 with Peter Girard, Headteacher, 9th from the left

After the Occupation, the Girls' Intermediate and the Boys' Intermediate School once again became single-sex schools. In 1950 they were permitted to retain students to the age of 18 and from 1955 they became known as Grammar Schools. Sheila Higgins, an English lecturer at Salisbury Training College in the 1960s, was a teacher at the Girl's Grammar School prior to coming to College. She remembered her time at the school and in Guernsey with much fondness.

It was a time of recovery and adjustment at College. By 1949 the number of College buildings began to increase – the development continued for nearly 25 years. Educational provision had expanded and the McNair Report set out plans for improved teacher training. Improvements were made to King's House and a new residential block, Maxwell House, opened in 1949. A gymnasium was ready for use in 1956 which even included showers and changing rooms. In 1952 a new science wing was opened. The library and chapel were enlarged and as student numbers increased, so did the lecture rooms. The Old Deanery, having been saved from demolition was restored and ready for use by 1963. At the end of the 1950s a music wing was added. Things were looking up for Salisbury students!

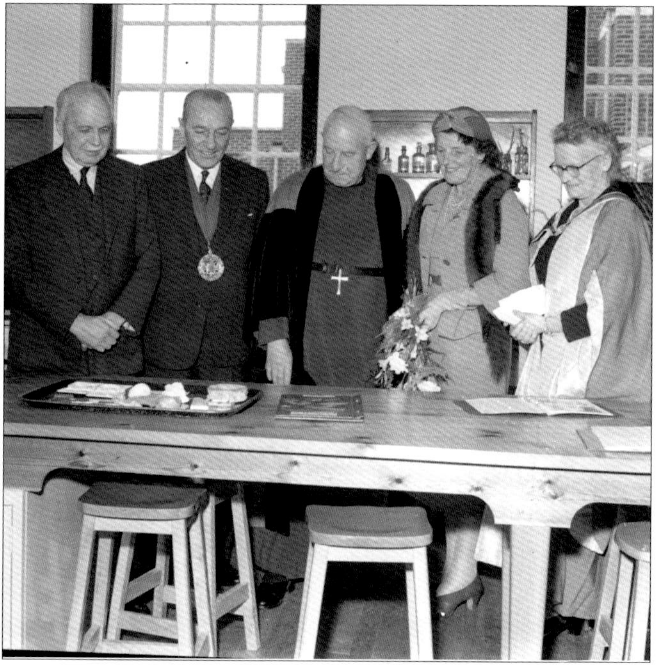

Fig. 9.3 The opening of the science laboratory in 1952.
Dr Grubb, College Principal, far right

In 1958 Shelagh Harris (see below) was a College student. Shelagh married a Guernseyman and lived and taught on the island. She recalled that when she was interviewed for a teaching post in Guernsey she was told: 'We know you were well trained because you come from Salisbury!'

Dr Grubb was the Principal at this time and is remembered as a charming but formidable lady who was always very well dressed in a suit. Shelagh had the job of delivering Miss Grubb's newspaper to her every morning and was once rewarded by being invited to tea – a formal and very polite occasion. This was a time when the two year course was changing to three years – there was so much studying to pack in. Students still tended to be treated as schoolgirls, for example, there was a weekly check of mattresses and rooms. The students were still minors at this time and if anyone became engaged they had to visit Dr Grubb to seek her approval!

Dr Grubb realised that times were changing and wanted College to be training for life. Living in the Cathedral Close meant there were certain rules. Students were not allowed out late except for a late pass once a term, with only two weekends away a term. Under Dr Grubb's leadership students began to gain confidence and to stand up more for themselves. By the mid-fifties permission was given for men to be allowed in rooms – a huge development!

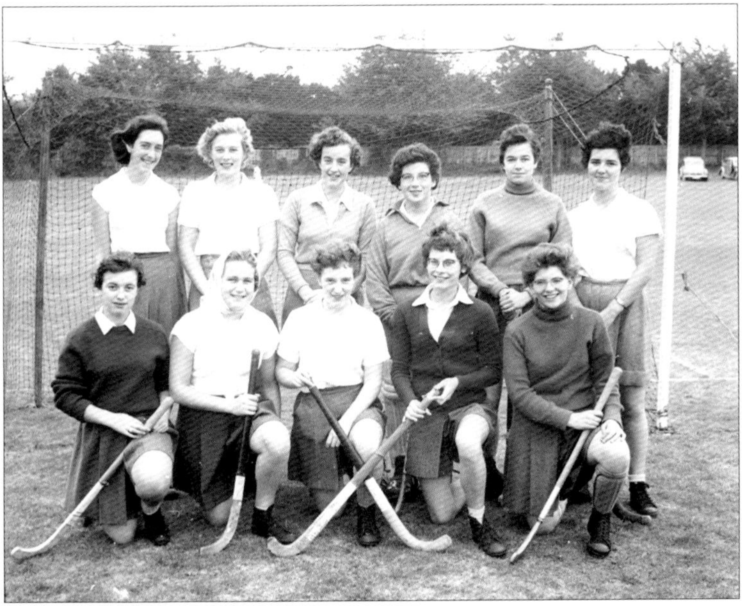

Fig. 9.4 Hockey team in the 1950s

Lucy Sanderson Taylor was a lecturer from 1946 until 1968 and was well ahead of her time. She had a positive and encouraging impact on many students. On difficult school teaching practices she provided invaluable support. On retirement she wrote a book about the College – 'The College in the Close'.

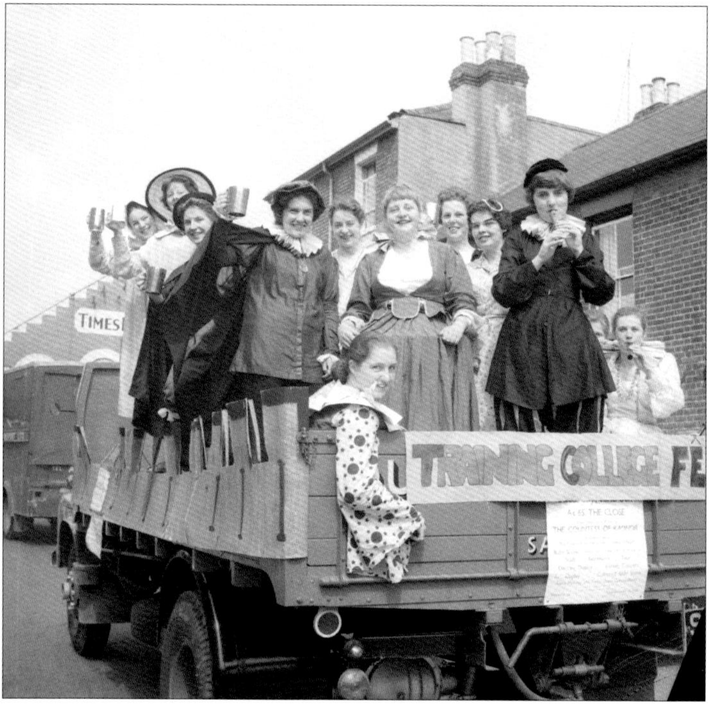

Fig. 9.5 Students publicising the fete in the 1950s

College food was unappetising and it was a treat for students to go to Woolworth's at the weekend. In the 1950s, post war stringencies were still very evident in Salisbury, so a trip to Woolworth's would have been much enjoyed.

The Cathedral Spire was in a precarious state and funds were raised to replace the cross, rebuild the top 30 feet and repair the rest. Citizens joined the nation in celebrating the Coronation of the Queen and ascent of Everest in 1953. Heavy floods hit the city in 1958 when canoes were launched in Fisherton Street. New schools were built and the decade ended on a more optimistic note.

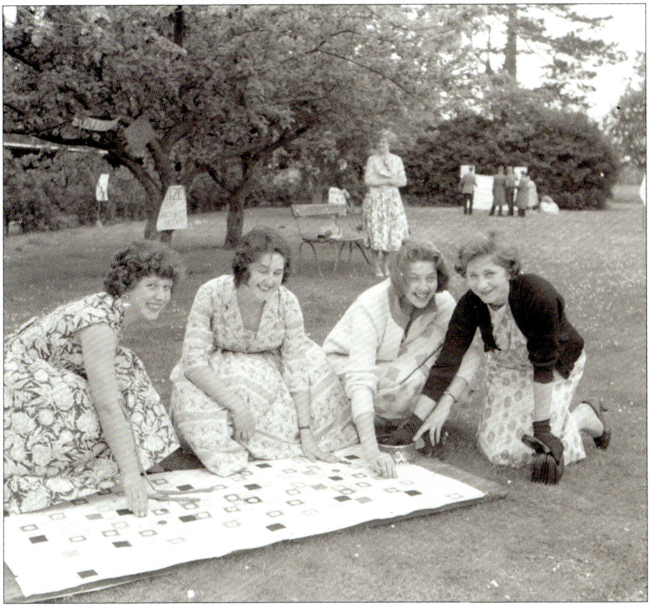

Fig. 9.6 Happy days at the annual College Fete 1959

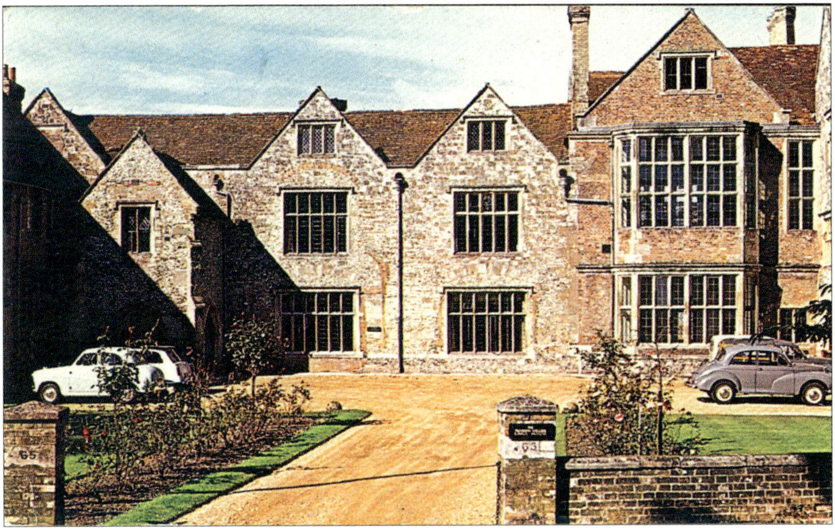

Fig. 9.7 King's House in the 1960s

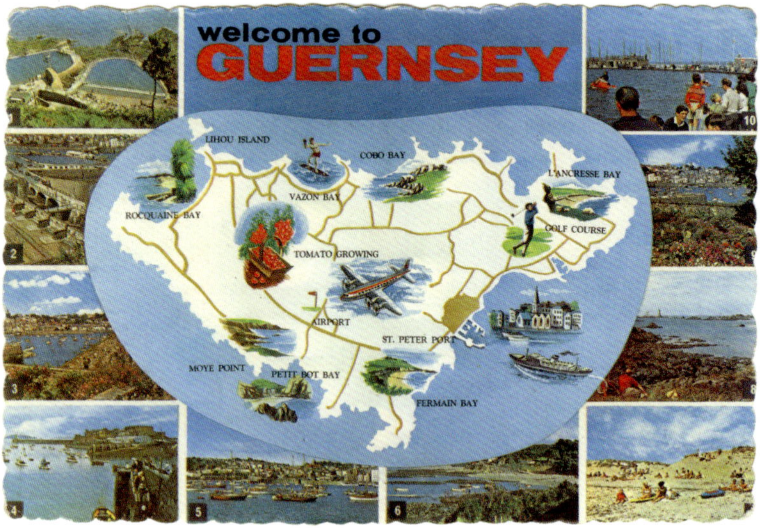

Fig. 9.8 Guernsey holiday postcard, 1966

The 1960s and 1970s saw a trickle of Guernsey students attending the College. By the 1960s Guernsey was well on the road to recovery. The late 1940s until mid 1960s were the heyday of Guernsey tourism. Tourists were once again visiting the island to enjoy the glorious scenery and beaches. Glasshouses flourished and 500 million tomatoes were exported annually.

Unfortunately there was then a financial 'Crash'. Due to the cheaper North Sea Fuel, tomato growers in the Netherlands were able to undercut the prices of Guernsey tomatoes. The decline of the tomato industry began

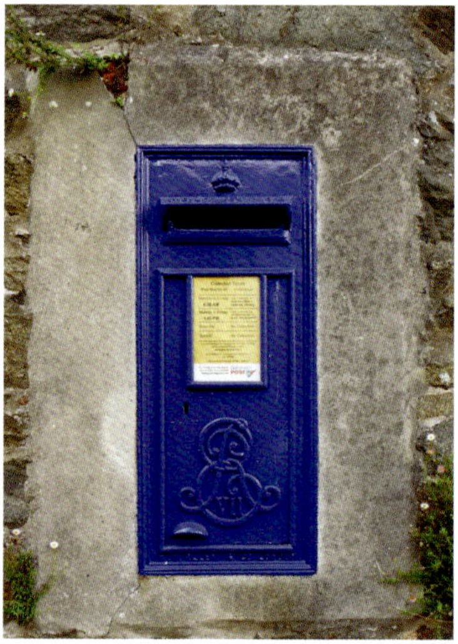

Fig. 9.9 A Guernsey post box

in the 1970s, although some growers continued after this decade, until the industry gradually ceased. Housing controls had been introduced in Guernsey in 1948 as some houses had been destroyed in the war and building materials were in short supply. Guernsey was unable to accommodate all the returning locals and the non-locals who were returning to the island. There was a fear of a huge population increase and measures were introduced to make it harder for people to move to Guernsey. Over the years the housing controls were modified.

In 1963 the first merchant bank had opened in Guernsey and this was the start of the finance industry which flourishes today. However, tourism declined as travel to the island was comparatively expensive when compared with other holiday destinations.

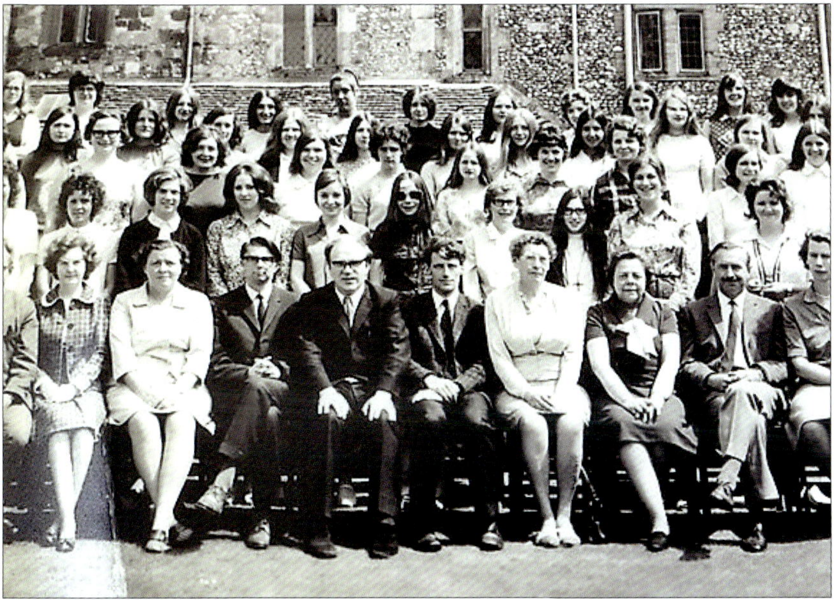

Fig. 9.10 Miss Ashley, the College Principal, seated front row with white sash. Jill Down back row far left, 1971

From 1968 to 1971 Guernsey students Jill Down and Madeleine Critchlow attended the College. Jill's main subject was Art and she has fond memories of working with David Neville, the art tutor, and even firing pots in a kiln down by the river. Jill has happy memories of her College days, but at first it was difficult to be away from the closeness of the island community. She had excellent 'digs' and opted to stay there for the three years. Throughout the years students were given College Mothers to help them settle in. This was a successful scheme and Jill remains in contact with her daughters today. Jill's College mother was also from Guernsey. Jill and Madeleine always missed the sea and felt relief to see it again. The journey home was by taxi to Southampton airport followed by a short flight.

Jill was the Chairman of the Rag Week Committee which also included students from Salisbury Technical College, the Art College and the Theological College. She remembers selling helium balloons by Salisbury Guildhall and being involved in setting up a 'mile of pennies' in Blue Boar Row. Many funds were raised by the students for local charities.

After her training Jill returned to teach at Amherst School, which she attended as a child. Times were hard for some of the island population and Jill remembers one boy in her class in 1972 being sown into his underwear for the winter.

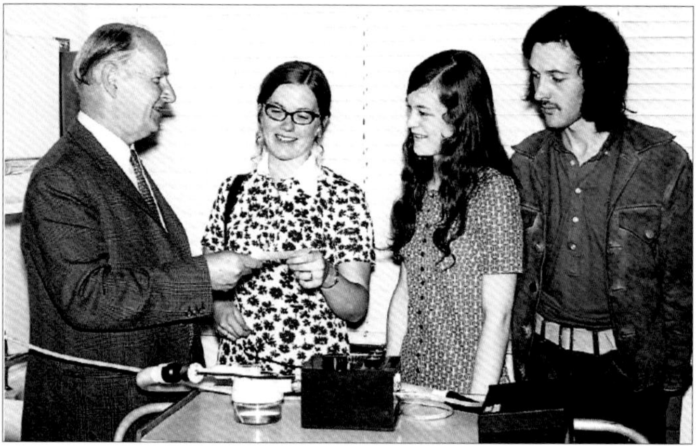

Fig. 9.11 Jill Down presents a Rag Week cheque of £250 to a representative from Salisbury Infirmary 1971

The early students used to collect ormers, a local shellfish delicacy, from the beaches at the lowest Spring tides. Unfortunately they were overfished (mainly by divers) and strict controls were introduced to protect stocks. Today the season is from January to April and Jill still enjoys her visits to the beach, turning rocks at the water's edge to find these elusive creatures. After beating the ormers to soften them, they are fried and then made into a tasty casserole. During the final years of the College at least three other Guernsey students trained in Salisbury and entered the teaching profession.

In 1970 an Education Act was passed in Guernsey which encompassed many aspects of island education. It heralded several years of more rapid development in education. The States supported students at further educational establishments in England. In 1975 the number of Guernsey students receiving grants was 276 – although very few of these were at Salisbury. In 1972 an HMI report recommended a Teacher's Centre for in-service training in Guernsey and in 1973 a Teacher's Centre was set up at Les Vauxbellets. It was used for teachers in their first year of training and also for regular in-service courses for all teachers on the island. Although this centre no longer exists, the Education services run a one year course on Guernsey, which is an initial teaching training programme supported by the University of Brighton. Current teacher recruitment in Guernsey is looking healthy.

Fig. 9.12 St Peter Port harbour 1970s

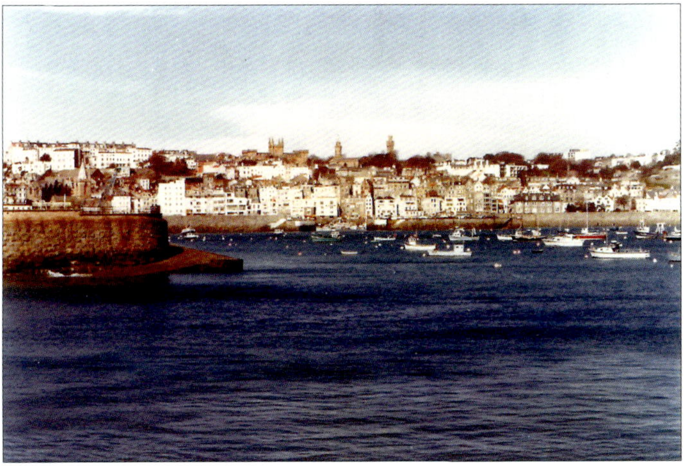

The States Committee for Education, Sport and Culture currently provide ten primary schools in Guernsey. As pupils come to the end of their primary education they sit the 11+ examination. At eleven, pupils transfer to one of four secondary schools, or a co-educational grammar school. There are also three fee paying colleges with lower schools, for which some scholarships are available for eligible pupils. In addition there are three schools for those pupils who need more specialist provision. The States is also responsible for the school on Alderney. Herm is a beautiful small island off the coast of Guernsey and is part of the Parish of St Peter Port. The primary school educates children up to the age of nine after which they usually become weekly boarders on Guernsey. Sark is completely separate from Guernsey administratively. In January 2018 the States voted for plans to introduce comprehensive education in 2019 and there will be significant changes to the whole education system.

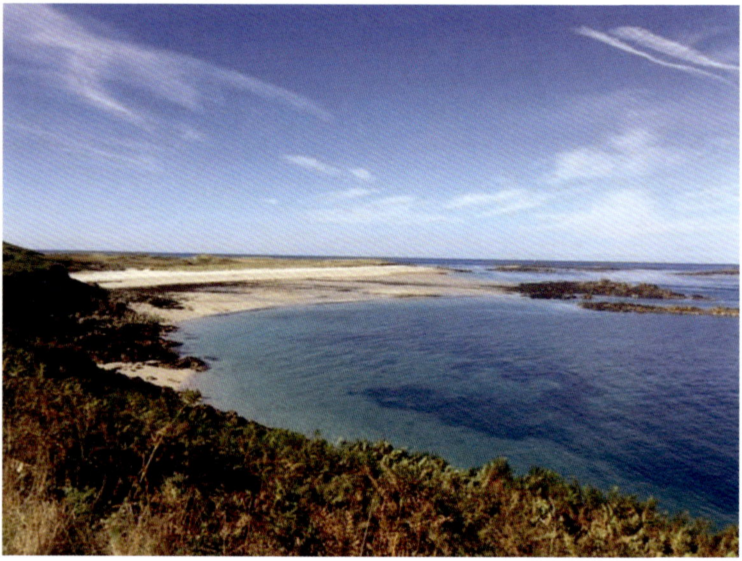

Fig. 9.13 Shell Beach, Herm

Salisbury Clubs linked to the Old Students' Association (OSA) existed until the late 1990s. Former students in Guernsey met regularly to enjoy each other's company. They met annually for a service in church, and tea or a picnic, and were sometimes joined by fellow former students from Jersey.

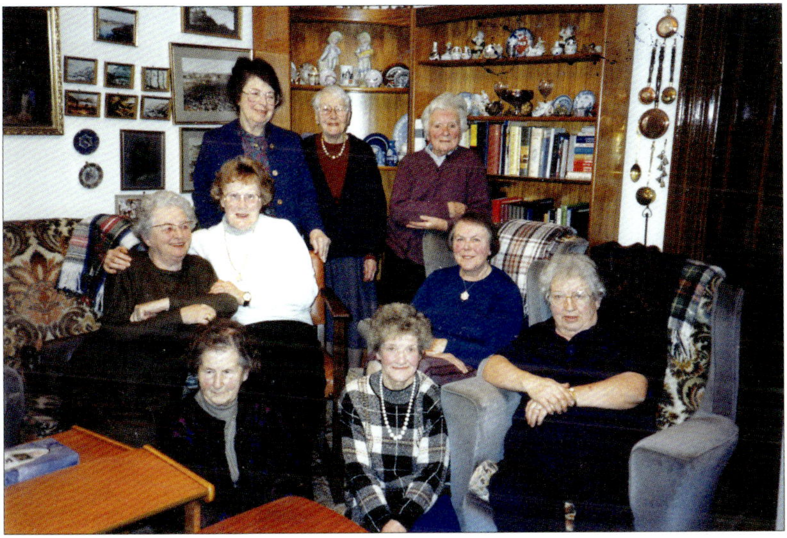

Fig. 9.14 The Guernsey Salisbury Club, 1991
From left to right: Mrs Marion Massey (Hamel), Mrs Joan Leeman (*née* Davies), name unknown, Miss Edith Albiges, name unknown, Mrs Pleasance Lihou, Mrs Bet Wilson. Centre, Audrey Oliver in checked dress, the other lady on the floor name unknown.

Members of the College staff would occasionally join them on these special occasions. A letter written in the College Newsletter indicates the importance of these meetings:

> Guernsey Club
> We plan to meet again in September this year here in Guernsey. On Saturday 29th September the Jersey branch of the Old Students' Association will be visiting our local Guernsey branch for a most enjoyable day together – our annual inter-island reunion, held alternately in Guernsey and Jersey. The next day the 1938–1940 group will be spending the day together. We would like you to join us'.
>
> Marion Massey (*née* Hamel) Betty Wilson (*née* Hippisley)

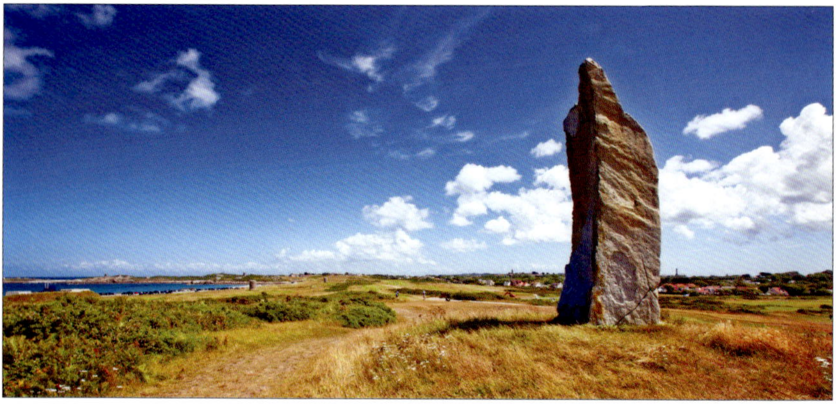

Fig. 9.15 L'Ancresse Common, a favourite picnic spot for former College students and one of the many idyllic locations on the beautiful island of Guernsey

The College Newsletter, dating from 1886, remains a much valued annual publication which still keeps hundreds of former students in touch.

Guernsey provided numerous students who trained as teachers in Salisbury. They chose Salisbury for several reasons: in the early days, although the journey was long and difficult, it was the most accessible college. Many were attracted by the beauty of the Cathedral and the peace and serenity of the Cathedral Close. Salisbury was not a huge city and the more rural aspect was a draw for some students, as it felt more like home. Others heard favourable reports of the comprehensive training and of the strength of friendships made there. Whatever their reasons for choosing to train at Salisbury, it provided them with an excellent foundation for their teaching careers and their lives beyond College.

2 Jersey

'We see there on the horizon a mirage of an Educational Utopia. Based on the solid foundations of the English Education Act of 1944, the structure of reorganisation is slowly but surely being built by experts. Once again, we are able to obtain supplies from England. Once again children have text books to interest and instruct them. Supplies may still be limited compared with pre-war standards …but to us, everything is ideal'. A.A.H. Downer: *The Channel Islands Schools 1940–45*

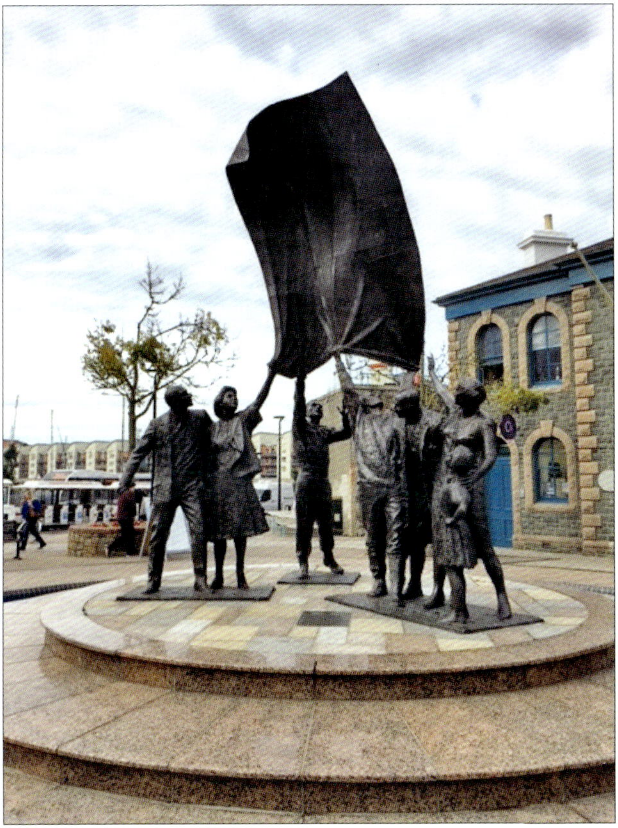

Fig 9.16 Liberation Square, St Helier

These words were written in 1946. The war was over. It was time for islanders to pick up the thread of their lives again and to put the past behind them. This was also reflected in a comment made by Muriel Le Breton, a former student, in 1945: 'After the first joy of freedom, the schools are now settling down to normal and although there is a great deal to make up in many ways, yet we all feel that there is now something to work for'.

It was Senator John Le Marquand who was credited with the development of Jersey's post-war education system, taking it out of a period of stagnation and into the 21st century.He was described in his obituary as the 'founding father of modern education in the island'.

The overall standards of island education in the 1930s had not matched those found in England and Wales. The German Occupation subsequently brought any progress to a total standstill. The provision of grammar schools was now long overdue. New secondary schools were needed for children whose families could not afford fee paying schools such as Victoria College, Jersey College for Girls (as it was renamed in the 1930s) and other private schools. Jersey Intermediate School was selective and only took pupils to the age of sixteen. The lack of secondary modern schools meant that over 60% of children were staying in their elementary schools until they were fifteen. The school leaving age had been raised to fifteen in the island in 1943, four years ahead of England. It was felt that pupils should remain in school for another year as they were unlikely to find employment during the Occupation and might therefore wander in the streets and cause trouble with the occupying forces..

After the war, the number of Jersey students applying to train in Salisbury dwindled. Higher education was beyond the reach of most young people. Moreover, there were once again work opportunities at home in banking, tourism and commerce and there may have been parental pressure to remain and to help to rebuild the island.

The strong family link which was a feature of the College was, however, maintained. Mothers were followed by daughters and sisters often followed each other. Two sisters who left their mark on Jersey's educational scene were Cecily and Evelyn Hoyles.

Cecily Myra Hoyles arrived at College in 1945, with Fay Arthur and Ruth Le Boutillier, a few months after the end of the war. She had asked whether she might be allowed to do a shorter course as she'd had considerable teaching experience during the Occupation and knew how short of leaders the Jersey schools were. This was not permitted.

Cecily spent her first year in Long South in King's House. This was a large room at the top of the stairs above the dining room. It was divided into cubicles, or horse-boxes, as they were affectionately known.

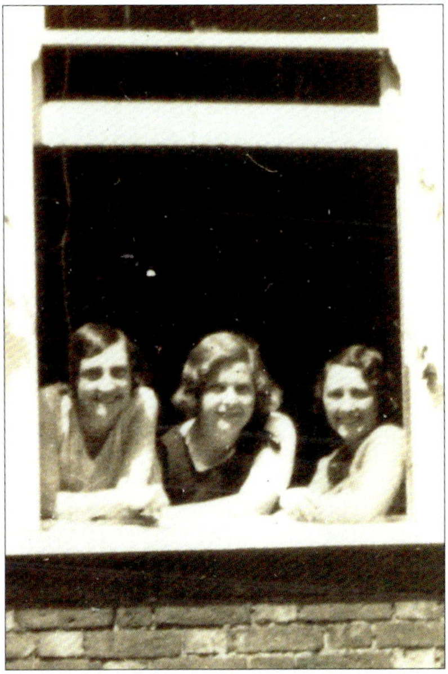

9.17 Students at Barnard's Cross

> 'After six years of war a miscellaneous group of students met in Long South to explore their curtained cubicles and curious attic bathroom up a winding staircase. As we made new friends we quickly realised that the pale, strained group of Channel Islanders (whose entry had been deferred from 1939) had not fared as well as us – from them we learned of tobacco-tin radios and home-made soap. Some of them wanted to talk of those times, others did not'.
>
> Jean Reynolds, 1945–1947

Cecily's main subject was History and she trained as a secondary teacher. Fellow students described her as 'intelligent, with a good sense of humour and a delightful way with words'. Cecily returned to Jersey after her training and most of her career was spent teaching children with learning difficulties and encouraging them to persevere. She taught first at St Helier Girls' School and later at Grainville when the school moved there. She was a loyal member of St Saviour's Church and her faith underpinned her life. Friends remembered her for her patience, her calm and practical common sense and her care for others.

Cecily was one of the many island old students who actively supported the Jersey branch of the Salisbury Club. The 1946 issue of the much

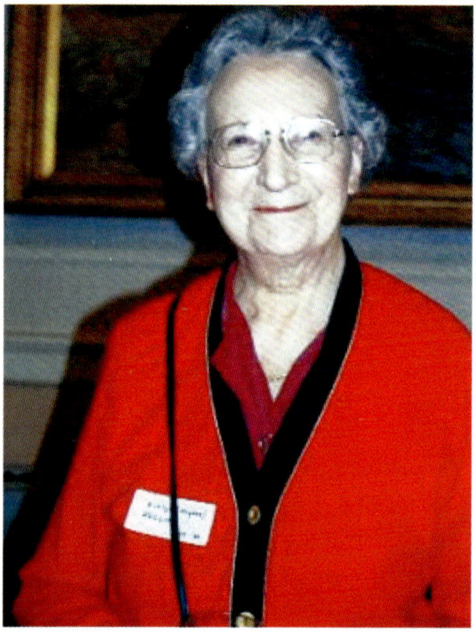

Fig 9.18 Evelyn Pullin (*née* Hoyles)

loved College magazine records a message from the forty members:

'It is with great joy and thankfulness that we are once more able to contribute to the Salisbury Magazine. During the years of occupation we found it advisable to remain inactive. It was with much pleasure that we received the telegram of greetings in June 1945 from the Club Meeting held 'under the spire'. We were deeply touched by the kind thought'.

Evelyn (Cecily's older sister) was educated at the Jersey Intermediate School before going to College in 1938. She returned to Jersey on the last boat before the Occupation and spent the war years there, teaching at the Intermediate School. She left the island after the war, having applied for posts on the mainland at the same time that Cecily started College. Evelyn spent the next twenty eight years teaching in England, during which time she held several posts, including that of Head Teacher at Vauxhall Manor Girls School in London. In 1974 she and her husband moved to the island and Evelyn (now Mrs Pullin) took up the headship of Jersey Girls' College (JCG). The school prospered under her calm, dignified but warm and supportive leadership.

'The overriding impression of Evelyn Pullin as a Head Teacher was of a calm, dignified woman, ram-rod straight who never appeared to hurry, but just glided down the corridors, never raised her voice and seemed able to command respect with just a look. Meticulous and severely self-disciplined, she also displayed much warmth, concern for others and a dry sense of humour'.

Margaret Stone, colleague at JCG

During her retirement, Evelyn embarked on a new career as a politician. This included some time as a member of the Social Security Committee and as President of the Education Committee. She was also on the Agriculture and Fisheries Committee, which led to much involvement in the fisheries dispute with France. Throughout her life, her sister Cecily was extremely important to her as a friend and confidante. Evelyn, like Cecily, had a strong faith and was a loyal member of St Saviour's Parish Church. She died in 2012, leaving a legacy that has enabled the renovation of the interior of the church.

Beryl Woodsford whose headmistress at the Intermediate School had been Miss Montgomery, was at College in the mid-1930s. Beryl loved her time in Salisbury and had vivid and lively memories. Her daughter, Jean Hanning, followed her to College in 1961 and whilst she was there, her mother attended reunions and enjoyed meeting up with teachers from Jersey and Guernsey. Beryl's two children were born during the Occupation. In 1953 she became the hospital teacher and enjoyed teaching children of all ages, as well as providing home tuition for pupils with difficulties such as school phobia. Beryl was 97 when she died and many former pupils attended her funeral, remembering her 'kindliness, vivacity and strong Christian faith'.

Kathleen and Sybil Ahier were both Salisbury students. Kathleen, who was born in 1897, initially attended St Clement's School. After her training, Kathleen was appointed in 1918 to teach at Grouville Mixed School. She spent the Occupation years teaching in Tottenhole near Dunstable, but returned to Jersey when the war finally ended. She was the Head at Halkett Place Girls until 1962.

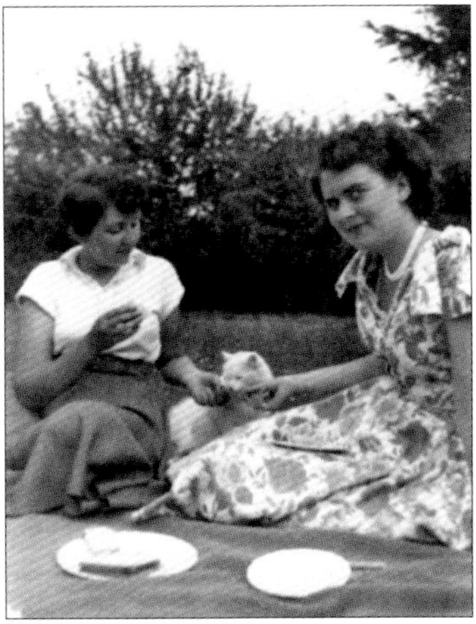

Fig 9.19 Olga Ozouf (right) and her friend Winifred

Olga Ozouf, who had spent the war years in the Southampton area with her mother, returned to the island after the Occupation and attended JCG before going to College in 1951. In the words of her friend June Rolfe, who first met her in Miss Taylor's Education class, 'Olga had a vibrant personality and was an adept and witty conversationalist'.

Olga was quite a linguist, speaking French fluently, but also speaking Jerriais, the unique local language. After training, she taught in England for several years before returning home and joining the staff of St Clement's Junior School. She left St Clements's in 1964. She had the distinction of being Miss Ozouf when she married Philip (no relation) the following year and became Mrs Ozouf. Writing in the 1965 College Chronicle, she says that she enjoyed every moment of her wedding and put it down to the 'quiet confidence gained during several years of teaching in front of far more critical audiences'. As well as bringing up their family, she threw herself into community and church activities. When the TV series 'Bergerac' was filmed in Jersey, Olga enjoyed being an 'extra' in many episodes. She was a keen member of the local Salisbury Club and loved returning to Salisbury for College Reunions. Her husband was a farmer and her friend June remembers that 'she always had to pop into Marks & Spencer in Salisbury to check the price of Jersey Royals so that she could compare it with what Philip had received for his crop'.

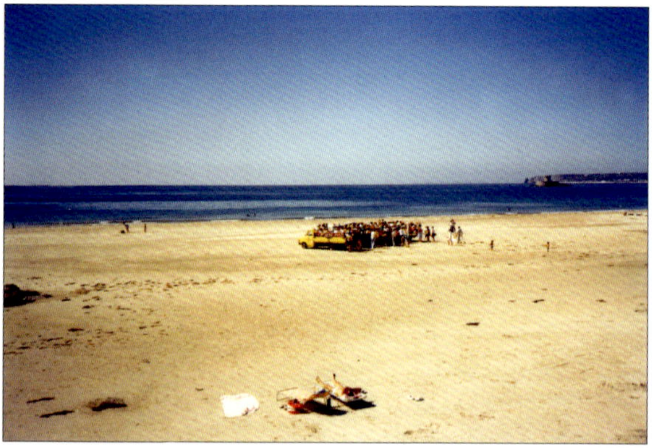

Fig 9.20 Sunday School outing to St Ouen

The decades following the end of the Second World War saw great changes in Jersey as the educational provision expanded. Two secondary modern schools, St Helier Boys and St Helier Girls opened in the 1950s, providing education for 11–16 year olds. The Jersey Intermediate School became St Helier Girls School (also known as Brighton Road Secondary Modern). Marguerite Le Chasseur, who had trained at College from 1939–1941 was appointed as Head of St Helier Girls. Two grammar schools were also opened at this time, Hautlieu for boys and Rouge Bouillon for girls, providing free education for children who had passed the 11+ examination. The building of these schools was bitterly opposed by people who were not convinced of the need for children to receive education beyond the age of 16. Enough work could be found in the banks and hotels and aspiration for higher education was at a low level. In 1966 Rouge Bouillon merged with Hautlieu, which became a co-educational school.

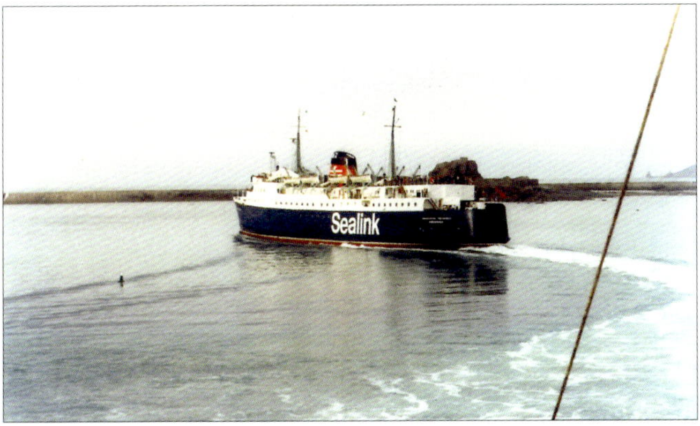

Fig 9.21 On their way to College !

By the time Betty Laurens and Heather Clarke went to College late in the fifties, the post war era of austerity was ending and life was improving. People were looking with optimism towards the future. Salisbury Training College, or the College of Sarum St Michael as it was renamed, was changing. There was an increasing demand for wider access to higher education and Training College courses were extended to three years in 1960. The College was growing in numbers. Whereas there had been approximately 98 students in 1950, by 1960 it was expected that there would be 240 students within two years. There were signs of greater prosperity in the country too. People were buying refrigerators and televisions and supermarkets were opening.

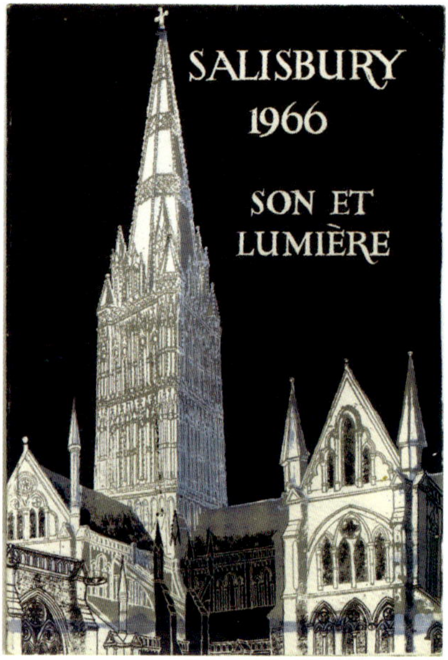

Fig. 9.22

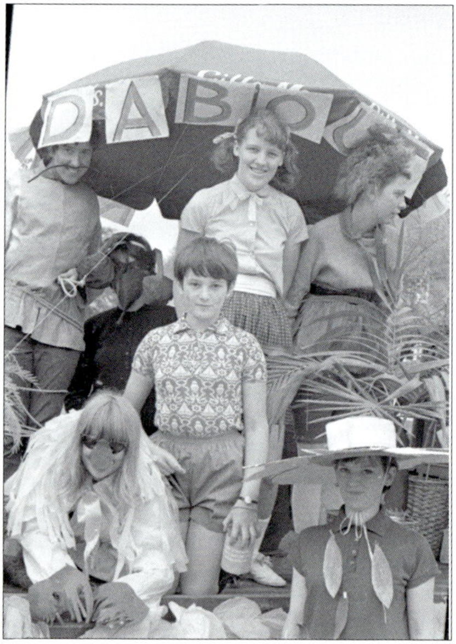

Fig 9.23 Rag Week 1960s

At the beginning of the 1960s, students dressed quite conventionally and some made their own clothes, often buying material in Salisbury market. As the decade progressed, hair grew longer and skirts grew shorter. Students wore their blue and white college scarves with duffle coats, and long boots. Gowns were introduced in 1960 and were worn in lectures and at Cathedral services. New buildings in The Close (behind King's House) were opened to accommodate the larger number of students and to provide facilities such as science laboratories.

Most of the island students travelled by sea as air fares were expensive. Jersey students in the sixties included Jean Hanning, Anne Priestley, Jane Houillebecq, Florence Houillebecq and Frances Bisson. Jane Houillebecq remembers her excitement at seeing the Cathedral spire for the first time and, on entering the Close, her feelings of awe at the size, grandeur and beauty of the Cathedral. Unlike Jean Hanning who had horse-box accommodation, Jane went to live in The Wardrobe (which is now the home of The Rifles Museum). Her initial reaction was that she wouldn't wish to stay for long, but, like many Wardrobe students, she quickly appreciated that what the 15th century building lacked in terms of home comforts, was more than compensated for by the privilege of living there. The Wardrobe was near the College, but separate from it and the 24 students relished their independence. Miss Mayo, the delightfully eccentric warden, interpreted the College rules in her own inimitable way: Students were not permitted to sunbathe in the genteel, ecclesiastical atmosphere of The Close. 'Be careful when sunbathing, ladies', said Miss Mayo. 'Remember there are canons to the right and canons to the left ...

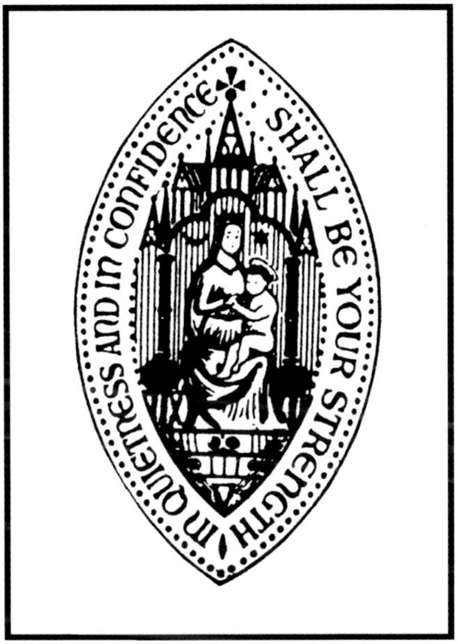

Fig. 9.24 The College badge and motto

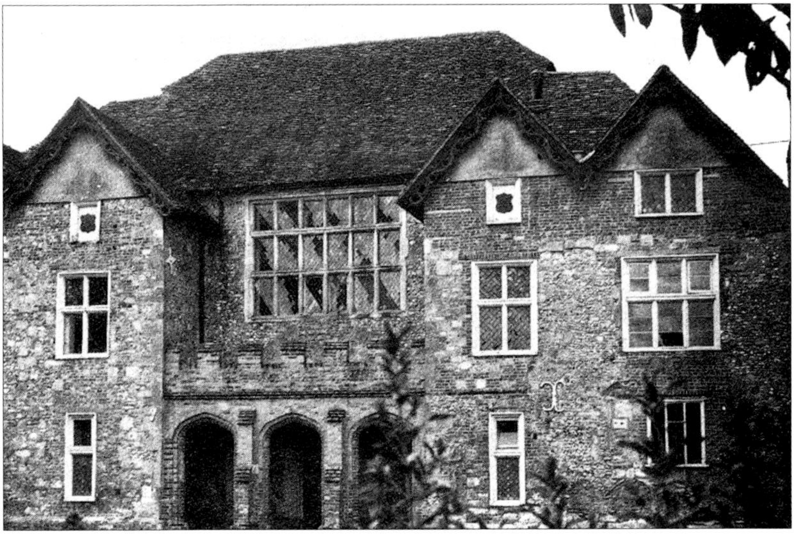

Fig 9.25 The Wardrobe in The Close, Salisbury

'The Times They Are a-Changin', sang Bob Dylan. Innovation was in the air and new educational ideas came thick and fast. Integrated days, open-plan schools, the child-centred approach, creative writing, Cuisenaire blocks and the introduction of ITA (Inishul Teeching Alfabet) were all discussed and debated by staff and students. A two year course for mature students started in 1967. It was based at a house in London Road and quickly became popular. In 1968 the B Ed degree started, entailing a fourth year of study and directed initially by the University of Bristol, but later by the University of Southampton. In primary schools, this was the era of nature tables, junk modelling, and project work. Climbing onto the Skylark coaches that took them to their school practice schools could be tricky for students clutching wild flowers, modelling materials, books –and often a guitar.

The College was flourishing, with numerous clubs, as well as sporting activities, music and drama. Many students watched the memorable 'Son et Lumiere' production at the Cathedral in 1966. The Students' Union organised Rag Weeks and there were College Balls and dances. Students were free to go into Salisbury, meet friends, visit local hostelries and sample the nightlife – but the High Street gate still closed at 11 pm, even in the swinging sixties.

Students whose homes were in Jersey returned from College to an island that was also booming. From the late 1950s onwards Jersey became a wonderful haven for family holidays. It had a gentle 'old world' charm and character, with unspoilt beaches, winding roads and rugged cliffs. Just a short hop from England, but Jersey was (and still is) another world. Tourists liked getting away from the mainland to somewhere that was a little different, but where English was still spoken, London newspapers arrived at breakfast time (unless there was fog) and there was the reassuring sight of policemen whose uniforms resembled those seen at home. Havre des Pas, with its Victorian seawater bathing pool, was no longer in its heyday, but still provided popular entertainment for families, as did the long established Sunday School outings.

Wealthy residents, attracted by the island's system of low taxation, were increasingly playing an important part in the island's growing prosperity. The economy, however, was still essentially agricultural, based on early vegetables, cut flowers and breeding of the famous Jersey cows.

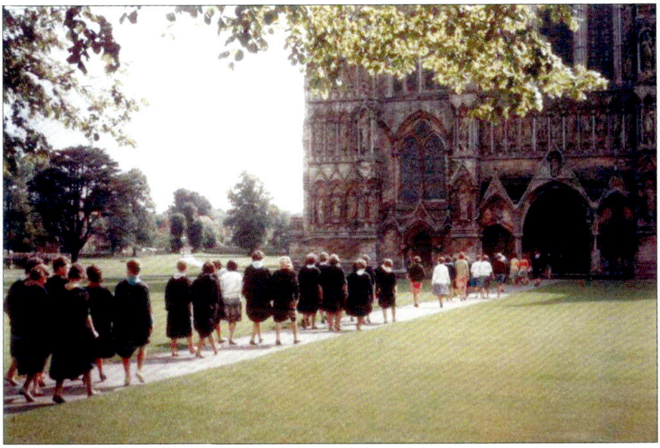

Fig. 9.26 Students going to a Cathedral service in the 1960s

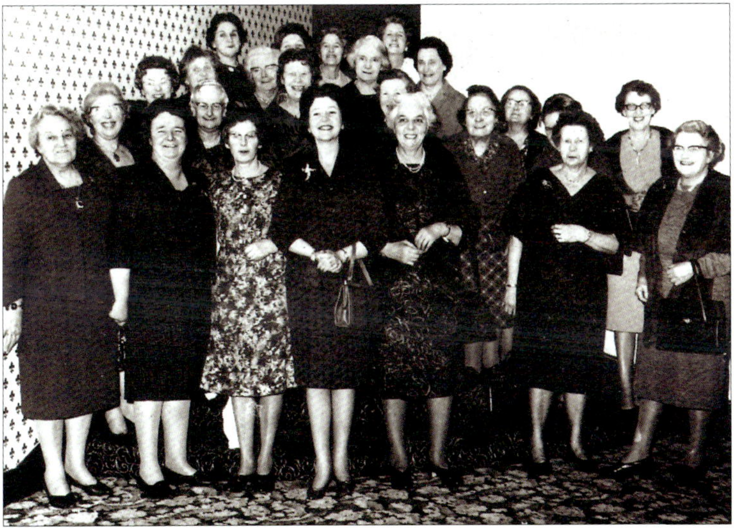

Fig. 9.27 Members of the Jersey Salisbury Club in the 1960s included Cecile Blacklin, Evelyn Pullin, Phyllis Perchard, Dorothy Duffett, Ethel Davy, Cecily Hoyles, Marjorie Starck, Madeleine Norman, Olga Ozouf, Betty Carter, Ruby Le Seelleur, Fay Arthur, Janet Tarr, Beatrice Le Huquet, Anne Mourant, Mary Renouf, Florence Houillebecq, Dora Hacquoil, Dorothy Mauger and others. There were 42 members in 1969.

Several of the Jersey students who were at Barnard's Cross during the First World War and the early 1920s went on to have long teaching careers in Jersey. During the 1960s more than 12 former students, retired from island schools, including Dora Hacquoil from Les Landes, Edith Le Marquand from Val Plaisant Infants and Mabel Ahier from Trinity.

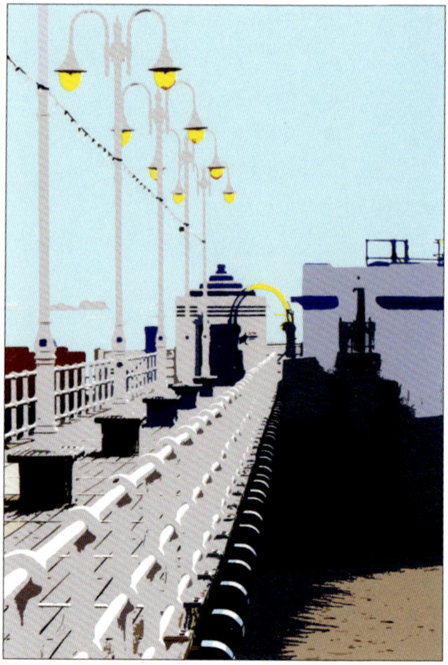

Fig 9.28 Havre des Pas, Jersey

The Jersey branch of the Salisbury Club played an important part in the lives of so many old students and the annual Old Students' Newsletter was also greatly appreciated. In 1972 the Newsletter recorded that Phyllis Perchard received an MBE in the Queen's Birthday Honours. Phyllis had taught at First Tower School for over 44 years and had set up and run the School Savings Bank for 34 years.

Keeping in touch with their Alma Mater was important to former students and the readymade group of 'Salisbury girls' was a real bonus. Members continued to meet until around the time of the Millennium. Ruth Le Boutillier and Cecily Hoyles were amongst the 51 former students from 1945–47 who attended the College Reunion in 2002.

Despite the fact that by the early 1970s the College was expanding, there were very few Jersey students. By now students could choose from a greater variety of colleges and universities. Travel was easier and single sex colleges possibly had less attraction.

The College of Sarum St Michael was, however, a buzzing, lively community in 1970, the year that eighteen year olds were given the vote. There were approximately 450 students, one of whom was Anne Blaine from Jersey. Unfortunately, things were about to change. The birth rate was falling and there were too many teachers. The state of teacher training was unsettled and, in retrospect, the future of small, single sex church colleges was unpredictable. Despite the gathering clouds, life went on as usual and in the early seventies students were unaware of the dramatic events that were to unfold. They continued to receive the excellent training for which the College was known, and to enjoy greater independence and fewer rules now that the College was no longer 'in loco parentis'.

The James Report in 1972 set the scene for wide-ranging changes, but it was a statement in the White Paper 'Framework for Expansion' later that year which really caused alarm: 'Some colleges may face the possibility that in due course they will have to be converted to new purposes; some may have to close'.

Staff at the College of Sarum St Michael were not too concerned. 'This was the only College of Education in Wiltshire and it was in good standing with the LEA and with the University of Southampton'. Events, however, moved quickly. There were letters, protests, discussions about a possible merger with King Alfred's Winchester, and an appeal to the Secretary of State. Dorothy Mauger wrote in the College Chronicle on behalf of the Salisbury Club in Jersey: 'Whatever may happen to Sarum St Michael, our College for which we have such deep affection, the Jersey Salisbury Club, with its membership of forty is still very active and intends to go on functioning under this name'.

In 1976 the Governing Body was informed by the Department of Education and Science (DES) that the College would receive no further intake of students and would close in 1978. Academic and professional standards, however, remained high right to the end. In the words of John Say, former lecturer in education:

> 'July 1978 rang down the curtain on 137 years of work in Sarum St Michael, the oldest residential teacher training college for women in the country. The overwhelming sadness that the ending of nearly a century and a half of life, work and culture engendered can only be imagined'.

Students and staff, past and present and including a contingent from the Channel Islands, gathered in the Cathedral for a service of reflection and thanksgiving. There was great sadness at the demise of a flourishing college that had built an enviable reputation, but also thanksgiving for the work of thousands of teachers who had taken the College's ethos and spirit into the schools where they worked.

The Salisbury link has not quite ended. Our stories have focused on the Jersey students who trained in Salisbury and returned to the island to teach. There were others who trained at the College before moving to Jersey. Sue Jones (*née* Wear) is one such person. She made the adventurous decision to accept a post in Jersey after finishing College in 1977.

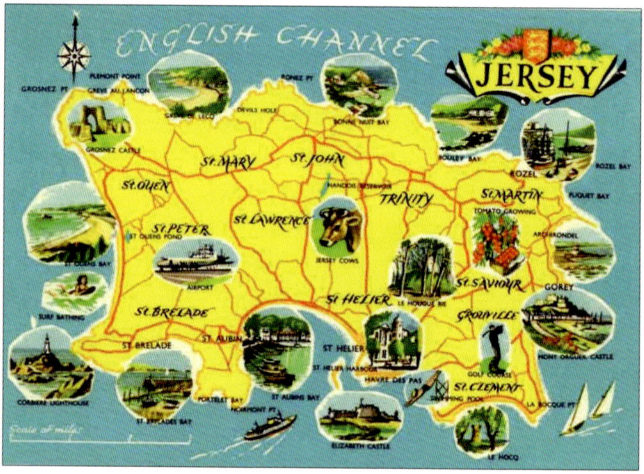

Fig 9.29 1970s postcard

Due to a shortage of housing, there was pressure from the States of Jersey to appoint local teachers, rather than applicants from the mainland. The fact that the post was given to a 'foreigner' rather than a local person caused Sue a few initial problems. Another challenge was that of taking the class register, as the correct pronunciation of Jersey names is notoriously difficult.

If people don't settle in the island, locals may remind them that 'there's a boat in the morning', but Sue settled down and taught in Jersey for many years. In 1978, the year after she arrived, the 11+ examination was replaced by 14+ transfer. Jack Worrall, former Headmaster of

Hautlieu, remembered that some parents were still not convinced that their sons and daughters (especially the latter) needed to pursue their education beyond the age of 16.

Today there are nine secondary schools in the island: Le Rocquier, Les Quennevais, Haute Vallée, Grainville and Hautlieu, Victoria College, Jersey College for Girls and the two Catholic schools, Beaulieu Convent and De La Salle College. Provision for children with learning difficulties includes Mont a L'Abbe School and specialist centres in mainstream schools. There are 22 States primary schools and seven private schools. Pupils generally further their education on the mainland, but Highlands College provides a variety of academic and vocational courses. Jersey also has a Graduate Teacher Programme for residents who would find it difficult to attend university on the mainland. The 'educational utopia' envisaged by A.A.H. Downer in 1945 has surely arrived!

More than forty years after she arrived, Sue Jones feels privileged to be part of this unique island community in which history and tradition are deeply embedded and where the sun is a little warmer and the summers linger.

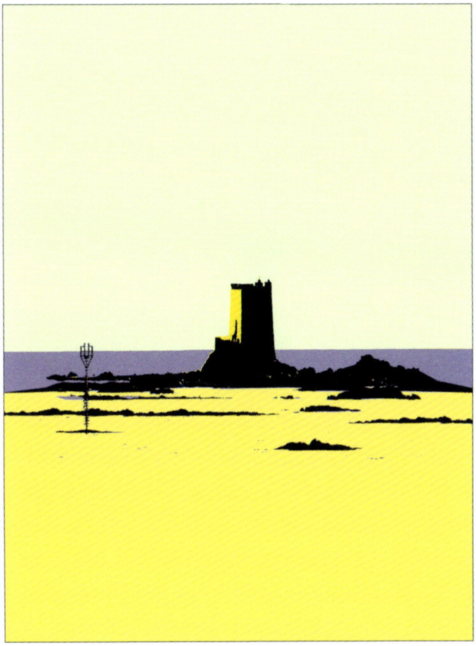

Fig. 9.30 Seymour Tower, Jersey

Reflection

'It was with mixed emotions that some two thousand people from all over the country, including the Channel Islands, and even Canada, gathered in Salisbury on June 25th 1978 to celebrate the life of the College of Sarum St Michael. The Chapel Bell rang out for the last time, but the final toll was not one of sadness, for it was a summons to us all – students and staff, past and present, to gather in the Cathedral for the wonderful Service of Thanksgiving for the life and work of a Christian College'.

College of Sarum St Michael Chronicle, 1978

From 1841 until 1978, Salisbury provided thorough teacher training and nurtured strength of character. Lasting friendships developed and, for many students, a deep love of the College. Reunions have taken place annually since the closure of the College.

In 2018, hundreds of former students from far and wide, including the Channel Islands, met for a memorable service in Salisbury Cathedral to mark the forty years since the College closed.

Between 1843 and the 1970s hundreds of Salisbury trained teachers contributed to education in the Channel Islands. Many local families have great aunts or great, great grandmothers who trained at Salisbury and returned to their islands. Their loyalty and affection for the College reflects the powerful influence of the years that they spent under the spire.

'In Quietness and Confidence shall be your Strength'

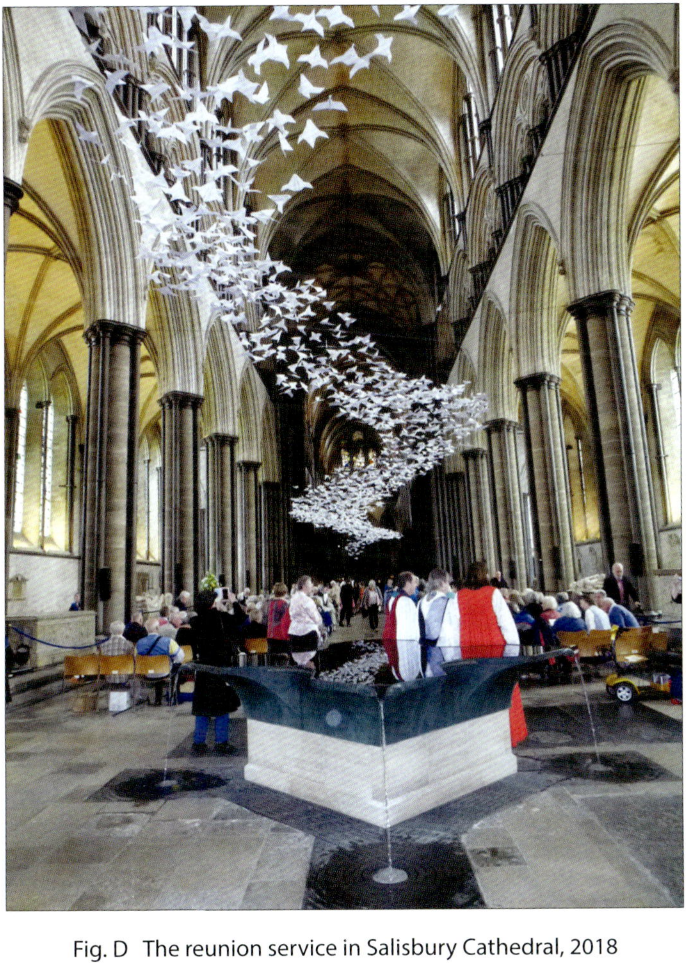

Fig. D The reunion service in Salisbury Cathedral, 2018

Roll Call

A record of some of the Channel Island students who trained at Salisbury Training College/The College of Sarum St Michael. The list is arranged in approximate chronological order and is as accurate as possible. The authors apologise for any inaccuracies and omissions.

GUERNSEY STUDENTS

Pre-1900

Eliza Smith
Mary Ann Beavan
Mary Dewey
Mary Anne Guillard
Florence Frampton
Ethel Anley
Gwendoline Rose Halse

1900–1930

Agnes Mary Le Huray
Dorothy Falla
Ethel May Hamel
Marjorie Falla
Edna Bisson
Dorothy Le Huray
Marion Cumber
Edith Rabey
Marjorie Sarchet
Linda Lucy De Broder
Winifred FlorenceLe Poidevin
Dorothy Bell
Ivy Dora Gillam
Nora Birch
Marie Louise Lanfesty
Kathleen Gertrude Beatrice Robilliard
Phyllis Weysom
Phyllis Kate Burgess
Edith Albiges
Kathleen Grace Clarke
Phyllis Margaret Ogier
Bertha Rose Gillam
Minnie Rachael Nevitt
Daphne Louise Carthew
Miss Le Blanque
Dorothy Mary (Joy) Carpenter
Marie Alexandrine Brigant
Daphne Edith Lacey
Ruth Le Boutillier

1930–1950

Freda Mildred Flambard
Margaret Harris
Renée Le Messurier
J. Hepburn
Lorraine Edith Le Page
Marion Knight
Francis Jay
Florence Foster
Marie Le Lievre
Marjorie Harkins
May Hamel
Marion Hamel
Audrey Hamel
Hazel Maplesden
Helene Gallienne
Betty Hippisley
Marie Swan
Pleasance Corbet
Louise Woolley
Enid (Nid) Falla
Joan Davies
Jeanne (Jonny) Guille
Constance Neve
Eileen Dorothy Connors
Beryl Evelyn Guille

I. Wilson
Gladys Mayo
J. Hepburn
Louise Brackley
Joan Leamann
Frances Jay
Mrs Robert
Mrs Woodman
Mrs Woolford
Miss Perchard

1950–1978

Nancy Lydia Ogier
Jill Down
Madeleine Critchlow
Helene Robert
Caroline Way
Sue Morgan
Susan Ann Marsh
Margaret Price

JERSEY STUDENTS

Pre-1900

Emma Jane de Gruchy
Maria Verner
Emily Hitchings
Susan Dowland
Caroline Dowland
Clara Webb
Annie Alicia Reynolds
Emily Mollet
Fanny Crouch
Sarah Baker
Mary Wheller Bryant
Ruth Maria Prigg
Virginia Butterall
Alice Smith
Marie Picot
Emma Clarke
Rachel Elizabeth Gillard
Louisa Saxby
Louisa Hutchings
Martha Stretchley
Delphina Coutanche
Malvina Gallichan
Elizabeth Jane Saxby
Emily Starck
Maria Vibert
Alice Stretchley
Annie Hennequin
Elizabeth Hunt
Ellen Ireland
Ruth Prigg
Frances Hallett
Anna Vibert
Harriet Jerry
Lydia Le Feuvre
Amelia Daniel
Ellen Pirouet
Marguerite Larbalestier
Florence Stone
Annie Dyer
Gertrude Le Feuvre
Nellie Couch
Ellen de la Mare
K.B. Adlam

1900–1930

Louisa Ellen Cudlipp
Elsie Cudlipp
Beatrice Russell
Alice Winifred Gruchy
Annie Kark
Ethel Raffray
Lucille Marett
Bessie Mollet
Marguerite Larbalestier
Evelyn Vaucour
Elsie Stanley Bowers
Jennie Gale

Lydia A. Pallot
M. Blackford
Louisa Aumont
Henrietta Heritage
Olivia Coutanche
Ellen Pirouet
Eunice Poignand
Edith Gray
Marie Picot
Eleanor K Falle
Edith Balleine
Ivy Le Cornu
Marjorie Sabrina Starck
Dorothy Ahier
Edith Balleine
Alice de la Haye
Margaret Fanny Cadiou
Gwendoline Bailey
Ivy Beatrice Boulanger
Muriel Olive Le Breton
Kathleen Ahier
Ruby Dorothy Dupre
Alice Hambly
Edith Margaret Smith
Alice Berry
Florence Le Poidevin
Mabel Annie Ahier
Dora Jane Hacquoil
Lydia Ann Pallot
Rose Boqueho
Iris Vera Le Brocq
Beatrice Prall
Edith Le Marquand
Kathleen Maher
Agnes Machon
Sybil Ahier
Ellen Le Feuvre
Kathleen Mundy
Norah Birch
Muriel Bishop
Linda Louisa Noel
Iris Le Brocq
Kathleen Robilliard
Muriel Bishop
Florence Hacquoil
Gladys Maud Gruchy
Christine Noel
Beatrice Le Huquet
Marjorie Collins
Doris Alice Noel
Dorothy Touzel
Ethel Gertrude Acourt
Florence Hallett
Marie Boqueho
Phyllis Perchard
Dorothy Stone
Ethel Davey
May Kathleen Agnes Durham
Jessie Brown
Constance Renouf
Gladys Le Moignan
Ivy Le Brocq
Kathleen Webb
Marie Francoise Boqueho
Dorothy Christiana Mauger
Florence Hacquoil
Vera May Le Seelleur
Irene Filleul
Eline Burman
Florence Mary Renouf
Ivy May Le Blanq
Kathleen Brookes
Lydia Bocqueho
Jessie Brown
Marjorie Collins
Roza Amy
Eileen Berry
Dorothy Touzel
Augustine Boqueho
Madeleine Louise Norman
Roza Alfreda Amy

1930–1945

Brenda Hallett
Cecile Nellie Blacklin
Frances Hallett
Dorothy Duffett
F. Turner
Marguerite Luce
Marion Knight
Muriel Hallett
Janet Tarr
Beryl Woodsford
Norah Bull
M. Cooper
Violet Le Maistre
Madeline Renouf
V.C. Hows
Phyllis Marsh
L.K. Darling
Phyllis Marsh
Miss Mould
Evelyn Hoyles
Joan Dymott
Betty Carter
Ruby Le Seelleur
Marguerite Le Chasseur
Augustine Boqueho

1945–1978

Cecily Hoyles
Fay Arthur
Jeanne Dorey
Ruth Le Boutillier
Doris Rolert
Daphne Ahier
Olga Ozouf
Betty Laurens
R. Le Seelleur
Heather Clarke
Frances Bisson
Jean Hanning
Florence Houillebecq
Jane Houillebecq
Anne Priestley
Anne Blaine

Photograph and illustration acknowledgements

The authors are grateful to former students and their friends and families, who have generously donated photographs. We thank the following for their kind permission to use the illustrations:

Front cover and Fig.1.1: *Ann Cardew and Helen Look*

Fig. A: *Sue Finniss*

Fig. B: *VisitGuernsey*

Fig. C: *Chris Lock*

Jerripedia: 1.5, 3.9, 3.12, 3.14, 3.15, 3.20, 3.21, 4.11, 4.13, 4.14, 4.19, 4.20, 4.21, 5.8, 5.9, 5.10, 5.12, 5.14, 6.2, 6.6, 6.16, 6.17, 7.13, 7.14, 7.19, 7.20, 7.21, 8.1, 8.6, 8.7, 8.14, 8.16, 9.29

The Salisbury Museum: 1.10, 3.30, 4.1, 4.2, 4.3, 4.6, 4.15, 4.25, 4.26, 5.1, 5.2, 5.3, 5.4, 6.4, 6.15, 9.18, 7.1, 7.2, 7.3, 7.4, 7.5, 7.6, 7.25, 7.28, 9.3, 9.4, 9.5.9.6, 9.7, 9.18, 9.23

Guernsey Museum and Galleries (States of Guernsey 2017): 1.6, 1.7, 3.1, 3.6, 4.4, 6.14, 6.26, 6.27, 6.29, 7.8, 7.10, 7.12, 8.8, 8.11, 8.18, 8.19, 8.20, 8.22, 9.1, 9.8

Jersey Heritage: 4.17, 5.11, 6.18, 6.19, 6.21, 6.22, 6.23, 7.18, 7.22, 7.24, 8.2, 8.4, 8.5, 8.15, 9.17

Wiltshire and Swindon Archives (WSA): 2.6, 3.8, 4.5, 4.6, 4.9, 4.27, 4.28, 5.6, 5.7, 5.13, 5.19, 6.1, 6.3, 6.8, 7.27

Rosemary Hampton: 1.3, 1.4, 2.1, 3.10, 3.11, 3.13, 3.16, 3.19, 3.23, 3.24, 4.12

The Priaulx Library, Guernsey: 1.8, 1.9, 2.3, 5.16, 5.17, 6.13, 6.28, 7.26, 7.29, 8.10

Pat Jones: 2.2, 3.18, 4.24, 7.11

Jools Holt (www.joolsholt.com): 8.12, 9.28, 9.30

The Science and Picture Library: 3.2, 3.3

Southampton City Council: 2.3, 2.4, 2.5

Guernsey Archives: 4.23, 7.9

VisitGuernsey: 8.23, 9.15

Barry and Rita Furse (painting by H.Canonbury): 7.7

Barrie Pictures: 8.26

David Guy: 7.17

Derby City Council and www.picturethepast.org.uk: 4.10

Dorset County Museum: 4.7

Kate Sykes: 8.25

theislandwiki: 8.33

Wikipedia: 1.2

Acknowledgements

Without the generous help and support of so many Channel Islanders, former students and their family and friends, this book would not have been possible. We are greatly indebted to them for sharing their memories, time and photographs. There are too many to mention everyone individually, but we give our heartfelt thanks to them all.

We are extremely grateful to Adrian Green, Director of the Salisbury Museum, for his ongoing support and for writing the Foreword.

Roger Jones, our publisher and graphic designer, has once again dedicated himself to our project with enthusiasm, skill and great patience.

Thank you to Ann Cardew and Helen Look for designing and painting the beautiful cover. Ann's great aunt was a former Channel Island College student, and she would be as thrilled as we are. As in our first book, *Inspired to Teach*, several people have kindly allowed us to use their work to add depth and colour to our book and we are grateful to them all.

We appreciate the support from staff at The Salisbury Museum, The Wiltshire Museum, and The Wiltshire and Swindon History Centre. Thank you Kevin Sanders for organising our website. Gomer Press has been excellent– Diolch! We value the backing of the Chalke Valley History Festival.

A special thank you to Lisa Burton at the Guernsey Museums and Galleries, The Guernsey Archives, The Priaulx Library and the Société Guernesiaise. Rose-Marie Crossan generously shared her research and writing, which provided invaluable insight into the background of Guernsey students. Richard Hocart was extremely helpful in checking facts and Alun Williams in sharing such useful information.

We are indebted to Henry Coutanche for his interest, encouragement and patient, thorough research in the Jersey Archive. His contributions provided the evidence that we were looking for and enabled us to add depth to stories of which we only had the bare bones. We would also like to thank the Jersey Archive and the Société Jersiaise for their interest and help.

Friends were an enormous help in reading the early proofs, advising on publicity and giving us lots of encouragement. Diana Davies did a meticulous proof read of the final copy. Thank you to Geraldine Beare for the skilful indexing. We are grateful to Sarum College for storing the books.

We thank everyone who pre-ordered a copy and to The College of Sarum St Michael OSA for the loan to get the project started and for their support.

Finally, thank you to Chris and Henry, our College boyfriends and now our very patient and understanding husbands, and to all our families.

Index